There is too much
depowerment and powerlessness,
especially for a human species having many
excellent powers and forms of intelligence and possessing
superlative sensing systems.

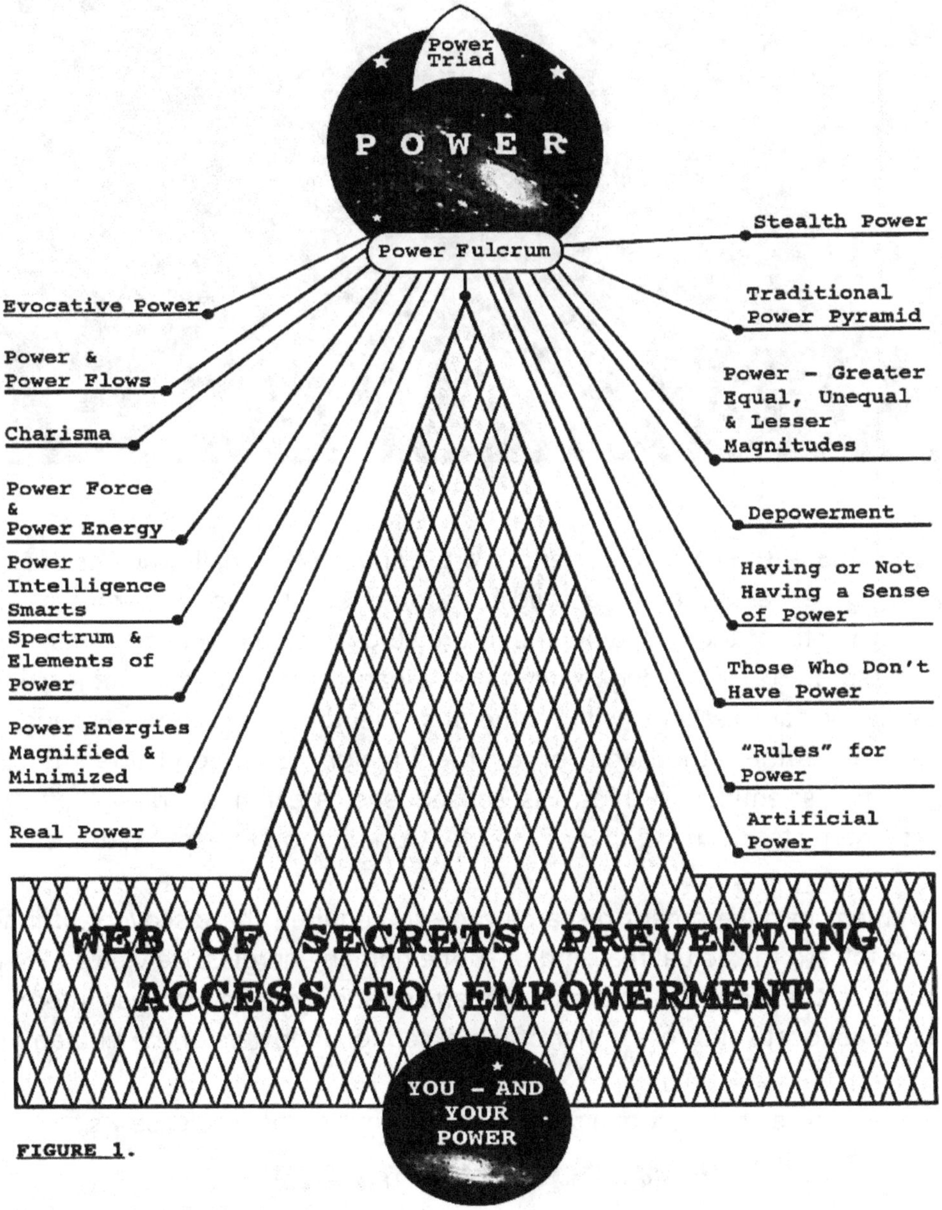

Power Triad

POWER

Power Fulcrum

- Evocative Power
- Power & Power Flows
- Charisma
- Power Force & Power Energy
- Power Intelligence Smarts
- Spectrum & Elements of Power
- Power Energies Magnified & Minimized
- Real Power

- Stealth Power
- Traditional Power Pyramid
- Power – Greater Equal, Unequal & Lesser Magnitudes
- Depowerment
- Having or Not Having a Sense of Power
- Those Who Don't Have Power
- "Rules" for Power
- Artificial Power

WEB OF SECRETS PREVENTING ACCESS TO EMPOWERMENT

YOU – AND YOUR POWER

FIGURE 1.

Ingo Swann (1933-2013) was an American artist and exceptionally successful subject in parapsychology experiments. As a child he spontaneously had numerous paranormal experiences, mostly of the OBE type, the future study of which became a major passion as he matured. In 1970, he began acting as a parapsychology test subject in tightly controlled laboratory settings with numerous scientific researchers. Because of the success of most of these thousands of test trials, major media worldwide often referred to him as "the scientific psychic." His subsequent research on behalf of American intelligence interests, including that of the CIA, won him top PSI-spy status.

His involvement in government research projects required the discovery of innovative approaches toward the actual realizing of subtle human energies. He viewed PSI powers as only parts of the larger spectrum of human sensing systems and was internationally known as an advocate and researcher of the exceptional powers of the human mind.

To learn more about Ingo, his work, art, and other books, please visit:
www.ingoswann.com

SECRETS OF POWER
VOLUME 1

Individual Empowerment vs The Societal Panorama of Power and Depowerment

A BIOMIND SUPERPOWERS BOOK
PUBLISHED BY

Swann-Ryder Productions, LLC
www.ingoswann.com

Copyright © 2000 by Ingo Swann; Copyright © 2015 by Murleen S. Ryder; Copyright © 2017 by Swann-Ryder Productions, LLC.

All rights reserved.
No part of this book may be used or reproduced in any manner whatsoever without written permission. For more information address: www.ingoswann.com.

Previously published in trade paperback by Ingo Swann Books and digitally by Crossroad Press.

First edition BioMind Superpowers Books.

Cover art: *Mandala* by Ingo Swann © Swann-Ryder Productions, LLC.

Lightening image from Pixabay (www.pixabay.com).

ISBN-13: 978-1-949214-31-4

SECRETS OF POWER

VOLUME 1

Ingo Swann

The best plan is to profit by
the folly of others.
(Pliny the Elder, 75 A.D.)

The shortest and best way
to make your fortune is to let people see
that it is in their best interests
to promote yours.
(La Bruyer)

The trouble with the world is that
the stupid are cocksure and the intelligent
are full of doubt.
(Bertrand Russell)

Everybody is a little bit of
a toady in the face of the very rich.
Even the rich to other rich.
(Thomas Hoving)

It is the business of the future to be dangerous . . .
The major advances in civilization
are processes that all but wreck
the societies in which they occur.
(Alfred North Whitehead)

Nothing is illegal if 100 business
men decided to do it, and
that's true anywhere in the world.
(Andrew Young)

The rules are . . .there are no rules.
(Aristotle Onassis)

Why level downward to our
dullest perceptions always
and praise that as common sense?
(Thoreau)

This book is dedicated in memorial
to my grandmothers
Marie Swan Johnson & Anna Gerboth Paul
who first nurtured my perceiving of the
workings of power beyond the merely
fashionable and conventional.

CONTENTS

Author's Notes x

Part One: Strategic Background Vistas Regarding Empowerment 1

   Chapter 1: THE COMPLEX LABYRINTH OF POWERDOM 2

   Chapter 2: TWO MAJOR CONCEPTS OF POWER 8

   Chapter 3: THE HIDDEN STATUS QUO RELATIONSHIP BETWEEN THE POWERLESS AND THE POWERFUL 13

   Chapter 4: OUR HUMAN POWER SPECIES 19

   Chapter 5: THE ROLE OF SECRECY IN DESIGNING A POWER STRUCTURE 25

Part Two: Societal Panorama of Power 31

   Chapter 6: SOCIETAL POWER vs THE ABSENCE OF POWER SCHOOLS 32

   Chapter 7: THE WEB OF SECRETS PREVENTING ACCESS TO EMPOWERMENT 39

   Chapter 8: THE TRADITIONAL POWER PYRAMID 47

   Chapter 9: FOUR GENERIC KINDS OF INDIVIDUAL AND SOCIETAL POWER 55

   Chapter 10: EMPOWERMENT AND DEPOWERMENT versus POWER GAMES 66

   Chapter 11: "RULES" FOR POWER DEPLOYED WITHIN POWERDOM 72

Part Three: The Situation of Power Personal 81

   Chapter 12: THE ON-GOING DICHOTOMY OF INDIVIDUAL AND SOCIETAL POWER 82

   Chapter 13: INDIGENOUS DEPOWERMENT AND PERSONAL EMPOWERMENT 88

   Chapter 14: POWER ENERGIES MAGNIFIED VIS A VIS THOSE WHO DON'T HAVE POWER 94

   Chapter 15: YOU - AND YOUR POWER 100

   Chapter 16: ON HAVING A SENSE OF POWER 106

   Chapter 17: PERSONAL POWER versus LOCAL CIRCUMSTANCES AND FRAMES OF REFERENCE 113

Part Four: Getting Beyond Societal, Group, and Individual Versions of Power 121

   Chapter 18: CLOSED-LOOP VERSIONS OF POWER 122

   Chapter 19: POWER - INTELLIGENCE - SMARTS 126

   Chapter 20: EVOCATIVE POWER, INTELLIGENCE, AND SMARTS 130

   Chapter 21: THE INTELLIGENCES AND THE INNATE POTENTIALS 143

   Chapter 22: TWO OF THE PRO-ACTIVE VEHICLES OF POWER: WILL AND DYNAMISM 151

Part Five: Subtle Contexts Relating to Empowerment _____ **159**

  Chapter 23: SUBTLE DISTINCTIONS BETWEEN UNFOLDMENT AND DEVELOPMENT _ 160

  Chapter 24: THE DIRECT CONNECTION TO POWER OF SIGNIFICANCE AND INSIGNIFICANCE _____ 167

  Chapter 25: EMPOWERMENT versus THE DUMBING-DOWN OF HUMAN SENSING SYSTEMS _____ 176

  Chapter 26: HUMAN SENSING SYSTEMS, POWER MOTION, AND POWER FLOWS ____ 187

  Chapter 27: THE FORGOTTEN CONNECTION OF POWER AND POTENCY _____ 196

  Chapter 28: WHERE DO INDIVIDUAL AND SOCIETAL POWERS BEGIN OR START? ____ 204

Suggested Reading _____ **210**

Ingo Swann

AUTHOR'S NOTES

"THE MORE things change, the more they remain the same" is an old adage that applies to many human activities.

But it certainly applies to the activities of human societal power. Its outer circumstances and formats change over time, but its inner workings remain remarkably the same.

One of the inner factors that remains the same consists of the ever-on-going distinctions between the powerful and the powerless that prevail through time and circumstances.

Thus, one may talk of ancient or modern civilizations and empires, and even of the forthcoming "globalization process," and still be talking of the powerful versus the powerless.

Two other factors also remain the same: (1) the general lack of interest in the nature of the powerless, i.e., why the powerless ARE powerless; and (2) the enormous fascination with the powerful, and with possibilities of becoming powerful.

This fascination is extremely prevalent, and is shared by the powerless and the powerful, the latter of which are fascinated with themselves and have little interest in the powerless.

Indeed, there is more fascination with the dramatics of power and achieving powerfulness than with the principal mandate of our species -- survival into the future, the prospect of which by now has become something of an unpredictable gamble.

There is another significant factor that needs to be taken into account, although it might at first seem quite distant from the problems of power.

This has to do with the enormous amount of discovered data, information, and knowledge that is avoided, forbidden, made taboo, swept under carpets, or simply trashed.

Brain researchers often say that we use only ten to fifteen percent of our brains. It's also quite possible to think that we use only ten to fifteen percent of discovered knowledge.

One may ask what these two somewhat unexplainable discrepancies have to do with power. Well, it's entirely possible that we know only ten to fifteen percent about the nature of power, and that we utilize only ten to fifteen percent of our innate powers.

Why a species equipped to function at higher percentages of everything should remain confined to ten percept performance is an awesome situation to meditate on.

Most information sources regarding power seem to end up giving two basic impressions about it:

1. That it is more or less straightforward and easy to understand -- IF one has the intelligent wherewithal to do so; and
2. That what is seen as power in both the individual and societal realms reflects some kind of natural order -- and which automatically establishes the legitimacy of the differences between the powerless, the relatively powerful, and the powerful.

It would be a great mental and emotional relief if the two impressions did reflect the basic nature of power. But they do not -- and cannot if the word "human" is prefixed to the term "power."

The two impressions are possible only if power is seen as one-dimensional -- i.e., seen either from the bottom up, so to speak, and/or from the top down.

But, as is well known, anyone who manages to think outside of the one-dimensional aspects of power soon becomes aware that power has very many dimensions. And, indeed, in many pre-modern cultures, it was often said that power has a thousand faces.

Whether discussed as being multi-dimensional or as having multiple faces, the inescapable meaning is that power, in its intrinsic nature, is complex.

This in turn means that any real examination of power will be fraught with problems having to do with uncertainty.

And indeed, if ever there was a realm of human activity totally encumbered by uncertainties, the realm of power activity clearly tops the list.

◻

Societal power is considered a very precious commodity, perhaps the most precious. Access to it is therefore a matter of ultra-intense competition. In turn, easy access to the competition itself must be guarded in order to limit the numbers of possible competitors.

There is only one really efficient way to guard against access to power, and that is to conceal, prohibit, and secretize all real knowledge about it.

It is unbelievable to think that real knowledge about the nature and workings of power is unavailable. But the ultra-precious commodity has been with us throughout history.

Thus, various long-term ways and means have been engineered to keep the majority dumbed-down about the nature of power so that it can be more efficiently sequestered in the hands of the few.

The long-term result is that most do not comprehend very much about power. But most do appreciate two well-known facts about it:

1. That power is what individuals can bump up against as they proceed through their lives; and
2. That power is also what, literally speaking, can thump across individuals attempting to proceed through their lives.

There is a basic fact that those aspiring to empowerment must face, sooner or later: societal power is almost always more powerful than the individual, even more powerful than groups of them.

Thus, in seeking empowerment, individuals WILL bump up against a variety of real-life societal situations already structured to control and delimit too much empowerment by too many.

Unless the aspirant understands something of what will be bumped up against along those societal lines, it is probable that not much will happen except a grinding of gears. Therefore, the first mandate for achieving empowerment is to become cognizant of those societal factors and forces already geared to preventing it on a very large scale.

In view of this unavoidable mandate, this first volume of SECRETS OF POWER is confined to twenty-eight chapters.

Each discusses some SOCIETAL aspect of power and depowerment, and all of which, in real-life feed-back, can defeat and even trash individual attempts at empowerment.

At the end of each chapter are some suggested items to observe in real life Out There, or some suggested exercises that might help increase awareness along those lines.

One seldom gets anywhere unless there is some kind of map to follow.

PART ONE
STRATEGIC BACKGROUND VISTAS REGARDING EMPOWERMENT

Ingo Swann

Chapter 1

THE COMPLEX LABYRINTH OF POWERDOM

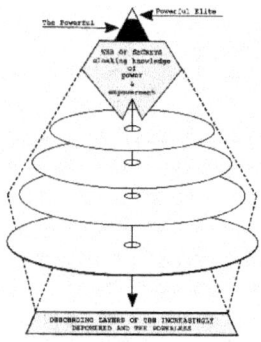

FIGURE 1: Societal power that incorporates large masses of individuals is achieved and held in place by the few not only by preponderant control of wealth and resources, but by control of information and knowledge that would activate empowerment among the masses of individuals. A "web of secrecy" that especially cloaks power and empowerment knowledge must therefore be brought into existence and maintained. The anticipated result of the "web" is that ignorance, social conditioning, and stupidity can better be managed in favor of the powerful few.

ONE OF the first things that can be observed and learned about power is that its workings are vast and enormously complex. The workings might therefore be compared to a labyrinth, constructed so as to be not only full of intricate passageways and blind alleys, but also containing secret doors as well as cleverly designed pitfalls and booby-traps.

In that labyrinth, one can expect to find accuracy and inaccuracies, inadvertent and deliberate misinformation.

One will also find an extensive variety of stratagems, ingenious devices, and episodic expediencies that usually go along with the "games" of power seekers and holders.

SIMPLIFYING AND VERIFYING ELEMENTS OF THE COMPLEXITY

The mix of the foregoing characteristics of powerdom makes it difficult to trust anything that is written about it.

In order to off-set this difficulty, I have elected to devote each chapter to specific situational aspects of power so that readers can observe or verify them in the open field of human activities.

It is very important to keep this verification potential in mind, because learning to observe and identify aspects of power is certainly a fundamental key regarding empowerment.

The personal verification potential is also important because large population segments have been socially conditioned to think of power only in given ways.

This conditioning factor is openly discussed in competent books about power structures -- for example, in John Kenneth Galbraith's THE ANATOMY OF POWER (1983).

Additionally, most people think about power from within the contexts of their personal realities, which may be governed not only by societal conditioning but by the limits of their experience and by flaws of knowledge.

SUBDIVIDING THE PANORAMA OF POWER

As complex and as extensive it is, the elements and factors of the entire panorama of power can be broken down, or subdivided, into numerous and increasingly complex categories.

In the first instance, however, power can be subdivided into three general categories as:

1. Power at the societal levels;
2. Power at the individual level; and
3. Power in relationship to intangible energetic phenomena that transcend the societal and the individual contexts.

The components of the first two of these categories are easily visible, but the elements of the third are more difficult to identify.

Taken altogether, phenomena of the three categories are quite extensive. So, it would be difficult to combine discussion into a single volume without truncating, or downsizing, each of them. And so, I have decided to consider each of them more extensively via separate volumes.

A second way of categorizing elements and factors of power is to distinguish between the powerful and the powerless. This constitutes the conventional approach to the "anatomy" of power.

That conventional approach, however, exclusively focuses only on the powerful and the anatomy of their power structures.

Thus, the general idea conveyed via the conventional approach is that power majorly concerns the powerful, with the powerless being considered as more or less inconsequential.

However, this volume especially focuses on empowerment, as contrasted to power. Thus, the issues involved must incorporate extensive discussion of the powerless -- and whose existence is more dynamically meaningful than can usually be imagined.

THE OVERRIDING IMPORTANCE OF SOCIETAL POWER

I fully realize that many readers would principally be interested in self-empowerment at the individual level.

However, and as is broadly understood, societal and individual power are frequently in conflict, largely because power at the individual level is conditioned and harnessed so as to serve not only societal power, but the power elites who govern them.

The scope of the ways and means of this conditioning and harnessing is, simply put, quite awesome and, all things considered, quite efficient.

As far as I have been able to determine, no book on self-empowerment comes anywhere near identifying and addressing the awesome societal elements involved, many of which are designed to suppress, thwart, or prevent individual self-empowerment.

It is one thing for a relatively powerless individual to wish for more self-empowerment. But such wishing can be thwarted if the individual is uninformed about the societal mechanisms designed to make wide-spread individual empowerment as complicated and as fruitless as possible.

There can be no doubt that efforts at self-empowerment must take place within societal contexts which contain ways and means to disarm empowerment, an activity that is a central objective of all power games. At the societal level, those ways and means have a long, but quite hidden history, and many of the methods involved have become not only institutionalized but secreted.

HIDDEN AND SECRET ASPECTS OF POWER

Whatever is deliberately "hidden" regarding power equates to some kind of secrecy.

And, as most realize, the wheels of power turn not only on the clever and covert manipulation of information and influences, but on a wide variety of secrets that are negotiated behind the scenes of public awareness.

To one degree or another, various versions of secrets of power have been deployed on behalf of all societal power structures everywhere, in all times, and in all cultures.

This clearly indicates that both the secrets and their deployment are generic to our species, and that such taken altogether and across time and cultures constitutes a class of activities with general characteristics.

It is not therefore necessary to single out various power institutions past or present in order to accuse them of wheeling and dealing in behind-the-scenes power stratagems or tactics.

It is more important to bring the generic hidden aspects of power into visibility, so that those who have empowering interests might gain whatever they can either in theory or by identifying or observing each aspect discussed.

THERE IS TOO MUCH POWERLESSNESS

The reader deserves to know why I have decided to compile these three volumes.

That reason, simply put, is that there is too much powerlessness everywhere, not only within the realms of the "official" powerless, but even among the powerful who often find themselves caught up in circumstances, trends, and affairs beyond their control, authority, or influence.

This is exceedingly strange for a species exceedingly rich in powers of all kinds.

Too much powerlessness, especially if artificially engineered by societal measures, really does equate to a profound waste of human potentials, and even of human life itself.

TWO NECESSARY TERMS

As has often been pointed up by linguists and semanticists, topics can be discussed only by utilizing the nomenclature a language contains.

Most languages contain a number of words than can be used to discuss power. But in the case of English, two important terms are missing, and which are important to the contexts of power everywhere.

DEPOWERMENT

The first of these is DEPOWERMENT, which is not found in dictionaries. Depower can be understood as the direct opposite of empower, a term that is found in dictionaries, and which basically means "to enable, to increase in power."

DEPOWER thus means to disable or to reduce from power, to deprive it of capacity or strength, to make incapable or ineffective, or to cut it back or down to negligible importance.

Empowerment and depowerment are terms indicating active change-of-state processes of some kind, and so they should not be confused with powerful and powerless which refer to states or static conditions.

GROK

The second missing term is GROK, coined by Robert A. Heinlein in his famous science fiction novel, STRANGER IN A STRANGE LAND, first published in 1969.

This term refers to grasping, or synthesizing, the larger or overall meaning, nature, or essence of something via an apparent mixture of empathy, intuition, and, sometimes, telepathy.

This activity does not necessarily imply a kind of extrasensory perception, but more refers to those cognizing abilities associated with the holistic and more speedy functions of the right hemisphere of the brain.

Groking is in contrast to understanding, the latter of which is usually achieved via the slower and more laborious linear functions of the left hemisphere. Groking reveals the sum of the lined-up parts, which is not revealed by the parts themselves.

While the processes of groking and understanding do contrast, they are not mutually exclusive, and can work in tandem. It can be pointed up, though, that one can learn to understand information by sequentially lining it up, but perhaps fail to make a groking synthesis of the sequence.

As a familiar example of this, one can prepare food by following how-to recipes laid out in sequence, and this, of course, is a linear left-hemisphere process. Without the recipe, however, food stuffs may remain a mystery.

Those who grok food stuffs can produce delectable delights without reading how-to recipes. Power of course includes both understanding and groking. But as with cooks, one probably should put one's money on the grokers.

ITEM TO CONSIDER

ENLARGING ONE'S POWERS OF OBSERVING MIGHT ACTUALLY CONSTITUTE THE BASIS OF EMPOWERMENT.

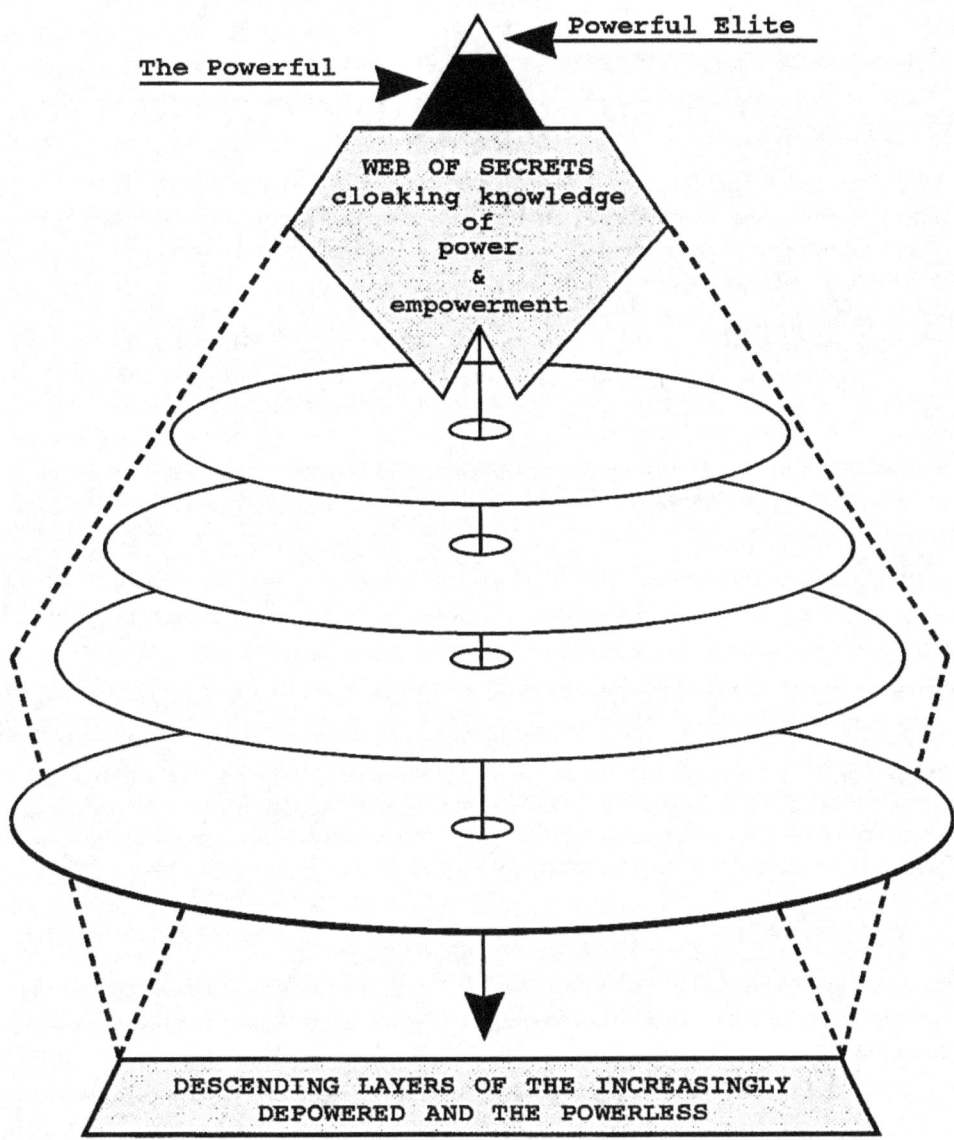

FIGURE 2. Societal power that incorporates large masses of individuals is achieved and held in place by the few not only by preponderant control of wealth and resources, but by control of information and knowledge that would activate empowerment among the masses of individuals. A "web of secrets" that especially cloaks power and empowerment knowledge must therefore be brought into existence and maintained. The anticipated result of the "web" is that ignorance, social conditioning, and stupidity can better be managed in favor of the powerful few.

Chapter 2
TWO MAJOR CONCEPTS OF POWER

THE COMPLEXITY of power and powerdom can be pictured in various ways: as a convoluted network; as a gigantic puzzle most of whose pieces are hard to find; or as an intricate labyrinth filled with fake doors, dead ends, and clever booby-traps.

THE USUAL FORMAT OF POWER STRUCTURES

This complexity makes it difficult to decide where to begin discussion and examination of what, in conventional terms, is sometimes referred to as the "anatomy" of power.

The anatomy of power can be, and indeed has been, mapped by a number of intrepid investigators. Their efforts reveal that power consists of some kind of hierarchical format whose structure contains orders or ranks, each subordinate to the one above.

It thus appears that power is a formatted arrangement of control, authority, and influence into a graded series ranging from the few powerful down to and including the many powerless.

If the formatted arrangement is all there is to power, then the case is more or less closed -- and all one needs to do is learn how to negotiate one's way among this or that power structure.

BEHIND THE CONVENTIONAL POWER STRUCTURE

However, deeper and more extensive examinations reveal that the anatomy (which is ardently accepted in conventional terms) is actually akin to the proverbial iceberg, only one-fifth of which is visible while the other four-fifths are hidden underneath the water.

Most people, even those tending toward intellectual idiocy, sense that the workings of power are composed not only of its visible factors, but also of factors hidden behind the scenes that are difficult to identify.

One factor is quite certain, however. Although the conventional concepts regarding power do reveal a great deal about its ever-changing vicissitudes, those concepts are also entirely inadequate with regard to many fundamental issues.

The principal reason for this is that the conventional concepts are NOT based in the probable totality of human powers themselves.

Instead, the conventional concepts are based within manufactured societal and sociological constructions, the contexts of which are set up to establish who is and who is not to have power.

In other words, the societal constructions set the margins between the powerful and the powerless, with the powerful thereafter maintaining those margins, and sometimes doing so with strength and enthusiasm that can be ruthless.

THE VISIBLE ANATOMY OF POWER AS SOCIETAL ARTIFICE

However, it can be seen that every societal construction is nothing more than some kind of sociological artifice -- i.e., "an artful stratagem, or an ingenious device or expedient" designed to incorporate individuals into some kind of sociological power structure.

And indeed, the well-known conventional definition of power as "control, authority, and influence over others" is closely linked to the definition of artifice -- in that the control is almost always gained by "artful stratagems, or via ingenious devices or expedients."

Only the very naive, lost in the illusions of idealism, will think that societal power does not incorporate ingenious devices and expedients. Most realize that societal power utterly drips with such.

But many do not realize the extent of the dripping -- and which, in accord with the infamous trickle-down theory, ultimately trickles down into the lowest echelons of the powerless.

SOCIETAL POWER ARTIFICE vs THE TOTALITY OF HUMAN POWERS

The structured power artifices do not at all reflect the entirety of human powers per se, but only the particular format of how control, authority, and influence over others is set up and then maintained for as long as possible.

This kind of thing sets up the distinction and well-known disparity between societal power systems and the relatively powerless individuals incorporated within them, the latter of which sometimes feel that their own powers are constrained and truncated by the devices and agendas of the power systems.

Attempts to view and understand this disparity from within the ranks of the powerless usually don't get very far, because it seems quite difficult to comprehend why societal power systems would WANT to constrain and truncate powers at the individual level. But viewed from the "top" of the power systems, it will logically be concluded that:

1. Control, authority, and influence over others literally means not only control, authority, and influence over the physicality of the subservient populations; but
2. Also over their minds, beliefs, emotions, education, intelligence, and any potential powers that might chance to emerge within the powerless individual levels.

There is an exact reason for (1) and (2) above, which will be discussed in the next chapter. It is first necessary to examine the contexts of the TWO major concepts of power, because they are in direct conflict with each other.

THE "ESSENTIAL" AND THE "AUTHORITARIAN" DEFINITIONS OF POWER

A central difficulty regarding enlarging one's comprehension of power relates to the conventional idea that the definition of power is "control, authority, and influence over others."

However, that definition is more aptly suited to the meaning of authoritarianism -- which is defined as "relating to or favoring a concentration of power in a leader or in an elite; also, relating to or favoring submission to authority. "

This author must hasten to point up that this linking of societal power to authoritarianism enjoys rather great precedence. After all, the term "authority" IS found in the accepted definitions of societal power. And those several authors, who have elaborated upon the anatomy of power, unambiguously refer to those who are subservient to authority.

Admittedly, there are various degrees and arrangements of authoritarianism, just as there are various degrees and arrangements of power elites. But if power is defined and accepted as control and influence over others, then the "others" are "subservient" in some sense at least.

The fact is that the conventional concept of power as control and influence over others is only a societal artifice set up and managed so as to incorporate the subservience of the "others."

In contrast to the authoritarian definitions of power are what can be called the "essential" definitions of it.

In most dictionaries, these are given as "ability to act; to cause or produce an effect; mental efficacy; a source or means of producing motive and transformational energy."

For clarity and ease of reference, these essential definitions can be thought of as causative ones -- as contrasted to the authoritarian ones which, by definition, are controlling ones.

If the distinctions between controlling and causative powers are meditated upon as calmly as possible, it can almost immediately be seen that the causative and the controlling definitions of power are in conflict. The most simple reason is because controlling powers would wish, or would find it necessary, to control causative powers at the random individual level.

It is certainly true that invested societal power structures can cause things to happen.

But causative powers belong more principally to our species as a whole. Those powers download into each and every specimen of our species, even into those many who find themselves powerless in the face of societal controlling powers.

As will be copiously discussed in the text, the essential, or causative definitions of power outlined just above are more or less the antithesis of authoritarian control, authority, and influence.

The more exact reason is that authoritarian control can act to suppress and defeat the phenomena associated with the emergence of the essential activities of power at the individual levels.

DICTIONARY DEFINITIONS OF POWER

Most modern dictionaries give first status to the authoritarian definitions of power, and second status to the essential definitions.

However, the Oxford dictionary of the English language reveals that the essential definition of "to cause to act" was first utilized around 1305.

The essential definition as "a particularly strong faculty of body or mind, of vigor, vitality, and energy" appeared around 1440.

The two somewhat authoritarian concepts of power as "personal or social ascendancy," and "controlling political or economic ascendancy or influence" did not emerge until about 1535.

In any event, in today's parlance there are two highly contrasting definitions of power. Both are mentioned, but the authoritarian one is given first, the essential ones given second.

This first and second place arrangement doubtlessly serves to impress that controlling powers are more important than the essential ones -- the latter of which (as will be intricately discussed in the chapters ahead) MUST be of some implicit worry to those who wish to have possession of control and influence over others.

THE POWER OF SOCIETAL ARTIFICES vs
ESSENTIAL POWERS OF THE INDIVIDUAL

Thus far, then, the complex topic of power breaks neatly into two parts -- the power of societal artifices, and the powers of the individual. These two kinds of power are not altogether the same thing.

A number of books on the subject of self-empowerment have appeared over time, and some contain very helpful information. But most of them are deficient with regard to one very important context: they give hardly any hint of what the individual is up against.

As a brief explanation, it can be said that it is true that one is born into physical and mental life, and that one is born equipped with a vast spectrum of innate powers. But one is also born into the environment of an existing power structure wielding control, authority, and influence.

For the most part, one is born into those power environments as a mere statistical unit having very little right to freely and fully develop innate powers in ways that do not accord with those power environments. Indeed, and as will be seen ahead, such environmental power structures, as societal artifices, wield enormous control and influence with regard to attempts for achieving self-empowerment.

THE BASIC PROBLEM OF SELF-EMPOWERMENT

Therefore, with regard to self-empowerment, one will not be attempting self-empowerment per se, but will be attempting it WITHIN a societal artifice which has established ingenious devices and expediencies to truncate too much self-empowerment.

If one is not at least somewhat cognizant of those societal devices and expediencies, one's self-empowerment efforts may end up being like a dismal, failure-prone war fought in unmapped territory where the societal devices have all the advantages.

If the foregoing seems harsh, just take a good look at the enormous number of the powerless throughout the world. Yet, our species existed here long before the societal power artifices that are controlled by the relatively few powerful.

And, indeed, if our species was not a power species to begin with, there would be little need to erect power artifices to control power in the first place.

In any event, it is now necessary to move into the next chapter in order to examine the enormous disparity between the powerful and the powerless -- and to point up at least one logical reason for the disparity.

ITEM TO REMEMBER

TRY TO OBSERVE DISTINCTIONS BETWEEN INDIVIDUAL AND SOCIETAL POWERS.

Chapter 3

THE HIDDEN STATUS QUO RELATIONSHIP BETWEEN THE POWERLESS AND THE POWERFUL

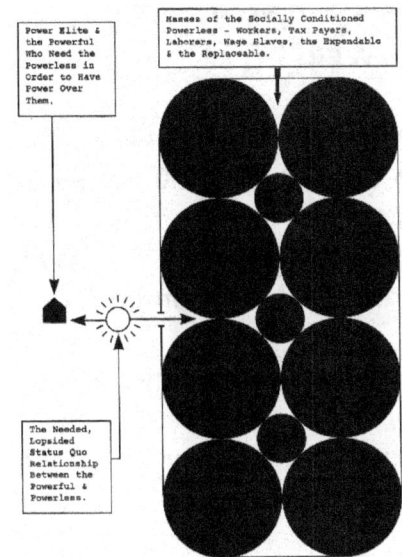

MOST BOOKS that map the conventional anatomy of power direct copious attention to the powerful, but hardly any attention at all to the powerless -- except to refer to them as the controlled, the influenced, the obediently subservient, and so forth.

Because of this, it is possible to find out a good deal about power via the power structures of the powerful.

But beyond that, it is really quite difficult to find out anything about the powerless, except that they are incorporated into the lower echelons of power structures where they are ranked as having relatively low or no power status at all.

In a general way, this is as much to say that the powerless exist because they ARE powerless, after which no further comment is necessary.

The above observations describe a rather fixed concept that seems to be taken as natural by the powerful as well as the powerless. The arrangement between them is thought of simply as the way things always have been, are, and always will be.

The whole of this can be diagrammed as the traditional power structure pyramid. The traditional power pyramid is usually shown in the neat format of an equilateral triangle, and it is this that gives the impression not only of balance throughout, but that the powerless are, in some way, an accepted benefiting part of the power pyramid.

A more real assessment of the total populations involved cannot result in the neat equilateral format.

So, with an eye on empowerment potentials, it seems necessary to establish the approximate real proportional differences between the powerful and the powerless, and then to point up a factor that is not found clearly mentioned in any book about power.

THE VAST PROPORTIONAL DISPARITY BETWEEN THE POWERLESS AND THE POWERFUL

Roughly speaking, the relatively powerful comprise about 10 percent or less of the total population, while the relatively powerless make up the remaining 90 percent or more.

This obviously cannot be neatly configured as an equilateral triangle. Perhaps the smaller power part of the population pyramid can be represented by an equilateral pyramid.

But the fuller, disproportional powerless population really needs to be represented by a vastly bigger and OBLATE design.

The less than 10 percent of the powerful can be further subdivided by considering the visible and the invisible power elite, the latter few of which are known to operate behind the scenes.

Of course, the exceedingly great attention paid to the powerful makes it seem that their proportional population is much larger than it actually is.

If the whole of our human species is considered, and if the vast proportional disparity is to be considered as real, then it seems that our species naturally produces the vast populations who are not meant to be powerful.

This, of course, is ridiculous in the extreme, if only because an allegedly intelligent species that produces over 90 percent of naturally powerless populations could not survive very well if at all.

Thus, it can easily be considered that the 90 to 10 percent disproportional relationship is little more than a societal artifice that is given artificial reality by various ways and means.

THE NEEDED STATUS QUO RELATIONSHIP BETWEEN THE POWERFUL AND THE SUBSERVIENT POWERLESS

A significant question that is never posed is that if the powerless did not exist, then who or what would the powerful have power over?

Thus, there is a real and a necessarily large lopsided dynamic status quo relationship between the powerless and the powerful.

There is every historical indication that the powerful are cognizant of this necessary status quo relationship, and that overt and covert ways and means are designed to perpetuate it at the general societal levels. In bygone centuries, this status quo was trenchantly assured by establishing class systems. There were the minority powerful and the majority powerless, between which there was no upward mobility. This was assured by denying literacy to the lowest class orders.

Simply put, people were born into a class, and there they stayed, regardless.

Historians explain this as a necessary method to ensure possession and inheritance of property and wealth.

But in fact, it also served the secondary, but equally obvious, purpose as a necessary method of limiting access to societal power as well as serving to perpetuate the powerless classes so that the powerful could have power over them.

By far and large, it is this needed status quo relationship that, in part, makes examinations of power so complicated, or at least renders such examinations into a puzzle whose pieces are very hard to locate.

Further, the perpetuation of the needed status quo relationship between the very few powerful and the very many powerless is itself a quite complicated affair, largely because it must be managed in macro and micro ways that prevent the collective powerless from becoming all that cognizant of it.

And in this sense, the necessary existence of the direct relationship between the societal powerful and the societal powerless probably qualifies as the first secret of power.

It is not really a secret, of course, and it is usually understood by the subservient masses incorporated into a given societal power artifice.

POWER IS NOT JUST POWER

In the light of the foregoing, it can be said that power is not just power. Rather, power over others can come into existence only in juxtaposition to the powerless, or at least with regard to something else.

What is amusing about all of this concerns the official definitions of societal authoritarian power. As already established, these are usually given as "control, authority, and influence over others," but the nature of the "others" is never identified. And for an apparently good reason.

If the nature of the "others," was openly and frankly identified, it would be perfectly legitimate to define power as control and influence over and among the powerless.

This definition would, of course, more efficiently reflect the necessary relationship between the few powerful and the very many powerless.

THE POWERLESS DO NOT GENERALLY THINK OF THEMSELVES AS POWERLESS

As it is, though, the topic of power is full of beastly glitches, and via the above it is possible to encounter one of them right away.

In general, the powerless seldom relish the idea of thinking of themselves as such

-- largely because the concept of being powerless is somewhat demoralizing and cannot easily be thought of as constituting anything like a cognitive comfort zone.

And it is indeed possible to evade the implicit issues here because power and powerlessness are always relative to each other.

Almost everyone has some kind of power, if only in their own local universe and their own reality sets.

But evading the implicit issues has another problematical quality that comes to light if and when one wishes to become more generally powerful than one actually is. In modern times, if individuals complain or grumble about not having enough power, they will quickly be told by one and all that the reasons reside in their own psychological realms: i.e., no self-confidence, not enough drive, problems with relationships, etc., and that these need to be corrected at the individual level.

These inadequacies perhaps have something to do with whatever is involved. But there is a larger reason why the powerless don't have much power. And the reason has something to do with the necessary relationship between the powerful and the powerless.

If the powerful need large reserves of the powerless in order to have power over them, it would be quite necessary to condition powerlessness into the masses via social and educational artifices. And so, the fault of powerlessness might not exclusively be one's own, but one of programming from external sources.

Perfectly legitimate books detailing the conventional anatomy of power do emphasize the importance of "social conditioning" so as to ensure at least subservience, if not complete powerlessness.

THE THREE HIDDEN PARTS OF POWER OVER OTHERS

If the foregoing is considered, the topic OF and the phenomena of power easily break apart into three fundamental parts having the following priority:

1. The necessary existence of the powerless;
2. The needed lopsided relationship between the powerless and the powerful; and
3. The powerful who surface from among the powerless and who thereafter must maintain the needed lopsided relationship.

The above three power parts suggest that the powerless must exist before the powerful can surface among them, to exert control and influence over the masses they have emerged from.

If this would be the case, then very few of the powerful would actually try to empower the masses, because doing so would default (2) above. But this is almost the same as saying that the powers of our species that could unfold among the vast populations are artificially contained by hidden societal mechanisms.

ITEM TO BE CONSIDERED

DOES OUR SPECIES NATURALLY PRODUCE GOBS OF POWERLESS INDIVIDUALS?

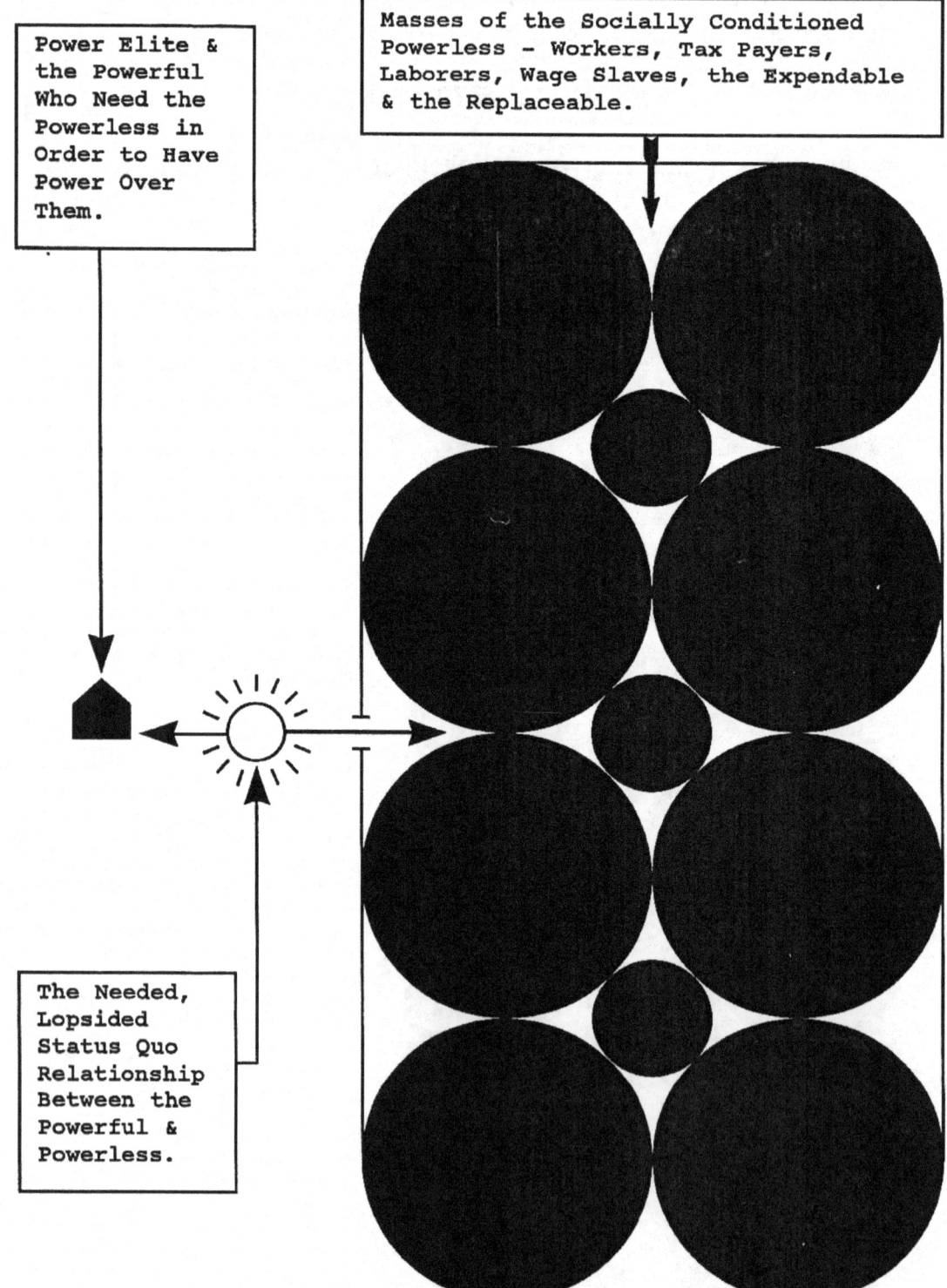

Chapter 4

OUR HUMAN POWER SPECIES

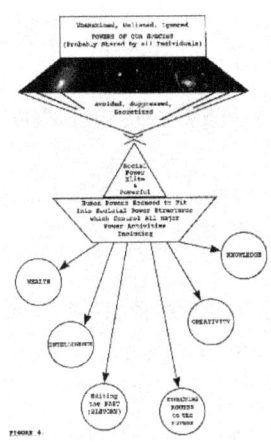

AT FIRST take, any effort to establish a functional link between power and our human species might seem uninteresting and quite distant from the subject of power itself.

And indeed, if one is thinking only in terms of power it is probably not necessary to make that link. But if one is thinking in terms of empowerment, then it is clear that empowerment involves a change of state from some kind of powerlessness into a state characterized by manifestations of more power.

THE DISTINCTIONS BETWEEN SOURCES AND MANIFESTATIONS OF POWER

One of the ultimate issues regarding empowerment has to do with where power comes from in the first place.

With respect to that issue, it is important to point up that there are meaningful distinctions between (1) where power comes from, and (2) what power is.

The foregoing also distinguishes between (1) sources of power, and (2) manifestations of power.

If one spends a lot of time surveying the literature about power, it is quite clear that most assume that manifestations of power are the same as sources of it.

But the term MANIFEST refers to whatever is "readily perceived by the senses, especially by the sight;" or to whatever is "easily understood or recognized by the mind."

MANIFESTATION refers to "something made evident, obvious, or certain by appearing, showing, or displaying."

SOURCE, however, refers to "the point of origin; a generative force; a cause; to rise up or spring forth."

Thus, if there is no point of origin for something, then there will be no manifestations of it. So, if there are no sources for power, then there will not be any manifestations of it.

As will become very clear, the foregoing discussion regarding sources and manifestations of power is absolutely super-loaded with implications having to do with groking not only the phenomena of empowerment but the phenomena of depowerment as well.

OUR SPECIES ERECTS POWER STRUCTURES

It is quite clear that people can gain access to positions of power within given power structures.

Thus, it is usual for individuals to think and talk about power within the contexts of their own local environments, where elements of the power structures impinge on them and condition their reality packages.

The general result of this is that those who want to climb societal or organizational power ladders within the power structures most likely see those structures as sources of power regarding manifestations of control, authority, and influence over others.

And so it is possible to think that this upward power mobility, as it were, consists of empowerment sequences. But this kind of thing is better described not as empowerment but as accessing into and playing power games within already established power structures.

At this point, it is reasonable to wonder from where and why power structures come into existence.

One plausible explanation hinges on the fact that scientists and philosophers accept the idea that our species is a social one and therefore erects structured societies.

SOCIETY is majorly defined as "an enduring and cooperating social group whose members have developed organized patterns of relationships through interaction with one another."

"Developed organized patterns" of course refers not only to local, or smaller, social scenarios, but also to the larger contexts of societal structuring.

There is no disagreement among scientists, philosophers, or sociologists that wherever people congregate for any length of time, they set about erecting, or formatting, social structures.

Indeed, this kind of thing is openly, and even proudly, acknowledged as a human species trait or as a species-wide characteristic. And this is exactly the same as saying that our species manifests societal structures.

However, what is NOT usually discussed, at least not in any clear-cut way, is that all societies erect power structures within their "developed organized patterns," and these power structures assume central control of whatever else the social structure consists of.

It is really quite fair to consider that if developing the elements of structured socialization is actually a species thing, then the developing of power structures is also a species thing. Indeed, where a social structure comes into existence, a power structure becomes formatted within it.

Thus, if it is possible to consider where power basically comes from, one will eventually have to conclude that it consists of important and strong elements within the human species as a whole, or within the general profile of the human species taken altogether.

Those important and strong elements download into each individual of the species, after which (1) the individuals express them if they can, and (2) also collectively design and set up power structures that can come to house large societies and even vast civilizations.

If one pursues this line of thinking, one can eventually encounter a number of cultural and knowledge oddities, the sum of which adds up to a surprising absence of considerations in this regard.

This is to say that although the topic of POWER obviously constitutes a very important element of our species as a whole, that element is hardly ever mentioned in philosophic or scientific descriptions of our species.

GIVING IDENTITY TO OUR SPECIES

The scientific classification of life forms did not begin until the mid-1600s, after which a species became identified by life forms that had common characteristics, and whose male and female specimens could mate and produce progeny.

In zoology and botany, the formal definition of SPECIES was established as "A group or class of animals or plants (usually constituting a subdivision of a genus) having certain common and permanent characteristics which clearly distinguish it from other groups."

Our species was eventually given the Latin names of HOMO SAPIENS SAPIENS. This name can be translated in a number of ways. Some options are:

Man (male & female) who thinks and knows that he does;
Man who knows and knows that he knows;
Man who has memory-intelligence and knows that he has.

In other words, intelligence -- not power -- was somehow considered as our species most distinguishing attribute.

But there is a rather enormous glitch in the above.

While it is certainly true that intelligence and power have some relationship with each other, it is also true that power can design ways and means to modulate and also suppress intelligence on behalf of this or that societal power structure.

This is what is meant by those authors who, attempting to describe the anatomy of power, refer to "social conditioning" of the masses which results in subordinating the vastly larger populations to the will of others.

Indeed, it is quite understandable that "conditioned power" refers to the educational persuasion of what the individual, in the social context, has been brought to believe is inherently correct.

Once this is achieved, in the societal context, submission to the authority of others reflects the accepted view of what the individual should believe, think, and do REGARDLESS of any intelligence that might be housed in the individual.

In any event, even though power and intelligence do have various kinds of relationships, they are not the same thing. It can always be seen that manifestations of power constitute a more central situation to our species than intelligence does. It can also be discovered that power only tolerates intelligence to the degree that the latter is not troublesome to it.

We of course need to think of our species as having intelligence, and probably as having creativity, too. But at our species level and immediately superior, as it were, to intelligence and creativity, is the consideration of Man who has and can make power and knows it.

As it really is, then, our species literally drips with power, far more than it drips with intelligence or even creativity.

And indeed, if the definition of power is accepted as control, authority, and influence over others, then that would naturally include the same with regard to the intelligence and creativity levels of those others.

OUR SPECIES ENDOWED WITH POWERS

In the biological and zoological sciences, it is assumed, as a dominant and unquestionable paradigm, that a species is basically designed for basic physical survival of itself within given environments.

But if this would be the case regarding the human species, then that species would not need the extraordinary line-up of additional endowments, powers, faculties, and abilities it is widely known to possess. (It is worthwhile pointing up one such power -- the power of discovering and accumulating knowledge and THEN the power of access and jurisdiction over it.)

This is the same as saying that our species is remarkably over-endowed with regard to mere survival -- indeed so over-endowed that there is an enormous scientific and philosophic gap between it and all other known species inhabiting this planet.

Our species is known to have powers and abilities it doesn't use, a good part of which fall into the category known as powers of mind -- but which could more correctly be referred to as power of powers.

It is perhaps a bit awkward to suggest that our species is a species having the power of powers.

Even so, it is our species that resolutely goes about erecting power structures of all kinds and shapes, the most basic and obvious purpose of which is to have control, authority, and influence over powers.

In any event, a species bereft of powers and power-making probably would not have an identifiable need to do any such thing.

ITEM TO BE CONSIDERED

WHAT POWERS DO SOCIETAL POWER STRUCTURES WORK TO CONTAIN, CONTROL, OR SUPPRESS?

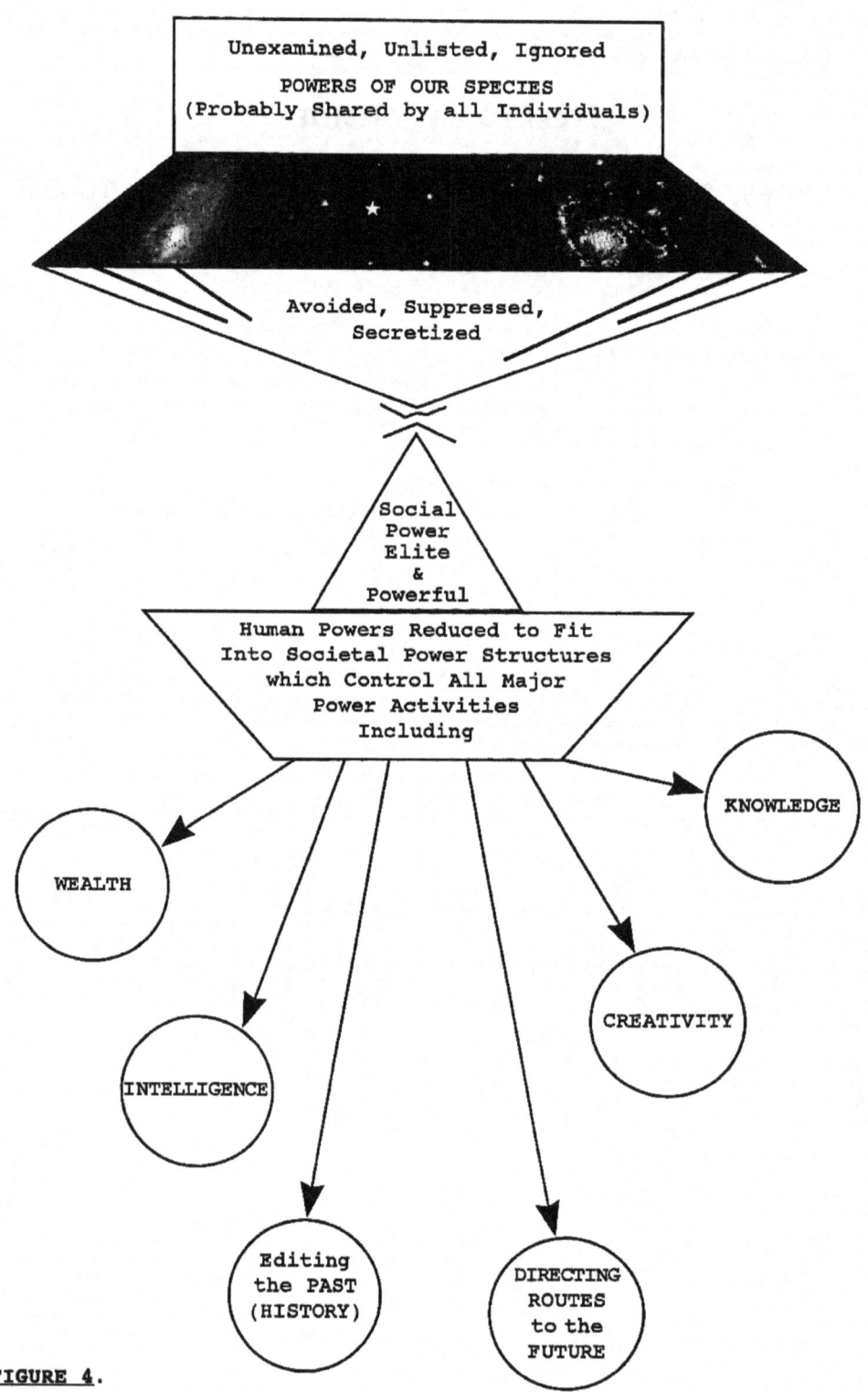

FIGURE 4.

Chapter 5

THE ROLE OF SECRECY IN DESIGNING A POWER STRUCTURE

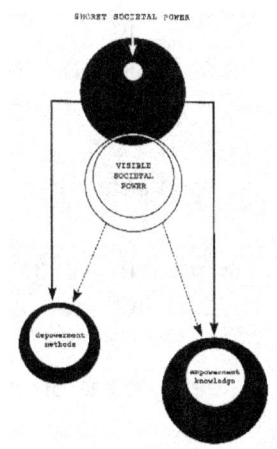

THERE ARE any number of ways of picturing the designs, or lay-outs, of societal power structures, and it is the function of this chapter to at least cast a brief glance at some of them.

Doing so will increase the dimensions of awareness among those who are interested in empowerment, and also be helpful in reversing subtle depowerment realities at work in most of those structures.

THE POWER PYRAMID DESIGN

As we have seen, power structures in modern times usually are pictured as having the shape of equilateral pyramids. The pyramids are then subdivided, showing the powerful few at the apex, the powerless masses at the broad bottom, with gradients of power between those two categories.

This, of course, is a neat way of picturing in that it can be groked all at once. As it stands, there is nothing wrong with this pyramidal presentation -- with two rather subtle exceptions.

First, the powerful themselves endorse this pyramidal presentation, since it establishes sequential gradients of order while at the same time letting everyone know that this is how it is. The pyramidal format also gives the subtle but explicit impression that access to power merely requires a vertical assent to the "top."

Second, and even more subtle, empowerment in the pyramidal format is to be understood AS that vertical assent and nothing else, and specifically so within the existing power structure and what it stands for.

In other words, notions of empowerment, and routes to it, are confined within the power structure, and this makes it possible and entirely probable that the top power echelons determine who is to ascend or not.

This particular power-structure design seems to present a fair and even hopeful description of power, implying, as it does, that those among the powerless ranks who can manage to do so CAN make the power-ladder ascent and possibly arrive at least in the vicinity of the powerful "top."

It is thus that the pyramidal design for a power structure, even if objectionable in many respects, exerts a somewhat hypnotic allure over the masses incorporated within it.

What is not expressly visible in the power pyramid design is a significant factor pointed up earlier.

This factor consists of the simple reality that the powerful NEED the presence of the powerless in order to have something to have power over, and this specifically in terms of control, authority, and influence.

Thus, ways and means must be discovered and implemented to keep the majority of the powerless as powerless as possible.

In that sense, if the powerless became aware of those ways and means, then significant numbers of the powerless would object to them. So those ways and means must at least be as invisibly subtle as possible, and even quite secret if necessary.

As will be dissected in Part Two, the power-structure design is more intricate than can ever be fully groked by simply picturing power as a neat pyramid.

THREE OTHER HELPFUL WAYS OF PICTURING POWER STRUCTURES

As already discussed in chapter 1, power structures can be pictured as intricate and confusing labyrinths.

It is proper to bear in mind the labyrinthine nature of power, largely because numbers of labyrinths will be found inside all power pyramidal designs.

Another reason has to do with the fact that power structures are rife with cleverly and deliberately engineered misinformation and disinformation activities. These activities are designed to be labyrinthine in character so as to mislead and confuse general cognitive awareness of what is really going on.

Everyone more or less understands this, of course, and so the engineering of such isn't actually too much of a secret. However, the activities within power structures that produce misinformation and disinformation are usually secretized.

Another way of picturing power structures is one that was fashionable in the late nineteenth and throughout the twentieth centuries.

Power can be pictured as a gigantic octopus having many-more than eight "arms." This image often appeared in the media, and was used to portray the powerful, their elite, and their offices in the act of grasping manifold elements, especially economic ones, which would reinforce their power status.

In slightly different formats, this image has had a long basis in history -- in that power was often pictured as having a thousand faces, arms, tentacles, currents of control, manifold secrets, and manipulating objectives.

And, as has already been discussed, one of the most functional ways of picturing power structures has to do with the proverbial iceberg, one-fifth of which is visible above the water in which it floats, while the other four-fifths are hidden in the water beneath the one-fifth.

THE GREAT ANTIQUITY OF POWER MACHINATIONS AND PROBLEMS

In its official definition, human history begins with the advent of some form of writing which makes it possible to recover a chronological record of significant past events. Anything that might have happened prior to that is officially referred to as pre-history or as prehistorical.

Writing is so closely associated with literacy that the two are considered the same thing.

As is so far known, the first literate civilization consisted of the Sumerians of the Near East and who, at some point around 3000 B.C., developed a type of writing now known as cuneiform script. And so, the historical period begins at about that date and place.

However, it is generally accepted that our species either emerged or appeared about 35,000 years ago. In that sense our species is referred to as Cro-Magnon Man, this name being taken from a location in France where evidence of a Cro-Magnon settlement was first discovered.

The so-called pre-historical period thus ranges from about 35,000 years ago up to the advent of writing at about 3,000 B.C., at which time human history begins.

This division is really quite silly, largely because throughout the long pre-historical period, Cro-Magnon Man possessed visual and three-dimensional arts. Many artifacts remaining from those arts can be carbon-dated, and they can reveal a chronology, albeit one not considered historical.

In any event, with the emergence of the great Sumerian and associated civilizations, one can find a factor which modern historians do not emphasize too much.

That factor is this: With the emergence of the historical period linked to the emergence of writing, it is dramatically found that the civilizations involved are already great, and ALREADY have developed and perfected what can easily be recognized as enormous power structures.

This can only mean that our species became preoccupied with the designing of power structures during the long prehistorical period and did so without writing and the particular kind of literacy associated with it.

This somewhat means that the designing, developing, implementing, and the maintenance of a human species power structure is not completely dependent on writing and the particular kind of literacy associated with it.

This is the same as suggesting that writing/literacy is not the key or central ingredient to formatting a power structure.

There are very few human elements that can equally and thus consistently transcend and link the very long prehistorical and the rather short historical periods of our species.

But certainly, the factor of secrecy is one of those elements, largely because secrecy can be conducted behind the scenes of writing and literacy, and even in their total absence.

And indeed, it is quite probable that writing, and literacy can be secretly managed on behalf of this or that power structure.

THE NATURE OF SECRECY

The nature of secrecy is, of course, to keep something hidden from others, and the modern definitions can altogether be groked accordingly.

1. Something kept hidden or unexplained;
2. Something kept from the knowledge of others or shared only confidentially with a few;
3. Something constructed so as to elude observation or detection;
4. Something revealed only to the initiated;
5. Working with hidden aims or methods;
6. Remote from human frequentation or notice;
7. Something kept unexplained;
8. Something hidden, but taken to be a specific or a key to a desired end;
9. Something done or achieved without attracting attention;
10. Action or behavior done with stealth, artful deception, or with skillful avoidance of detection and in violation of usage, law, authority, or established knowledge;
11. The habit or practice of keeping secrets or maintaining privacy and concealment.

The foregoing definitions are, of course, modern and consist of contemporary understanding as to what comprises the whole of secrecy.

It is usually dangerous to project contemporary understandings backward in time -- the process is called anachronistic application -- and superimpose them on by-gone peoples, societies, and civilizations, thereby arriving at a sometimes gross misinterpretation of the past.

However, projecting the contemporary definitions of SECRECY back into the past, even into the very distant past, probably is not too much an anachronistic application.

Indeed, it seems quite likely that our species, either as Homo sapiens sapiens, or as Cro-Magnon Man, understood elements of secrecy from the get-go 35,000 years ago, and also groked that secrecy was opportune for designing power structures.

EMPOWERMENT ITEMS TO IDENTIFY

CONCEPTUALIZE FIVE GENERAL AREAS OF SOCIETAL SECRECY
THAT WOULD BE NECESSARY TO PERPETUATE
POWERLESSNESS AMONG THE POWERLESS.

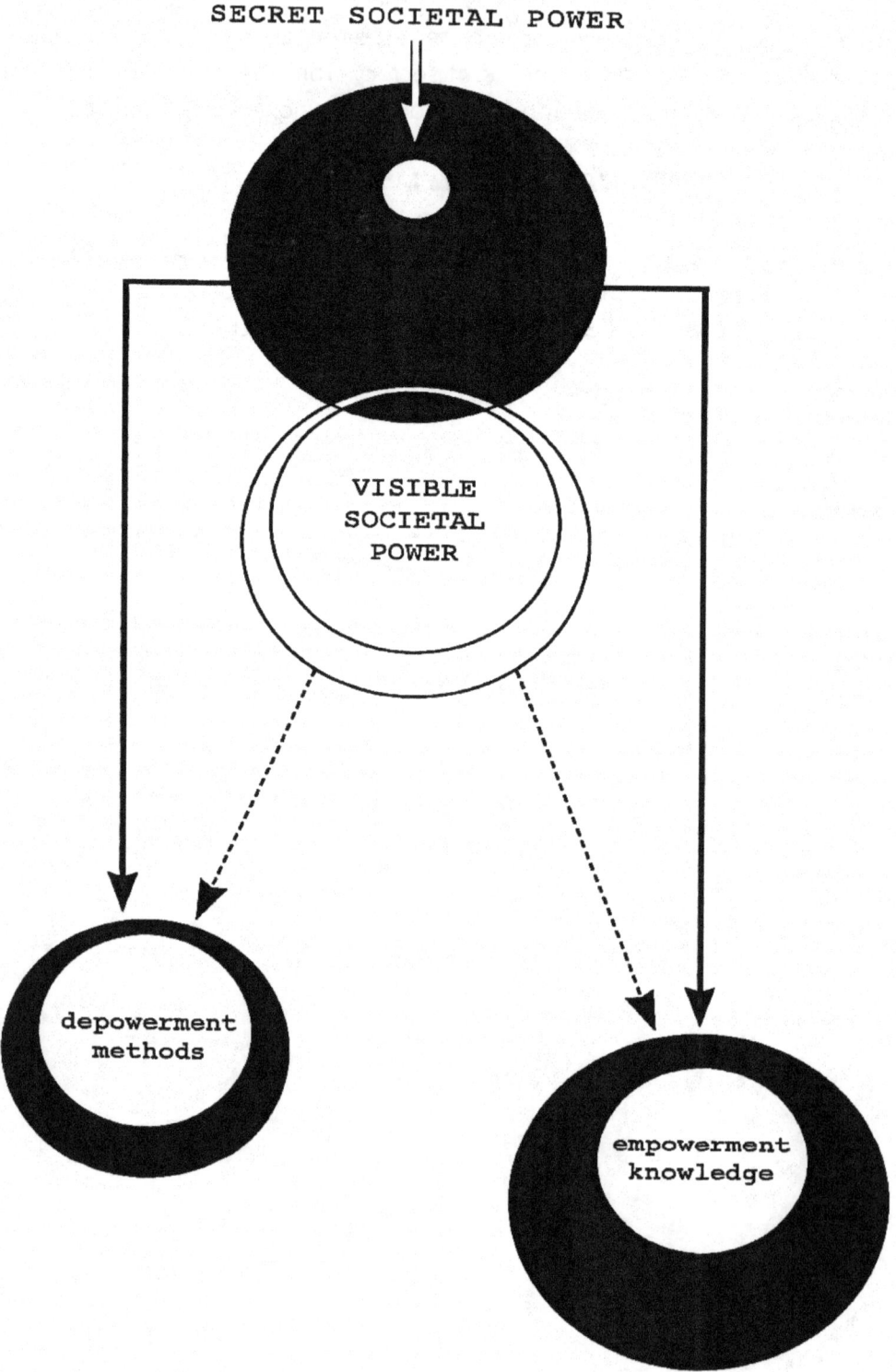

PART TWO
THE SOCIETAL PANORAMA OF POWER

Chapter 6

SOCIETAL POWER vs THE ABSENCE OF POWER SCHOOLS

MANY INDIVIDUALS want to discover ways and means that might lead to some kind of empowerment.

But if they have very little comprehension of the vast and enduring societal panorama of power, then their empowerment efforts might end up resembling a candle undergoing meltdown until the flame extinguishes.

There are two principal reasons, which can be thought of as barriers to gaining empowerment.

The first barrier consists of the easily recognizable fact that power is considered extremely precious by the powerful, and so gaining access to it is made as difficult and as complicated as possible.

The second barrier can also be easily recognized, IF one somehow chances to notice its existence.

It is never mentioned by those examining the anatomy of power, and it is never identified and talked about even by those advocating ways and means of empowerment.

Simply put, there are no socially endorsed power schools in which the general public might educationally enroll in order to learn about the nature of power, its manifold elements, and its workings among the populations in general.

As has already been discussed from different perspectives, the activities and problems of power have been present within our species from time immemorial -- so much so that like life and death themselves, power can be thought of as one of the major implacable facts of human existence.

It is not altogether out of order to suggest that wherever humans are or wherever they go, they transport with them not only the human power principle in general, but especially those activities and problems of the kind of power specifically defined as control, authority, and influence over others.

As also discussed earlier, the "others" have to be present in order to have power over them. So wherever humans go they will transport with them the techniques of ensuring the presence of the "others."

Logically speaking, in terms of empowerment and depowerment, the others need to be kept in conditions of depowerment, so as to not become empowered enough to become troublesome to the powerful.

So, techniques rigged to guarantee their depowered existence range from brute force to elegant and subtle conditioning that can produce what is called "co-operative obedience or submission."

SOCIETAL TECHNIQUES AIMED AT PREVENTING WIDE-SPREAD EMPOWERMENT

In modern times, the whole of the techniques is also sometimes referred to as social engineering. Such engineering always has two faces or two sides; the visible or obvious one; and the invisible or not obvious one.

It can be said, without too much error, that most people naturally focus on what is visible, or at least upon what they can perceive.

Thus, it is possible (and logical) to suppose that societal techniques to prevent too much empowerment must contain some kind of expertise that influences perception not only toward the visible aspects of power, but also away from its invisible aspects.

The major societal power dynamics of the modern period do not differ all that much from earlier historical ones. This is to say that while power contexts might change in the historical sense, the essential power structures remain much the same, especially with regard to their visible and invisible faces.

If the above holds water, then it is reasonable to expect that modern books about power will focus only on examinations of its visible aspects.

This focus on the obvious aspects tends to establish what power IS in ways that are both explicit and implicit, with the result that both adherents and detractors of societal power support or attack the visible aspects.

Even those among the powerless seeking some kind of empowerment conceptualize the routes to empowerment in ways that are consistent with the visible aspects.

Having said this much about the visible and invisible aspects of power, it is now necessary to point up what might qualify as the "top dog" invisible aspect of power and societal power structures.

MODERN KNOWLEDGE BY-PASSES IN-DEPTH INFORMATION ABOUT POWER

This top-dog invisible aspect is slightly complicated, so it is necessary to erect some kind of reality basis for it. Thus, it is first necessary to indicate a singular and important fundamental premise supporting the idea of the Modern Age.

This fundamental premise had to do with the objective amassing of knowledge based in organized study and scientific categorizing achieved against the background of the formal techniques of reasoning (i.e., the techniques of logic).

LOGIC itself is defined as the science that studies the formal principles of reasoning.
Thus, in the short time span of about 25 modernist years, there appeared:
TECHNOLOGY - defined as applied science.
BIOLOGY - the science that studies living organisms and vital processes.
BOTANY - a scientific branch of biology dealing with plant life;
ZOOLOGY - a scientific branch of biology concerned with the animal kingdom and its members as individuals and classes of them, and with animal life;
PSYCHOLOGY - the science that studies mind and behavior;
SOCIOLOGY - the science that studies society, social institutions, and social relationships.

The modern age also eventually developed SEXOLOGY -- the study of sex or of the interactions of the sexes, especially among human beings.

The suffix LOGY is taken to mean the organized study and the science of something. And so in keeping with its foundational premise, the modern period produced the several OLOGIES mentioned above.

THE ABSENCE OF THE SCIENCE OF POWEROLOGY

However, among its gigantic amassing of all kinds of organized knowledge, the modernist period DID NOT establish and develop anything akin to POWEROLOGY -- and which, if it existed, would refer to the organized study of power, its science, and the applications of that science.

The crucial reasons for the absence of powerology are not hard to grok.

If power might be thought of as the most important thing in the world, then obtaining it will also be one of the most competitive enterprises in that world.

If that is so, it must follow that how to get power must become shrouded not only in confusions, but in secrecy, and which secrecy needs increasingly to be refined into various deeper and deeper operative levels.

If THAT is so, then logically speaking there must somehow exist an organized study, a science, and an applied technology regarding ways and means to defeat the arising of powerology (and empowerment), and to eradicate whatever might somehow get it started.

THE ABSENCE OF POWER SCHOOLS

This is clearly to say that IF educational powerology is persona non grata within the panorama of societal power structures, then it should of course be taken for granted that anything resembling power schools will never see the light of day.

To repeat for clarity, there are no societally endorsed public educational courses that might be called Power Studies 101 whose curricula would teach students HOW TO understand and gain control, authority, and influence over others.

Of course, such studies would also have to include important information that distinguishes between visible and invisible aspects of power as well as information about functionable methods not only regarding empowerment, but also workable techniques regarding depowerment.

Indeed, and by necessity, the powerology curriculum would obviously have to include important information regarding methods of depowerment, in order to ensure the continuing presence of "others" to have power over.

It can easily be established, with rather convincing obviousness, that power schools do not exist -- at least of the kind that are open to the public.

That this aspect of power is not noticed in a large-scale way is quite remarkable. However, one explanation might be that those who examine and write about the anatomy of power are so conditioned to and fixated on its visible aspects that they cannot espy ANY of its invisible ones.

In any event, if there is a monolithic societal absence of power schools, then by extension there would also have to be an important absence of power studies within other meaningful socializing activities, such as philosophy.

THE ABSENCE OF PHILOSOPHICAL POWER STUDIES

The issues and circumstances of power should have taken on extreme philosophical importance ages ago, for the question might well be asked: How can human societies consider themselves philosophically without figuring out the central meanings and importance that power has?

The three major activities of PHILOSOPHY are:

1. The pursuit of wisdom;
2. A search for truth through logical reasoning rather than factual observation; and
3. An analysis of the grounds of and concepts expressing fundamental beliefs.

If these activities are connected up with power and power-making, then any actual and real pursuit of wisdom has immediately to be jettisoned.

The reasons for this are plentiful. But certainly, one of them, as almost everyone already groks, is that any real pursuit of wisdom will surely be inconvenient to the pursuit of power, and which pursuit is not notable for wisdom questing.

With regard to the second activity of philosophy, a search for truth through logical reasoning can often be in conflict with a search for power based on factual observations -- for example, those of factual force, cunning, deceit, and social conditioning.

And surely the goals of power with regard to control, authority, and influence over others HAS to be ascertained via factual observation rather than by logical reasoning.

With the third activity, there has probably been no societal power structure that would relish and endorse an analysis of either the grounds or the fundamental beliefs concerning power -- unless such analysis proved favorable to it.

Human history is full of narratives about many past philosophers who undertook such analysis which turned out unfavorable, and those philosophers swiftly met with bad ends.

So, philosophers decidedly belong among the "others" that the powerful have control, authority, and influence over. And indeed, it would be logical that the workings of power structures must obtain control and authority over anything that is mind-influencing -- such as philosophy.

It is thus that philosophy, in its purest and ideal sense, must not only be of perpetual, but of serious concern to power structures -- with the result that smart philosophers have long understood that frank philosophical discussions of power as such are not only taboo but can be dangerous.

And so there is almost a complete absence of philosophical studies regarding power. And what does exist along such lines usually does not constitute a study based in logical reasoning, but merely a note about the visible aspects of power.

For example, in 1967, Macmillan, Inc., a major publisher to be sure, brought out THE ENCYCLOPEDIA OF PHILOSOPHY, a tremendous work many years in preparation. It consisted of eight volumes, altogether amounting to just over 2,120 oversized pages. Every conceivable philosophical topic and philosopher was given lengthy write-ups in it.

In this comprehensive compilation, the topic of POWER could not be avoided altogether. So the entry for it consists of only two and a half pages, the short length of which is surely indecent for a topic which is otherwise of such enormous importance.

The entry tells not much more than a streetwise individual will already know about power. It more or less concluded that:

> "To possess power or to be powerful is, then, to have a generalized potentiality for getting one's own way, or for bringing about changes (at least some of which are intended) in other peoples' actions."

Well, what has been quoted above surely reflects what the powerful WISH to be openly known and accepted about power, and the compilers of the encyclopedia did their duty.

THE SOCIETAL FATE OF POWER STUDIES, POWEROLOGY, AND POWER PSYCHOLOGY

If, from the perspective of invested power structures, there are to be no power schools, then it generally must follow that there is to be no knowledge of power either -- at least of the kind made openly available to the powerless who might empower themselves thereby. These, then, are required to be socially conditioned so as to conform and exist within the design and needs of this or that power structure.

But it also must follow that any significant empowerment activities that somehow get going, and which are intended for mass consumption, must swiftly be deconstructed.

There are many horror stories having to do with the deconstruction of such fated empowerment efforts. But one of those efforts is quite significant, precisely because it directly involved making the powerless more powerful.

Early in the twentieth century, various efforts grouped together as power psychology got going in Europe. One of the chief exponents was Alfred Adler (1870-1937), who founded the school of individual psychology.

Adler was among the first to reject the Freudian emphasis upon sex. He maintained that all personality difficulties have their roots in feelings of inferiority (power-lessness) derived from physical, intellectual, or from conflict with the natural and social environment that restricts an individual's need for power and self-assertion.

In Adler's terms, feelings of inferiority (diminished power) were the opposites of feelings of superiority (enhanced power). Adler thus saw behavior disorders as over-compensation for power deficiencies and socio-environmental depowerment.

He founded the school of individual psychology in order to treat and cure individuals suffering from the inferiority complex manifested as diminished power, thereby restoring them to their natural powers of self-assertion. As might be imagined, Adler's school of power psychology got off to a brilliant start.

This kind of thing, of course, constitutes something akin to a nightmare among stalwart managers of power structures.

Within those structures, the existence of diminished and enhanced power is not only of on-going fundamental relevance, but anyway are always delicately balanced even at the top of all power structures.

Alder's goal of re-empowering the depowered thus required subtle deconstruction efforts that would achieve two effects: making him seem foolish in the eyes of his professional peer group, while at the same time tacitly warning that group against pursuing power studies that might lead toward empowerment techniques.

Adler might have understood inferiority complexes quite well, but he clearly did not understand the machinations of power structures.

So, to make things worse for him and his mission of empowerment, in 1927 he produced a seminal book entitled UNDERSTANDING HUMAN NATURE.

Human nature had long been thought of as containing, among its other qualities, the famous or infamous Power Drive, elements of which presumably dwelled in everyone, just as human nature did.

Adler's book came out just when the modern West was scientifically deconstructing the very existence of human nature as something which had any bearing on human fate and destiny.

Thus, in his book, Adler posited that the urge to power was a constituent of human nature itself. As such, power should be dissected to be better understood and managed.

As might be imagined, such an effort, if it ever got underway, could have serious implications to any number of power structures.

Indeed, discovering how to understand and manage power in an organized and presumable scientific fashion threatened to bring the rules and methods of power into fuller disclosure -- something few really wanted because it might give undue advantage to just anyone.

As a result, both the workings of human nature and the pursuit of power psychology disappeared as such. Even so, and if a little dated by now, Adler's books are well worth reading by anyone grappling with the problems of empowerment.

ITEM FOR INVESTIGATION

TRY TO LOCATE A POWER SCHOOL OPEN TO
THE PUBLIC THAT IS ENDORSED AND FUNDED BY A MAINSTREAM POWER
STRUCTURE.

Chapter 7

THE WEB OF SECRETS PREVENTING ACCESS TO EMPOWERMENT

THE ELEVEN most obvious definitions of secrecy have been discussed in chapter 5. Via those definitions it can be supposed that the term secrecy represents the ways and means of hiding things from others.

But in a larger picture, it seems that secrecy is not only a process of hiding things, but an aspect of collective human nature overall.

By way of explanation, if we can think that the "urge" to power is a species-wide aspect of human nature, then it is possible to place the "urge" to secrecy quite close to the power urge. Almost anyone can discover that power and secrecy are always found together or working in tandem.

It is important to point up this factual relationship, because conventional books that review the most obvious anatomy of power NEVER introduce the aspect of secrecy as part-and-parcel of power games always on-going within societal power structures.

THE CONCEPT OF A WEB

Taken from Old Norse into English, the term WEB refers to weaving something so as to snare, entrap, or entangle.

Three of the major definitions of TANGLE are given as:

1. To unite or knit together in intricate confusion;
2. A complicated or confused state or condition;
3. A state of perplexity or complete bewilderment.

It is logical to think that if all the elements of power and empowerment stood revealed to everyone, it would then be difficult to format a power structure of any kind because everyone would more or less be equivalent.

The obvious reason, as already discussed, is that power as control, authority, and influence over others requires the factual and extensive presence of those others who must be maintained in some unequivalent condition of depowerment.

So, the elements of power and empowerment cannot be allowed to stand revealed to everyone, and instead must broadly be cast into a complicated or confused condition.

A power structure can then be designed and formatted which does incorporate the relatively powerless and the powerless who are perplexed within webs of bewilderment, especially with regard to empowerment.

THE CLOSE LINKAGE OF SECRECY AND POWER

The reason for the close linkage of power and secrecy can now be seen as obvious, in that there is no supportable reason for secrecy unless it is used to deny information to others for the empowering benefits of those who instigate the denial.

Power over others can, of course, be achieved by brute force, and there is no secret about that method.

But power over others is also achieved by preventing the others from acquiring real information and knowledge about empowerment.

If this is successful, then the others end up as dysfunctional and bewildered not only regarding a fuller understanding of power itself, but with respect to gaining empowering access to it.

The foregoing refers to affairs of power and power structures that are quite complicated. But to aid in beginning to sort through it, two principal kinds or uses of secrecy can be identified.

Most are familiar with the fact that power structures utilize secrecy to gain or obtain advantages with respect to other power structures, especially regarding militant, economic, and, sometimes, ideological goals.

All those who are incorporated in the power structure, including the relatively powerless, will more or less tolerate and support that kind of secrecy. The other option is to perhaps be conquered by another combative power structure.

But there is another principal use for secrecy, and it is one shared in common by almost all power structures.

In terms of its total population, a power structure is roughly composed of a very small cadre of the powerful and a very large cadre over which the small cadre exert control, authority, and influence.

This very large cadre is often referred to as "the masses" of individuals incorporated in some subservient way into the power structure. But, and to emphasize, without the presence of the incorporated masses, the powerful would not have much to have power over.

There is thus a quite dynamic relationship not only between the relatively powerless and the confirmed powerful, but also between power and secrecy.

Many sociologists have examined this dynamic relationship, but only within the contexts of the belief that the powerless are naturally powerless and so nothing further about them needs to be understood.

It is rare to find any sociologist even hinting that the status of powerlessness among the masses must be maintained as such in order that the power structure remain complete.

There is a useful analogy via which the powerful can be pictured as the head and the powerless as the body. If the powerless suddenly abandon the head, then the head has nothing to be the head of.

DEPRIVING THE MASSES OF POWER KNOWLEDGE

Thus has emerged the central dual situation of power rulership throughout history having to do with the powerless masses.

1. The powerless masses must be kept content and non-combative with regard to the powerful, but in a mental state within which they are acceptive of the powerful; and
2. At the same time, the masses must also be deprived of all knowledge that has any relevance regarding how to become powerful.

This dual situation IS a problem because all individuals of our species are born with a mind that can organize information and figure things out.

This is to say, if only in the generic sense, that all individuals are innately born with a large number of awareness and intelligence faculties. It would be obvious that the on-going existence of such faculties also poses an on-going problem for the managers of power structures.

If these innate faculties were to be nurtured and developed among the powerless masses, then the head of a power structure would be faced with all sorts of problems regarding whom to have power over. Indeed, dramatic revolutions can ensue if the masses become too dissatisfied with the assigned lot as the powerless.

In modern times, those who study and write about the anatomy of power do indicate that the masses within a given power structure must be made to undergo "social conditioning" so as to become "subservient to and acceptive of" the powerful.

However, those investigating the anatomy of power do not penetrate very deeply into what "social conditioning" consists of, how it is instigated, or how it is managed.

There is a reason for this. If they are not exactly the same, social conditioning, behavior modification, and mind-control are at least depowerment siblings having many similar aspects and results.

Social conditioning can, of course, be imposed by abject and overt force, and history is full of such occasions.

But that kind of conditioning usually leaves a residue of resentment, desires for revenge, and, ultimately, rebellion. It can cause quakes within any power structure and even pull down the powerful -- who then are quite likely to be subjected to abject force such as assassination, beheading, and so forth.

Thus, use of overt force on behalf of establishing social conditioning has not proven very workable in the long run, largely because those targeted for the conditioning can recognize it for what it is.

This leaves the option of achieving social conditioning via hidden and secret techniques so as to prevent and inhibit the conditioned from recognizing it for what it is.

This type of activity becomes noticeable not by studying the obvious anatomy of power, but by examining the not-so-obvious anatomy of the powerless together with the ways and means of achieving and maintaining them as such.

THE MAJOR STRUCTURE OF DEPOWERMENT

Those seeking some kind of empowerment usually focus on what they imagine to be its seemingly obvious processes, and usually pay no attention to the processes of depowerment. However, depowerment processes can more factually account for the origins of their perceived powerlessness, and thus their feelings of inferiority.

Alfred Adler, whose empowerment efforts have already been discussed, clearly put one finger on the machinations of depowerment.

He indicated that a principal source of feelings of inferiority, and thus of feelings of powerlessness, were to be found not exclusively within the individual.

The more likely source had to do with societal environments that deconditioned empowerment not only among the masses, but even within given power structures as a whole.

But with this, Adler touched only upon the concept of empowerment and re-empowerment, but not upon HOW societal conditioning toward endemic depowerment proceeds -- and does so with an almost unparalleled and unexamined efficiency.

THE BEST KINDS OF DEPOWERMENT PROCESSES

We might assume that most individuals incorporated into a power structure would not want to undergo conditioning toward depowerment and would probably fight against it if the conditioning became easily identifiable.

Therefore, in order to achieve even a modicum of efficiency, the processes of such conditioning clearly require formats of secrecy that are not easily recognized as such, or even recognized as existing in the first place.

Depowerment processes must not only be secret and subtle, but invisible as well. After all, most will not think to discover and recognize what is apparently not there to recognize.

THE ABSENCE OF POWER SCHOOLS

As already reviewed, hardly anyone seems to recognize the ABSENCE of power schools.

In visible fact, however, attempts to establish what equate to power schools, such as Alfred Adler tried, are shot down and given odiferous reputations.

Indeed, the absence of power school and power-enhancement curriculums is an unmistakable clue regarding the existence of a depowerment agenda of no mean proportions.

THE ABSENCE OF ENCYCLOPEDIAS REGARDING THE SCOPE OF HUMAN POWERS AND ABILITIES

But if absences of power schools might be identified, it can as well come to light that no encyclopedias have ever been compiled that list and describe the whole of known or suspected range of human powers and abilities.

The existence of this important vacuum is almost never identified, and so individuals have no real way of identifying their own powers and abilities.

This vacuum is exceedingly strange, especially with regard to modern scientific and psychological times.

During those times, concise and comprehensive encyclopedias of seashells, slime molds, architectural edifices, of toys and antiques, and of and distant star systems have been produced.

Extensive encyclopedias of psychiatric and psychological disorder have also been produced. But no encyclopedias of human powers and abilities have seen the light of day.

THE ABSENCE OF STUDIES REGARDING THE NATURE AND SCOPE OF HUMAN AWARENESS

The nature of awareness, and its full scope, must constitute a key factor not only in respect to empowerment potentials, but also as a factor for basic survival.

Indeed, those of minimal or deconditioned awareness are likely to become easy victims of just about any agenda or insidious activity.

Expanding one's awareness potentials certainly plays a crucial role with regard to empowerment and to power. Indeed, one has to become aware of something in order to even begin dealing with it. But there are no studies regarding awareness, much less studies regarding how to expand its fabulous spectrum.

THE ABSENCE OF STUDIES REGARDING INTUITION, TELEPATHY, AND FORESIGHT

The attributes of intuition, telepathy, and foresight are so visible among our species and in all cultures, so much so that most at least tacitly accept without question their real existence.

It is true that many books about these three elements have appeared. But extensive and efficient studies of them have NEVER been officially sponsored by any invested societal power structure.

The obvious reason concerns the real possibility that real knowledge and development suggestive of applied technology could come about.

Thus, any full magnification of those three attributes would not only have significant, but decidedly nightmarish implications regarding empowerment and invasions of secrecy webs.

PERPETUATING A STATE OF UNKNOWING REGARDING EMPOWERMENT

When the majority of people are kept in a state of unknowing, they are easier to influence, control, or dominate by the managers of power-structure systems.

The best way of defeating empowerment among the masses is to keep absent ANY knowledge that has real implications toward empowerment. And almost anything along those lines can be rendered invisible, or at least cast into confusion.

The whole of this process can be referred to as the web of secrets preventing access to empowerment. Those who aspire to some kind of empowerment might take more than just a passing interest in this deadly web and its secrets.

THE LONG HISTORY OF DEPOWERMENT BY SOCIETAL DESIGN

The societal prohibition against real and workable power-knowledge is so long-enduring, so long sustained, and so LOGICAL to power-holders, that it need not even be put into print as a directive. It is practically INTUITIVE among power-holders; it is unspoken, it is silent -- and well maintained.

Just imagine, for example, that you are a power-holder of a high office or position.

How would you like to see thousands or millions of the powerless become awakened to their own empowerment -- and turn their eyes toward your power position?

What would you do in such a case? In any event, there is no power structure that can afford to have even a small portion of our species become awaken to our species power faculties. Theoretically awakened, perhaps. But never dynamically awakened.

The best way to accomplish this negative power engineering in the long term is:

1. To permanently hide all effective knowledge concerning empowerment;
2. To permit, even encourage, the production of disinformation about empowerment which won't result in empowerment;
3. To make the issues of depowerment so completely invisible that the term itself is not linguistically present and is not therefore to be found in dictionaries.

The three items above more or less characterize the web of secrets that efficiently prevent access to empowerment.

ITEMS TO CONTEMPLATE AND VERIFY

NO POWER SCHOOLS.
NO ENCYCLOPEDIAS OF HUMAN POWERS AND ABILITIES.
NO STUDIES REGARDING THE NATURE OF AWARENESS.
NO PRODUCTIVE STUDIES REGARDING INTUITION, TELEPATHY, AND FORESIGHT.

KNOWLEDGE MANAGEMENT
BY SOCIETAL DESIGN DURING THE MODERNIST PERIOD

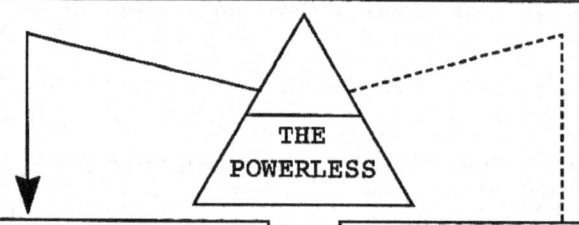

KNOWLEDGE "YES" LIST	KNOWLEDGE "NO" LIST
ACCEPTED EXTENSIONS OF THE SOCIETAL POWER PYRAMID	NOT ACCEPTED EXTENSIONS OF THE HUMAN INDIVIDUAL
SOME KNOWLEDGE ACCUMULATED AND EDUCATION AVAILABLE	NO KNOWLEDGE ACCUMULATED AND NO EDUCATION AVAILABLE
Business Banking Economics of physical substances Politics Limited literacy Media Military Physical sciences Group Sociology studies Social control & conditioning techniques Psychology formats that avoid "B" List items Memory based in physiology Conventional formats of spying	Human power spectrum Scope of awareness The nature of power Kinds of intelligence Types and real extent of human sensing Types of intuition Dynamics of creativity Nature of the individual Subtle human energies Types of perceptions Telepathy Mind Over Matter Exceptional human experiencing Non-conventional method of spying
CONSTRUCTED AND SPONSORED BECAUSE NEEDED BY SOCIETAL POWER STRUCTURES	DECONSTRUCTED AND NOT SPONSORED BECAUSE OF THREAT TO POWER STRUCTURE CONTROL
KNOWLEDGE ACCESS ON "NEED-TO-KNOW" ONLY	CONFUSE AND PUNISH ALL ATTEMPTED KNOWLEDGE ACCESS

YOU - AND YOUR POWER?

FIGURE 6.

Chapter 8

THE TRADITIONAL POWER PYRAMID

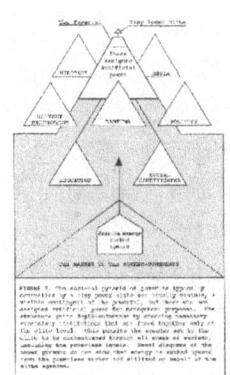

OF ALL the possible designs for societal power structures, the shape of the structure as a pyramid has been most prevalent throughout history.

Therefore, that design has long been accepted not only as traditional, but as inherently natural within our species as a whole. So, the pyramidal power structure is assumed to be emblematic and symbolic of power itself.

One of the subtle results of this is that writers seeking to reveal the anatomy of power end up assessing not the anatomy of power itself, but the anatomy of the conventional power pyramid.

This is an important distinction to be made by those who can grok it, in that a societal power pyramid can house power, but the house is not power itself.

Even so, societal power pyramids are quite real enough, and within the contexts of this book their anatomy needs to be examined.

SOCIAL CONDITIONING ON BEHALF OF A PYRAMIDAL POWER STRUCTURE

As we have seen, the concept of "social conditioning" is pointed up in conventional discussions of power, which also establish that it is generally achieved by two visible methods:

1. Affirmative rewards to those who agree to work on behalf of supporting the power structure;
2. Condign punishment of those who go against the power structure.

Condign punishment refers to punishment that is thought to be deserved and appropriate within the contexts of any given power structure. Examples of it range from mere social and professional condemnation to serious imprisonment or terminal execution.

Such punishment of course is designed to rid power structures of real or imagined misfits. But in terms of social conditioning contexts, it is also quite helpful in demonstrating to the potentially obstreperous, and to everyone, what can happen if they step outside of social conditioning norms. It is a powerful tool.

But beyond mentioning that social conditioning is achieved by affirmative reward and condign punishment, none of the conventional assessments enter into extensive discussions regarding how wholesale depowerment is subtly achieved. So it is exceedingly difficult to discover the ways and means employed to achieve that particular kind of conditioning.

As seen in the foregoing chapter, those processes need to be so entirely subtle that they are enmeshed in invisible, but nevertheless strong, webs of secrets.

However, there is more to social conditioning than punishment and reward -- such as subtle formats of general behavior modification and mind-control of the masses. In this sense, the traditional power pyramid needs to be examined afresh.

THE CONVENTIONAL CONCEPT OF THE POWER PYRAMID DESIGN

As briefly mentioned in chapter 3, the design of the conventional power pyramid is usually presented in the neat shape of an equilateral triangle.

At the top of the power pyramid, called the Apex, will be found either an individual or a small elite group who exercise, demand, and receive obedience from the increasingly large strata beneath them.

Descending from the apex toward the broad base of the pyramid, one will find what are commonly called citizens and workers.

They, of course, owe allegiance and support to the apex occupants who are guiding or controlling their society, supposedly on behalf of the pyramid entire.

The "top dogs," as they are often referred to, are those few apex dwellers who exercise ultimate control, authority and influence throughout the entire pyramid collective.

The underdogs consist of the increasingly larger masses beneath the apex who volunteer or are conditioned so as to respond to and be managed by the top dogs.

The chief VISIBLE vehicles for the conditioning of the underdogs consist of some kind of affirmative rewards together with examples of condign punishment when necessary or needed.

In this sense, the societal power pyramid can be seen as incorporating and enforcing the two most famous aspects of stimulus-response behaviorism -- pain if in error, and reward if in agreement.

INVISIBLE ASPECTS OF THE CONVENTIONAL POWER PYRAMID

If the anatomy of the conventional power pyramid design is studied in depth, it turns out that certain, but exceedingly important and more complex, factors are conveniently smoothed over by casting the design into the neat shape of an equilateral triangle.

This smoothing over more or less renders certain factors relatively invisible. As it is, though, if they are studied in depth, there is no societal power structure that can really be rendered as a neat equilateral pyramid.

Power-holders within the pyramid are almost certainly aware of this, and so it is to be wondered why the idea of the balanced equilateral shape is publicly offered up in the first place.

One possible reason is that the neat shape presents an apparently complete, authoritative but exceedingly simplified visage of power which, on average, can be understood by the simple-minded and accepted by the naive.

If so, then the neat shape, endorsed as accurate and valid by the powerful, and offered up to the public, serves some meaningful function in the social conditioning of the public. Indeed, the neat shape serves to occlude easy perception of various problems and inconsistencies always present in any societal power structure. These, then, remain invisible.

NUMERICAL POPULATIONS INCORPORATED INTO A SOCIETAL POWER STRUCTURE

Perhaps the first of such inconsistencies has to do with the actual numerical count of populations thought to be incorporated into the pyramidal schematic.

This numerical count has briefly been alluded to in chapter 3, where it was indicated that the subservient and powerless masses conventionally seen as incorporated into the structure can be exceedingly greater than the small, even tiny, numerical powerful at the power apex.

The numerical differences can be tremendous, as in the cases of those present-day nations in which the small cadre of the powerful exert control over massive populations of many hundreds of millions.

It might be thought of as splitting hairs if one considers the difference between "incorporated into" and "controlled by."

But if this difference is examined, it can be understood that the powerless masses are not actually incorporated into a power structure. They are merely controlled by it either by agreement or by force.

The term INCORPORATE is defined as:

1. To unite thoroughly with or work indistinguishably into something already existent; and

2. To blend or combine thoroughly to form a consistent whole.

Technically speaking, then, the vast populations of the powerless cannot actually be incorporated into a power structure in order to form a consistent whole.

The reason is obvious enough. Doing so would erase the important distinctions between the powerless and the powerful.

Furthermore, it can easily be verified that nowhere will the small cadres of the powerful wish, desire, or accept any such thing.

In this sense, a power structure has a more limited definition which refers to the very small populations of the powerful themselves, who structure control over the enormously extensive powerless masses.

If the foregoing can be considered, then the conventional idea of the incorporative power structure feasibility breaks apart into two structures:

1. The controllers - the actual power structure of the small minority powerful; and
2. The controlees - the actual powerless structure of the enormous majority powerless.

The latter, of course, cannot be incorporated into the former. As already pointed up, permitting this would erase the important boundaries between the powerless and the powerful.

Those who truly have power to determine which way things should or should not go "like" to keep their participating numbers as limited as possible.

This is easily verifiable and seems to have something to do as a whole with human nature and our species unshakeable idea: that it is feasible that one singular individual COULD rule the entire species, i.e., the known human world.

THE MULTIPLICITY OF POWER STRUCTURES WITHIN A POWER STRUCTURE

The idea that the entire nature of a power structure can be understood or groked as a neat equilateral pyramid definitely conceals the fact that a given power structure contains numerous power structures that are vitally dynamic -- each of which seek dominance over all the others.

In this case, if one of these is to achieve dominance, it IS necessary to somehow incorporate all the other contenders, or to eradicate them.

The powerless are usually irrelevant in this, since what is involved is a power-trip-thing among the already powerful or the potentially powerful.

In reality, a power structure cannot be thought of as one singular structure. In actual terms, "a" power structure is a multiplex construction or ensemble made up of numerous power structures, all of which can, and often do, have their separate areas of control, authority, and influence.

The idea that these can be internalized or incorporated so as to seem a unified whole makes it difficult to identify from where the real control, authority, and influence of power actually emanates and downloads.

In that sense, many conspiracy theorists build good cases for the existence of real controlling power always being behind-the-scenes of visibly perceived power.

POWER WITH REGARD TO MEANINGFUL AREAS OF ACTIVITY

To get more intimately into what is involved in the multiplexity, if power is defined as control, authority, and influence over others, it surely needs to be defined in an additional aspect: control, authority, and influence over meaningful areas of activity.

Some of these areas of activity can easily be identified as military, economic, political, socio-cultural, educational, and last, but not the least, secret intelligence and "workings" typically associated with secrecy.

Within the neat pyramidal concept, these are often indicated as "arms" of power and the powerful. But in actual fact they either are, or can be, power structures in their own right. Each can also have covert or behind-the-scenes power of sometimes enormous magnitude.

All things considered, most consistently real power is probably closely associated with:

1. The very few of our species who hold economic and financial influences of some magnitude;
2. Providing they also possess or have covert access to significant intelligence networks; and as well
3. Are insulated in some productive fashion from the problems associated with that ephemeral factor called philosophical ethics.

Wealth is always associated with power, but wealth alone does not automatically grant access to societal power, an access which many who are not wealthy often achieve.

THE "ARM" OF POWER STRUCTURES INVESTED WITH
THE POWERS OF EDUCATING THE MASSES

The point of all of the foregoing has been to dissect the conventional picture of a societal power structure, and to do so in a manner that more accurately distinguishes between the collective powerful entity and the collective powerless entity.

Each of these can be thought of as "civilizations" in their own right, with the minority powerful civilization controlling the massive powerless one.

The central purpose of working toward identifying this distinction is that if the powerless are to be controlled, then they, as a recognizable collective entity, must somehow be made knowingly or unknowingly amenable to the control.

Beyond the comical aspects of this, there is a serious societal element involved.

The best vehicle for implementing and maintaining control is the socio-cultural factor called education -- and which, from the viewpoint of the really powerful, can be designed to consist of anything and everything except real knowledge regarding ways and means of empowerment.

It is a given that a fairly high percentage of all people eagerly subscribe to and take advantage of societally approved education if it is made available to them.

But behind-the-scenes of this enthusiasm, it is to be wondered who decides what societally approved education is to consist of. This deciding includes:

What textbooks are to be designed and published;
How histories are to be written according to which slant;
What is considered appropriate to philosophical, scientific, and sociological teachings;
And, as well, what is to be educated toward and what is, so to speak, to be de-educated away from.

In his book, THE ANATOMY OF POWER, John Kenneth Galbraith all too briefly discusses the necessity of social conditioning with regard to educationally formatting the masses so as to establish among them a broad consensus acceptance of organized power structures.

He observes that the conditioning has two faces, one having to do with what the masses need to be educated toward, and second, what they need to be educated away from. Beyond that observation, Galbraith then leaves it to the imagination of the reader what the two faces more deeply consist of.

Obviously, the social conditioning leads toward installing acceptance of power and the powerful -- and leads away from installing knowledge about power and empowerment, and about depowerment as well.

It is not too much to say, then, that societally approved educational formats will contain vacuums of knowledge regarding anything that explicitly or implicitly might have to do with empowerment and depowerment.

Indeed, omitting certain factors from the overall human knowledge pool is clearly one excellent way of keeping them invisible and inaccessible.

But WHAT is efficiently to be omitted is certainly understood by societal power structures. Otherwise, how could anyone know what to omit?

With exceptions to be discussed ahead, it is thus possible that the web of secrets preventing access to knowledge of empowerment is subtly implemented via the deliberately selected parameters of societally approved education.

By far and large, humans usually and unquestionably assume the authenticity and truth regarding education downloading from approved societal power sources.

Whatever they have NOT learned via such sources will be considered as unreal to them -- and they will castigate it as such.

This means that if the officially educated of a given power structure have not learned of the existence of empowerment and depowerment processes, then they, themselves, will be of tremendous assistance in denying the possibility of such processes.

Thus, efforts to keep the powerless in conditions of depowerment are rather exquisitely designed.

AN EXERCISE TO IMAGINE

OUTLINE FIVE OR MORE PROCESSES THAT DEFEAT EMPOWERMENT AND ENHANCE DEPOWERMENT.

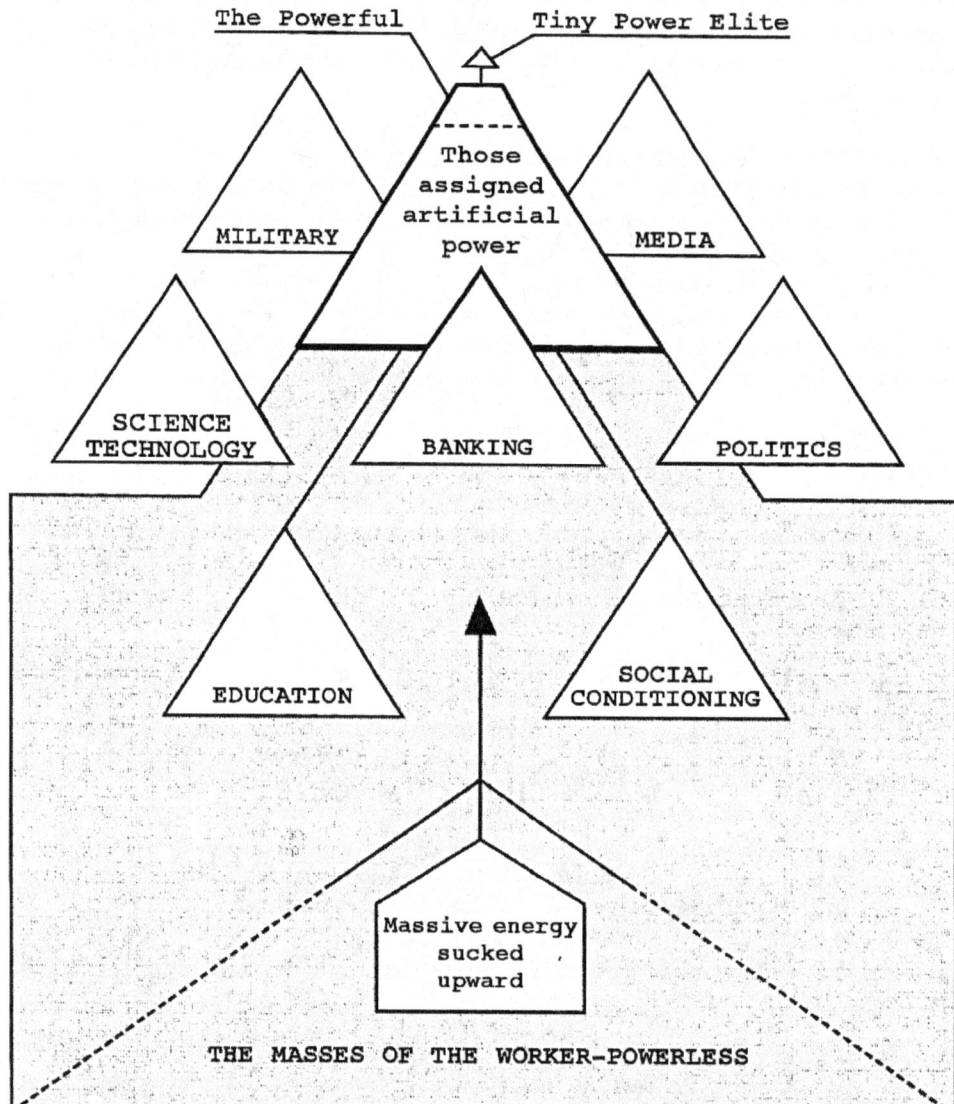

FIGURE 7. The societal pyramid of power is typically controlled by a tiny power elite not usually visible, a visible contingent of the powerful, and those who are assigned artificial power for management purposes. The structure gains depth-endurance by erecting necessary subsidiary institutions that are fused together only at the elite level. This permits the agendas set by the elite to be orchestrated through all areas of society, including the powerless levels. Usual diagrams of the power pyramid do not show that energy is sucked upward from the powerless worker and utilized on behalf of the elite agendas.

Chapter 9
FOUR GENERIC KINDS OF INDIVIDUAL AND SOCIETAL POWER

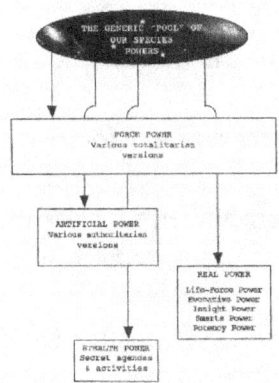

FIGURE 8. The human species has many powers some of which have been identified, while others remain undiscovered, perhaps deliberately so. The four powers described appear to be generic. They emerge in all cultural settings, and are thus easy to recognize.

IT IS generally understood that "power games" go on within societal and corporate power pyramids.

It therefore seems that those games denote where the power action is at, and so those seeking to ascend to the heights of the power pyramid feel obliged to take part in the games.

But any action that can be perceived is probably quite superficial and belongs to the fifth of the power iceberg that is visible above the water line. The visible aspects will always obscure subtle aspects and problems.

AN OBSCURED PROBLEM THAT CAN DEFEAT EMPOWERMENT

Power games will be discussed in the following chapter. Before getting into that topic, it is necessary to point up a problem that is central to power games, but which is never mentioned in conventional discussions about power.

The lack of discussions of course tends to obscure the existence of the problem and render it into at least quasi invisibility.

It has to do with what kinds of power are involved within this or that power game -- and if there ever have been problems characterized by massive apparencies and illusions, this is certainly one of them.

The precise function of this chapter is:

1. To at least bring to light some of the dimensions of this problem; and
2. To forewarn that if one wishes to enter into power games, but cannot identify the kinds of power involved, one will shortly find oneself in some kind of clobbered condition.

WHY THE PROBLEM BECOMES OBSCURED

The first dimension of the obscured problem has to do with why it is obscured in the first place.

Most people realize that different kinds of power exist, and this is more or less in keeping with the old axiom that power has a thousand different faces.

Anything having so many different faces as its essential nature is a vast multiplex of some kind and will therefore be quite complex.

A very important aspect having to do with achieving more empowerment is that the thinking patterns of the depowered are usually limited by what they think power consists of.

One really can't assign blame to the powerless for this deficiency, because what they do think power consists of has been conditioned into them by socio-environmental factors.

Their frames of reference regarding power will therefore be mostly responsive to the conditioning rather than to the dynamic kinds of power itself.

FRAMES OF REFERENCE REGARDING WHAT POWER IS THOUGHT TO CONSIST OF

To help grok this overall panorama better, just imagine a large movie multiplex having fifty small theaters each showing a film that portrays a different kind of power.

On average, people will gravitate toward the theaters showing the kind of power with which they are most familiar.

One likely reason for this is that they have mental frames of reference for that kind of power, but not for the other kinds. It is their conditioned frames of reference that make that kind of power real to them.

This overall situation is important when it comes to the processes of empowerment at the individual level -- because most people who would like empowerment will attempt to achieve it within the contexts of their existing frames of reference.

This situation is important if viewed from the panoramic level of the powerful, and who, as history attests, are not all that receptive to any wholesale real empowerment at the individual level.

One way to prevent, or at least to complicate, the individual kind of empowerment is to keep the frames of reference regarding power as limited and as simple as possible.

If something, such as power, IS complex, but people are conditioned to think it is simple, then the chances are very good that they will never penetrate into the complexity.

The chances are also very good that those who can deal with the complexity will achieve control, authority, and influence over those who cannot.

Another observable way to limit these frames of reference regarding power is more subtle, but equally effective. This involves setting up intellectual and educational frames of reference, each of which apparently identifies different types of power.

On closer inspection, however, those allegedly different types of power turn out to have quite similar societal power structures.

INTELLECTUALISMS MISTAKEN AS DIFFERENT KINDS OF POWER

For example, most will intellectually assume that socialism, democracy, communism, capitalism, authoritarianism, totalitarianism, anarchism, revolutionism, fundamentalism, individualism, and even utopianism, represent different kinds of power.

The typical pyramidal power structure can be superimposed with great ease on all of those intellectualisms. Yet they are not kinds of power, but merely refer to methods or ways whereby wealth, influence, belief, and information are to be managed within the structure.

Power still belongs to the elite at the tops of the pyramids.

Most frames of reference and intellectualisms regarding power are, of course, only fabricated ideas that shift about and come and go.

The only three aspects about them that remain similar and familiar over time are the pyramidal formats themselves, their internal power ladders, and how empowerment and depowerment are to be managed.

Indeed, there is upward power mobility to be had even among anarchists and Utopians, and certainly among intellectuals themselves, and so there will be power ladders to climb in order to gain proximity to chief anarchists, Utopians, and intellectuals.

If one conceptualizes empowerment within the contexts of shifting, fabricated ideas about power, then it is little wonder that the processes of empowerment remain elusive, if not dumbfounding.

GENERIC KINDS OF POWER

It is interesting to note that most writers attempting to establish the conventional anatomy of power do not distinguish very well between the kinds.

A possible explanation for this omission is that books about power are written from the viewpoint of the powerful AFTER their control/authority over others has become consolidated AS societal power.

All formats of consolidated societal power quickly assume the power pyramid design, after which they all look relatively the same. And so it is easy enough to assume that kinds of power need not be distinguished in the conventional sense.

But if the anatomy of power is examined from the viewpoint of the powerless, as well as from any viewpoint relevant to empowerment and depowerment, then identifying actual kinds of power takes on strategic and tactical meaning.

The reason is that different kinds of power require the implementation of different kinds of depowerment in order to disarm the masses.

As has been mentioned in chapter 2, societal power formats are artifices designed to acquire and manage power by the few.

Within the contexts of this chapter, it can now be somewhat groked that the management is obtained by the few via whatever frames of reference or intellectualisms are deemed by them as necessary or convenient. It is obvious that the powerless do not set up frames of reference for power.

Yet, although the societal power structures are designed social artifices, basic human power per se is neither an artifice nor an intellectualism. Indeed, the artifices and intellectualisms are merely attached or appended to the real existence of our species innate and indwelling powers.

If this is the case, then our species must have generic powers so that the artifices and intellectualisms can become attached to them. Indeed, if the generic powers did not exist, then the artifices and intellectualisms would have nothing to attach to.

The term GENERIC refers to whatever relates to or is characteristic of a whole group, class, or species.

It would be somewhat comical to assume that our species is not a power species. Indeed, our species physically, mentally, and creatively displays, even flaunts, its power concomitants.

Thus, our species must have many generic kinds of power, of which the following four are the most obvious and easily identifiable:

1. FORCE POWER;
2. ARTIFICIAL POWER;
3. REAL POWER;
4. STEALTH POWER.

On average, it is not too stressful to isolate at least the parameters of these four generic kinds of power -- because they are always being experienced in a social sense at all levels and within given social frameworks.

The only real difficulty is that the four kinds are usually found superimposed or intermixed in some fashion, which makes it a challenge to establish descriptive definitions for them.

There is an advantage, though. People generally realize that the four kinds do exist.

FORCE POWER

The most familiar generic, and thus most obvious kind of power is force power because:

1. Force power is encountered on a daily experiential basis; and
2. Force power enjoys a vivid and rich historical and educational background, and also has high entertainment value.

In its more overt format, and bluntly put, force power is the power of the fist, gun, club; the power of armies; the power of take-overs.

More subtly, it is the power of persuasion by force, of mind-conditioning, educational programming; of group or peer pressuring, of conformity; it is also the power of apprehension, terror, fear, and reprisals.

Force power can be either overt or covert. Usually it is overt, even if subtle, since most merchants of this kind of power want it to be clearly and unambiguously recognized.

Force power probably should be more clearly understood as some kind of enforcement-power via fear, since its key word IS enforcement combined with fear of duress and punishment if the enforcement by itself does not succeed.

Force power is distinguishable from artificial power and real power because the latter two are based upon some hind of social agreement. But force power is based in nonagreement, which is to say in some kind of duress or threat of it.

It must again be pointed up that if there is no one to have something enforced upon them, then force power cannot exist.

Doubtlessly, force power draws or sucks upon the weaknesses, incompetence, or ignorance of others, especially if they are in a depowered condition, or are rendered into it by force power.

This societal power arrangement is perfectly logical. If there is nothing or no one to dominate, then domination by force cannot exist either. And so domination is but one of the many formats of force power.

So force power seems majorly to be composed of enforcement of some kind. But whether it is composed of enforcing opinions, beliefs, or realities onto others, or of aggression of armed military take-over might, it can easily be viewed as parasitic.

In other words, force power "feeds" on enforcement, and thus those who are victims of force power constitute the "host" that force power parasites feed upon.

Just imagine yourself as a force power merchant with nothing or no one to enforce something on. You might get the idea that force power is a parasite always looking for something or someone to feed upon in order to sustain its own sense of why it is existing.

Manifestations of force power almost always end in disaster of some kind, later if not sooner. It is the largest contributor on this planet to what is referred to as "conflict."

Therefore, it is not surprising that force power is ultimately experienced as destructive -- even though its opening shots, so to speak, may seem to be mounted on glory, success, and that particular ecstasy that arises out of domination ideas.

Clever force power managers realize that they can thrive if they engineer general conditions of depowerment and maintain them as such.

ARTIFICIAL POWER

It is a generic aspect of our species to engineer and erect societal power structures, within which are different gradients of power management. These range downward from the most powerful to the least powerful.

The gradients, however, are delegated by the powerful, and so they do not consist of powers unto themselves.

Delegated power can therefore be thought of as artificial power -- as something contrived, produced, or effected by art or artifice rather than by nature.

In any event, those gaining access to artificial power are managing it on behalf of the powerful.

The distinction of artificial power may be a little difficult to work with, but it is necessary in order to help distinguish real power.

If control, authority, or influence are inspected closely enough, it can be seen that they represent not power itself, but status within an organized societal power framework.

Status may automatically bestow certain kinds of authority, but only in temporary or artificial ways.

This is to say that power is attributed to the status, not to the occupant of the status.

Those trying to climb power ladders within a power structure are more actually climbing status ladders.

There is thus a persistent confusion between status and power in that they are mistakenly seen as much the same thing.

However, status can easily come -- and just as easily go. Many do achieve this or that kind of status, but when they exit or retire from it, they are suddenly without power (authority) again.

If one subtracts the status from apparent power-figures, they are seen as having no power at all. They are again nobody.

And here is the chief scenario within which power is said to be a fickle thing -- when in observable actuality it is status that is more fickle.

Power that temporarily comes and goes with the status cannot really be said to constitute real power. It is artificial power, temporarily gained or bestowed.

REAL POWER

The basic distinction between artificial and real power is that the former is socially contrived and engineered whereas the latter is not artificial, contrived, fraudulent, or illusory.

It isn't so easy to identify and discuss real power -- largely because it is a human species attribute that can escape, and give the finger to, the control, authority, and influence that most societal power structures are based upon.

So most societal power structures are perpetually nervous at the possibility of real power. As a result, educational and social conditioning steps are taken to make general understanding of it as convoluted and impenetrable as possible.

The term REAL is defined as:

1. Of or relating to fixed, permanent, actual, or immovable things that have self-manifesting existence;
2. Something that is neither derivative, dependent, nor contrived, but exists necessarily of and in itself.

More intimate discussions regarding real power will commence in Part Three ahead. But here it needs to be pointed up that while artificial power can intellectually be recognized as such, real power seems to be a felt or a sensed thing.

This is to say that it is felt or sensed by OTHERS in some kind of empathic, intuitive, or telepathic manner, and in ways that go beyond the contexts of mere status-holding.

Those manifesting real power can of course achieve status, too. But it doesn't seem to matter if status is conferred or not.

One of the major reasons it is difficult to recognize and identify the contexts of real power is that they extend beyond the physical and the tangible.

Within conventional contexts, power is judged almost exclusively as control of the tangible, or what represents it such as wealth, property, and money.

The conventional contexts of power are therefore expressed via trenchant materialism and whatever can be seen as fitting into that particular philosophy.

The principal methods that advocates of materialism seize upon to deal with and control the intangible is to deny it exists and then to socially condition against any knowledge about it.

From the viewpoint of materialism, this is a logical thing to do regarding power.

Indeed, within the contexts of power over the tangible, it is easy to know what there is to have power over -- and this includes the powerless in the form of their physical bodies, not in their form as beings of our species.

If the existence of the intangible, including the intangible nature of real power, was to be admitted as a real reality, then impressive confusions would immediately surface regarding what, exactly, one is to have power over.

The best way to avoid the emergence of such confusions is to deny the existence of the intangible altogether -- and, of course, to somehow punish those who seek efficient enlightenment along those lines.

Thus, power can be seen as only having a direct relationship to the tangible material, and which power can be managed by contrived, artificial, and artful cunning.

STEALTH POWER

If our species is a power species, then it must contain generic faculties and mental mechanisms via which power can be efficiently manifested, implemented, and controlled with regard to specific usage.

It is possible to assume as much because all other remarkable attributes of our species that have achieved recognition are understood to have "routes" and "functions" through which they manifest.

Indeed, the human body/mind systems seem designed for utter efficiency in all of their aspects, and when that efficiency is not apparent the reasons must be judged as originating from factors other than in the systems themselves.

It is completely understood that any system, no matter how efficiently designed to function, can become downgraded by factors imposed so as to distort and disarm the efficiency.

Such distorting factors can be imposed, for example, into the efficient systems by social conditioning, mind-control, and by deliberate destimulation of the intelligence and accompanying awarenesses required for the efficient functioning.

Of course, the efficiency can also be deformed by deleting or prohibiting cognitive knowledge packages needed for high-stage power functioning.

Ideally speaking, a truly intelligent power system would be obliged to recognize that it must protect itself against such distorting factors.

There may be many ways that are important in that regard. But there is surely one truly efficient way to effectively achieve that protection.

In both essence and in fact, the truly intelligent power system must take measures so as to conceal its existence from other intelligent power systems which might undertake steps to degrade its functioning.

This means that the truly efficient power system must remain hidden, secretive and, above all, concealed. If this measure is successful enough, then that system can deploy its powers by stealth.

Everyone at least suspects that hidden and secret power exist. The terms HIDDEN and SECRET principally refer to WHAT is kept from observation, view, or recognition.

The term STEALTH, however, is defined as:

1. The act or action of going or proceeding furtively, secretly, or imperceptibly;
2. The intent to escape observation, notice, or identification.

STEALTH, therefore, is a cut above the hidden and the secret, although causing things to become hidden and secret obviously are adjuncts to it.

Additionally, whatever is imperceptible takes on invisibility. Imperceptible stealth therefore can proceed in the clear light of day without being noticed because it is being conducted imperceptibly.

If human history was not full of confirmed examples of stealth power, then it might be easy enough to think that stealth is artificially designed into power games simply as yet another flimsy societal artifice.

But because of the copious evidence attesting to the real existence of stealth power, it is possible to think of it not as mere societal artifice but as a natural and necessary factor innate in any intelligent power system.

This signifies that stealth power is a generic kind of power within our species as a whole.

Indeed, any intelligent power system that becomes visible and identifiable enough to be shot down by other intelligent power systems might be referred to as a stupid power system.

Historical evidence more than suggests that stealth and power somehow go together very closely. And anyone attempting empowerment should always bear this in mind.

If it is possible to suppose that stealth power is an innate factor in our species, then it is to be understood that how it is utilized on behalf of this or that constitutes issues that are clearly separate from the innate factor itself.

THE MOST DISTINCTIVE CHARACTERISTIC OF THE FOUR GENERIC POWERS

Perhaps the most distinctive characteristic of the four generic powers so far identified is that one doesn't need to intellectually study them in a book in order to sense or intuit their presence.

Indeed, even those whose awarenesses and intelligence have been grossly truncated or diminished by negative societal conditioning can still retain a good chance of sensing their presence.

If this is adequately groked, then we are finally talking about awareness and intelligence rather than about intellectualisms and societal artifices. Intellectualisms and societal artifices belong to social activity which can be conditioned in various ways.

But generic forms of awareness and intelligence belong to our species itself.

EXERCISES TO EXPAND AWARENESS OF THE FOUR KINDS OF GENERIC POWERS

MAKE STEALTHY LISTS OF PEOPLE WHO SEEM TO FALL WITHIN EACH OF THE FOUR KINDS OF GENERIC POWERS.

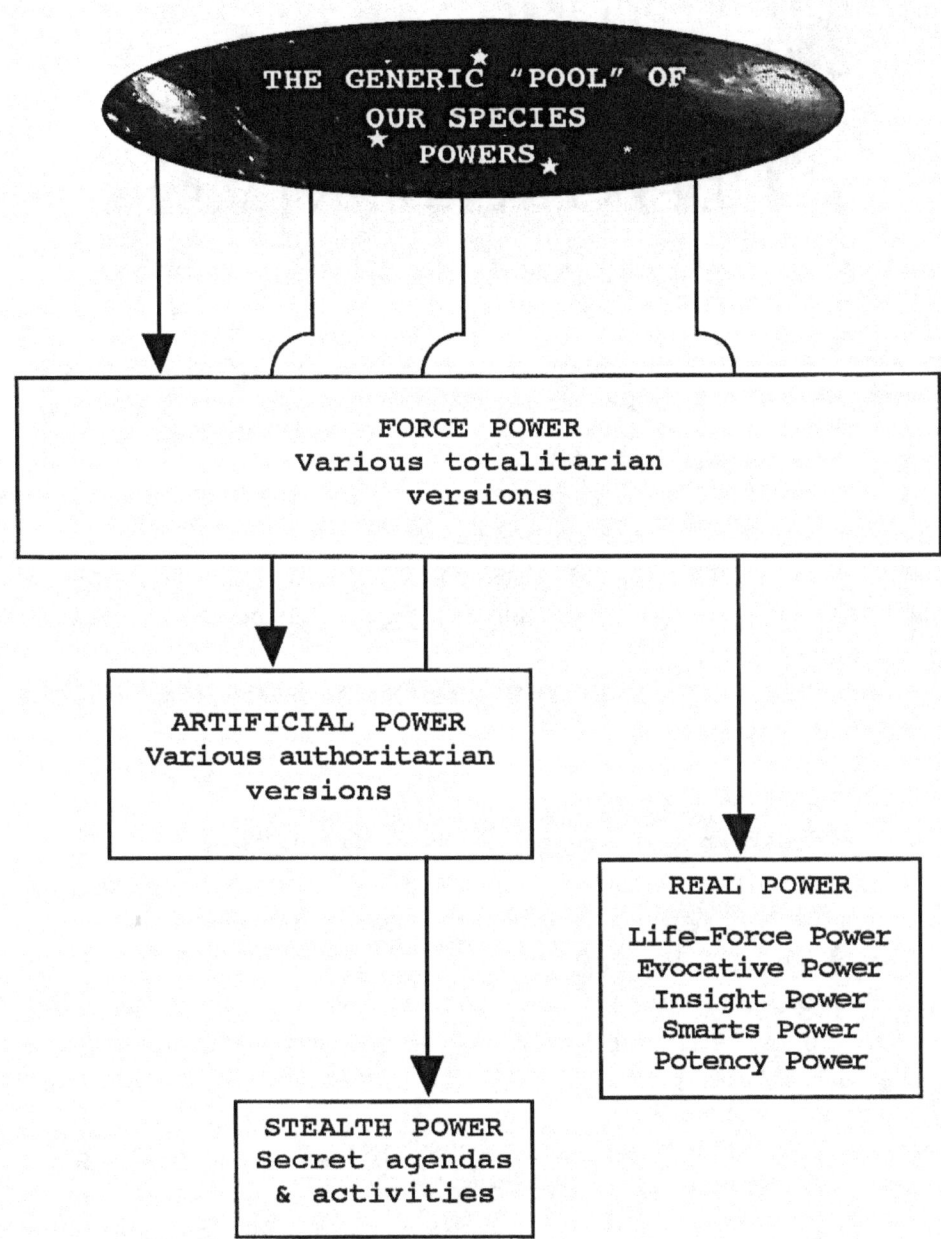

FIGURE 8. The human species has many powers some of which have been identified, while others remain undiscovered, perhaps deliberately so. The four powers described appear to be generic. They emerge in all cultural settings, and are thus easy to recognize.

Chapter 10

EMPOWERMENT AND DEPOWERMENT versus POWER GAMES

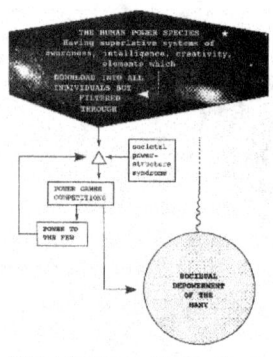

FIGURE 9. On the surfaces of societal power artifices, the concept of "power games" requires the concept of "winners" and "losers," achieved via the concept of "competition rules." Beneath the surface, the actual activity is the "winning" gain of power via depowerment of "losers" by any means possible. Societal power games thus require hidden stealth expertise in achieving societal and general depowerment with the result that depowerment is endemic. This is seen as rational within societal power contexts, even though societal engineering of endemic depowerment cannot be thought of as rational for a species having superlative systems of awareness, intelligence, and creativity.

THE IDEA of power games is a popular and standardized frame of reference, easily thought of as having relevance to empowerment.

So it is generally assumed that all one has to do in order to climb this or that power ladder is to learn to play the power games well enough.

However, the concept of power games has limited application not only with regard to empowerment, but also to what actually goes on within power structures, especially the larger societal ones.

To get into this, it is first necessary to review the official definitions of GAME as found in any competent dictionary:

1. Amusement, diversion, fun, sport;
2. A procedure for gaining an end, or a field of gainful activity;
3. A physical or mental competition conducted according to rules, with the participants in direct opposition to each other;
4. A set of rules governing a game;
5. A situation involving opposing interests given specific information and allowed a choice of moves with the objective of maximizing their wins and minimizing their losses.

Please etch into memory (5) above, especially the ideas of being "given specific information" and being "allowed a choice of moves."

This is important because control, authority, and influence over others largely depends on what types of information can and cannot be given in order to achieve and maintain, yes! the control, authority, and influence over others.

POWER GAMES vs NO POWER GAMES

As discussed in chapter 7, there is one generic type of "specific information" that is hardly ever given to anyone.

That information is specific to knowledge of power itself, and to the ways and means of gaining empowerment.

Information NOT given regarding power and empowerment of course sets up a condition that can be referred to as no-game.

NOT giving information helps ensure that no-games regarding them will come into efficient existence.

In this light, definition (5) above can be slightly rephrased in order to help better grok no-games power situations:

NO-GAMES can be thought of as a situation of opposing interests, such as the powerful vs the powerless, the lesser of which (the powerless) is not given specific information so as to minimize or obviate a choice of moves against the greater (the powerful).

In that sense, the OBJECTIVE of the powerful is to erase and prevent games situations from developing between them and the powerless.

The implications of THIS can perhaps be thought of as a games situation between the powerful and the powerless.

But in so thinking, one can easily miss recognizing the validity and real existence of the no-games objectives -- especially if those objectives are made so imperceptible via stealth powers that they will not be noticed in the first place.

Because of the foregoing, whose reality-making elements can easily be identified by anyone, it is rather certain that power structures contain both games situations AND no-games situations.

If one thinks that learning to play power games is all one has to do, one will, at some point, be in for some surprises and painful defeats.

GAMES AS RACKETS

Most competent dictionaries give RACKET as one of the definitions of games, but they do not elaborate upon that meaning.

With regard to power games, the functional definitions of RACKET are:

1. A fraudulent scheme, enterprise, or activity;
2. A usually illegitimate enterprise made workable by bribery or intimidation (i.e., a version of force power);
3. An easy and lucrative means of livelihood.

The etymology of GAME is not certain, but it seems to derive, at least in part, from GAMMY, and which term is not found in most contemporary dictionaries.

However, the OXFORD dictionary of the English language indicates it early referred to hunted animals and, as slang, to the smell of over-ripe dead flesh.

At about 1890 or earlier, GAMMY was drawn into English from "tramps' slang" with the meaning of "bad, not good" regarding activities or situations that "stink."

It is possible that GAMMY was derived from the French word GAMBI, meaning "crooked."

Dictionaries of modern slang refer to GAME as ON THE GAME, the original meaning being associated with prostitution. William Shakespeare referred, in his work TROILUS AND CRESSIDA (1606), to prostitutes as: "Set them down for sluttish spoils of opportunity, and daughters of the game."

At about 1739, ON THE GAME was given another nuance as "actively engaged in burglary."

POWER GAMES AS GAMMY POWER GAMES

If one examines the general anatomy of power games, it is impossible to think that they, as a whole, can ideally be fitted into the official definitions of games, at least of the type that are played within obedience to and the limits of established rules and guidelines.

Thus, while there is a widely shared perception that power games ARE games, there is nevertheless a large consensus that they tend to be Machiavellian in their working premises.

MACHIAVELLIAN POWER GAMES

The concept of Machiavellianism is of course drawn from the political observations of Niccolò Machiavelli (1469-1527).

In his writings, and especially in his famous book THE PRINCE (which is still kept in print), he advocated the view that politics, from its foundations upward, is fundamentally amoral and that any means however unscrupulous can justifiably be used on behalf of the objective of achieving political power.

He suggested numerous principles of conduct that could justifiably be utilized on behalf of achieving that objective.

The principles are largely characterized by secrecy, cunning, duplicity, clever management of corruption, opportunizing on bad faith, and so forth. His principles along such lines have been assiduously studied ever since he presented them.

And so, Machiavellianism has come to be a synonym for amoral cunning and for justification by power.

In other of his works, however, Machiavelli also attempted to propound a general theory of politics and government that stressed the importance of uncorrupted political culture and vigorous political morality.

His general theory along those lines is not as widely studied as are his principles regarding cunning and duplicity.

POWER GAMES WITH REGARD TO DEPOWERMENT

Power games ultimately imply outcomes involving winners and losers.

While it is true that people do realize this, it seems that the emphasis of interest usually gravitates toward the optimistic potentials of winning -- whether by means fair or foul.

What is not usually considered is that the opponents of a power game must somehow be made to undergo some type of technical depowerment.

In this sense, power games are not really linked too closely to the concept of "May The Best Man/Woman Win." Everything considered about them, such games provide equal opportunity for the worst who can also win.

A full part of power games therefore requires an in-depth working knowledge regarding depowerment of others, especially if they could turn out to be contenders and opponents.

It is possible to consider that THIS type of working knowledge is even more important than a working knowledge of empowerment.

But, as has been discussed, the term DEPOWERMENT doesn't exist, does it?

POWER GAMES vs POWER OBJECTIVES

One of the principal reasons for discussing the more complete contexts of power games is to be able to point up that the idea of games consists of frames of reference that are probably useless in the open fields of power, of power-gaining, and of power-making.

All things considered, it is logical to think that power is not gained, made, or achieved merely in order to play games with it.

In a more actual sense of it, power is not only pursued but is proven and made apparent by gaining objectives. If the objective is seen as important enough, then there is justification for gammy methods and means to be utilized.

As a noun, an OBJECTIVE is defined as:

1. Something toward which effort is directed, or an aim or end of action; and
2. A strategic position to be obtained, or purpose to be achieved, usually via militant design and planning.

Given those definitions, frames of reference for games, and acquisition of objectives will not mesh very well.

The concept of power games is therefore something of a ruse to socially obscure the more serious aspects of power objectives.

It is not too much to say that the concept of power games will interest and fascinate only the naive.

But it is also fair to observe that power games and pursuit of power objective do intermix at certain points.

ITEM TO IMAGINE

IMAGINE/DESIGN SIX METHODS OR MORE TO DEPOWER POWER OPPONENTS -- BEYOND THE FIRST MOST OBVIOUS AND PERMANENT WAY.

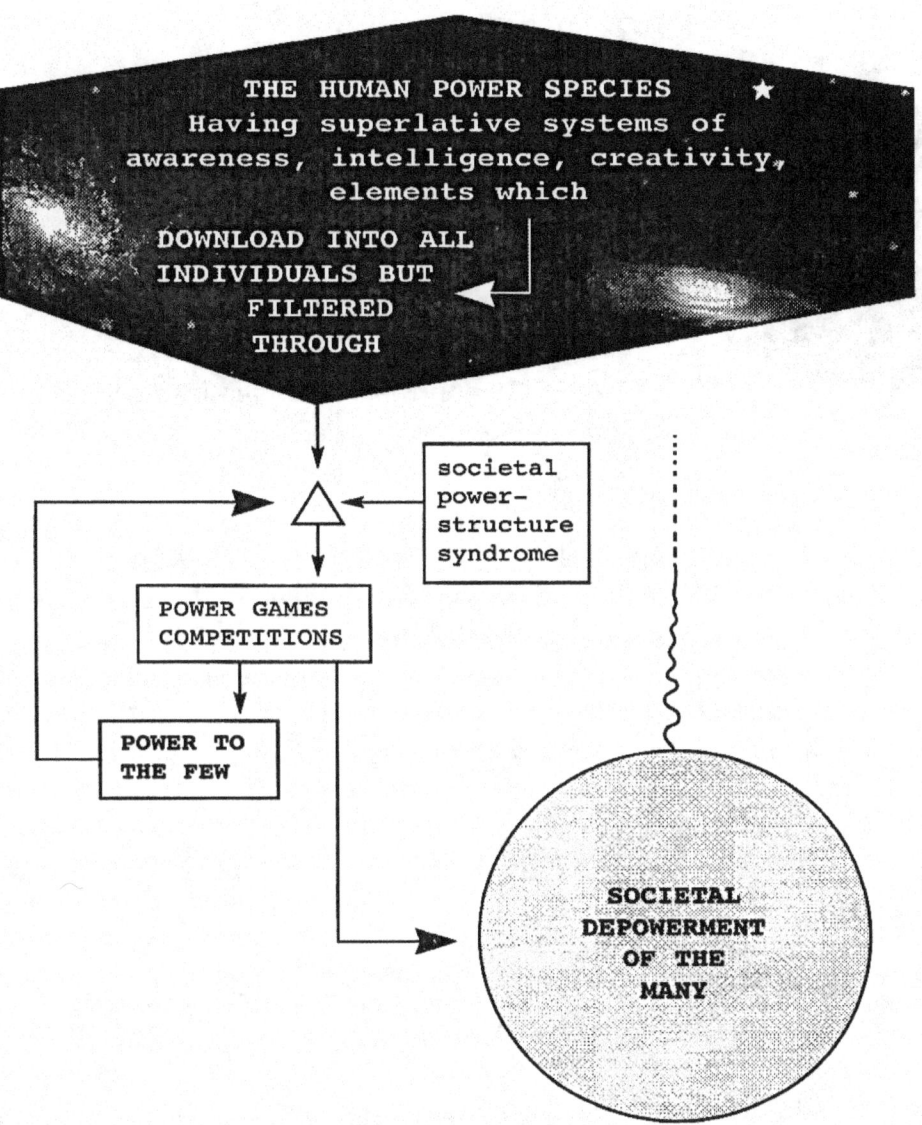

FIGURE 9. On the surfaces of societal power artifices, the concept of "power games" requires the concept of "winners" and "losers," achieved via the concept of "competition rules." Beneath the surfaces, the actual activity is the "winning" gain of power via depowerment of "losers" by any means possible. Societal power games thus require hidden stealth expertise in achieving selective and general depowerment with the result that depowerment is endemic. This is seen as rational within societal power contexts, even though societal engineering of endemic depowerment cannot be thought of as rational for a species having superlative systems of awareness, intelligence, and creativity.

Chapter 11

"RULES" FOR POWER DEPLOYED WITHIN POWERDOM

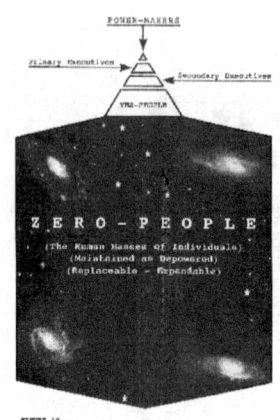

FIGURE 10.

THE ASPECTS of power so far identified contribute to a mix of information bits that can help unfold a larger grasp of the nature of power per se and societal power in particular.

But it is necessary at this point to consider a particular tendency that is lavishly spread throughout human nature. This has to do with the widespread assumption that all things have "rules" and that if the rules can be identified and aligned, then one can hope to achieve some kind of straightforward mastery over the works or functions of whatever is involved.

This is often referred to as "playing by the rules," or "playing by the book."

It is thus that many seeking empowerment try to find out what the rules of power are.

This seems a perfectly logical thing to do, largely because the first need of the powerful is to establish and enforce order so that a power structure can take shape and be maintained in an orderly fashion. Therefore, such order naturally implies the existence of orderly rules.

As it is, though, any given power structure is ordered principally to suit the desires and goals of the top level powerful. And it is in this sense that all power structures, large or small, are malleable artifices via which power over others can take orderly shape and be maintained -- IF "the others" follow the orderly rules designed for THEM.

POWER COMPONENTS AS PLASTIC AND MALLEABLE

MALLEABLE is defined as:

1. Susceptible of being fashioned into a different form or shape; and
2. Capable of being shaped by beating with a hammer or by the pressure of rollers.

It is worth mentioning here that the hammer is, of course, the universal symbol of force power, while images of pressure rollers have often been used to picture social conditioning.

The components can also be thought of as being PLASTIC, i.e., capable of being molded or modeled, capable of being adapted, and easily bent, folded, twisted, or manipulated. Manipulation is of course the chief frame of reference for societal power itself.

Thus, power and its components are plastic and pliable. And it is this situation that makes it so difficult, especially for the powerless and the depowered, to identify the "rules," if any, of power and power-making.

This particular difficulty also confuses frames of reference as to what empowerment or re-empowerment processes might consist of.

THE NATURE OF RULES

In order to plunge into this plastic complexity, it is advisable to point up official definitions of certain terms that have significance to the entire power puzzle.

The several definitions for the term RULE as the noun establish that there are different types of rules, not all of which are consistent with each other:

1. A prescribed guide for conduct or action;
2. A generally prevailing quality, state, or mode;
3. An accepted procedure, custom, or habit;
4. The laws or regulations prescribed by the founder of an order for observance by its members.

Those who are naive or innocent of powerdom's internal workings might assume that such rules would be based on the first definition above.

This can be partly the case, especially with regard to artificial power whose contours tend to be defined by prescribed guides. However, exponents of force power and stealth power probably think such prescribed guides are mere laughing matters.

"Rules" derived from accepted procedures, customs, or habits tend to be more universal within power structures, because they are groked sort of instinctively or intuitively.

For example, it is customary or habitual to stand aside or make way for the powerful, and certainly one accepted procedure is not to bother them too much lest one attract their ire.

THIS kind of thing holds true from the bottom upward of most societal power structures, and even those invested with high artificial power tread softly in the presence of the truly powerful.

The fourth definition given above is relevant to many aspects within any power structure or organization. For example, there are usually several, or even many, power cliques and elites within any given power structure, the leaders of which establish behavioral regulations for members of their camps.

DEPLOYMENT OF RULES FOR POWER

It would be obvious that if rules regarding power cannot be deployed, then they consist of not much more than smoke or pillars of air.

And indeed, if power itself cannot be deployed with respect to power objectives then like many intellectualisms, power ultimately remains something akin to an illusory figment, no matter how attractive the figments seem.

If power is examined and studied in the open field, it is surprising to realize that most people have very little or no idea of what deployment consists of.

This lack permits a significant deficit in groking not only power itself, but the processes of empowerment and depowerment.

TO DEPLOY is taken into English from the Latin DISPLICARE which means to scatter or to display. The official English definitions are:

1. To spread out or arrange strategically;
2. To place in battle formation or appropriate positions;
3. To extend (a military unity) especially to achieve width and depth.

By its suggestive nature, deployment of power and power rules tends to be achieved via some covert method. But if power rules are to become perceptible enough so that everyone can know what they are, such rules need somehow to be overtly displayed.

The term DISPLAY is also taken from the Latin DISPLICARE, but rather means to scatter in ways that are visible. A DISPLAY, then, refers to:

1. An eye-catching arrangement;
2. A device that gives information in visual or linguistic form on behalf of communications and understanding.

It turns out, based on the above discussion, that there can be (and always are) at least two major types of rules for power: Those made visible to one and all, and those cocooned in secrecy.

The visible rules are important only to those who assume that their authenticity applies to everyone within a given societal power structure. However, those seeking empowerment within the contexts of the visible rules are in for some surprises and not a little stultification.

As it is, then, covert rules for power, and their equally covert deployment behind the visible scenes of power, constitute one of the major secrets of power.

Because of their secret nature, it is somewhat difficult to identify and piece them together. What follows are some general outlines, to which others can doubtless contribute much more because of their own knowledge and experiencing.

THE CONCEPT OF POWER-MAKING

As has already been emphasized, our species, in addition to its many other remarkable attributes, is a power species.

This implies that elements and faculties having to do with power are innate in each of us, at least to one degree or another. Those elements, however, are conditioned by socio-environmental forces, which, on average, can deploy factors that decrease empowerment and increase depowerment.

This conditioning engulfs the entire question of human powers in fog so thick it almost achieves the texture of mud. But it also serves to obscure a certain factor that is important to any thinking about power.

Our power species may have innate endowments and faculties regarding power. But visible and tangible MANIFESTATIONS of power have literally to be made (fabricated, produced) in both objective and subjective terms in order to take on presence, visibility, and meaning.

Indeed, the first four definitions of TO MAKE are entirely relevant to power-making:

1. To cause to happen or to be experienced;
2. To cause to exist, occur, or appear, or to create;
3. To favor the growth or occurrence of;
4. To bring into being by forming, shaping, or altering materials [i.e., materials physical or psychological.]

If no one ever set about manifesting-making power, then it and its resulting issues would never come up into visibility.

Looking at the above definitions as a whole, and if ramifications of power-making are contemplated slowly and long enough, it can ultimately be realized that rules for power are most likely not only designed or set up by power-makers, but also enforced by them.

That this is the case can be determined by what happens to the rules when a visible power-maker is caused to undergo denouncement or rejection or is suddenly removed from the scene. A period of "power transition" follows, during which rules for power become wobbly or entirely uncertain.

A study of the French Revolution is a very revealing example of this.

By using power-makers as a starting point, the following five-part scenario can be unfolded regarding rules for power. This scenario can be confirmed by direct observation, and it can also be added to and enlarged by others.

MAKERS OF POWER

Based on the evidence, it can be supposed that power-makers are above all rules but make the rules for all others. The only real distinction here is that visible power leaders must at least appear to follow certain rules. The invisible elite power-makers have no such need. Power-makers have no rules. They establish rules for others.

PRIMARY EXECUTIVES OF POWER-MAKERS

Power-makers of course need executives so as to have a cadre through which their power can be established and exercised. Here is the first realm of artificial power, in that various aspects of power are delegated to the primary executives providing that they accept, know, obey, and enforce the rules set by the power-makers.

SECONDARY EXECUTIVES OF POWER-MAKERS

Secondary executives of power-makers obey the primary executors, but seldom know all or even any of the rules -- and, as well, might have no idea of who the power-makers actually are.

The two foregoing categories usually make up much of what is referred to as the power bureaucracies of given societal power structures.

YES-PEOPLE

In general, yes-people respond to the secondary executives or their spokespersons. And, as can be immediately understood, yes-people obey rules as decided or dictated, but usually only those which the primary executors mean for them to understand.

Yes-people usually suffer from some form of social conditioning and depowerment, so they rarely become power contenders.

But by the well-known systems of social conditioning, including reward and punishment, they are otherwise encouraged to become productive enough to get the work of the power-makers done.

Thus, yes-people are ideal to have power over because of their anticipated and agreeable obedience to the rules of power, even if they don't know exactly why or what they are.

As a large collective, yes-people conventionally accept the visible aspects of powerdom and are reluctant to consider powerdom's invisible and hidden aspects.

ZERO-PEOPLE

It is difficult to describe zero-people, because their enormous populations are not all of one piece, fabric, or pattern. It can collectively be said that they are the bottom of the line, socially subjected to trenchant formats of depowerment, and generally have not the least idea of what is going on.

It can also be said that they feel powerless, and, in some sense at least, hate power or care very little for it.

But they are also the largest source of the cheapest labor productivity and tax collecting income for the power-makers and their objectives.

In the contexts of the four categories above, zero-people as individuals are usually considered not only as nothing, but as expendable. They are mere statistics.

However, zero-people collectively have enormous power because their populations number in the high thousands and millions. If they get collectively upset, as was the case during the French Revolution, they can pull down an entire societal power structure.

In order to avoid, or at least limit, such activity, informed power-makers and their primary executors are obliged to offer up palliatives to the masses, or at least illusions of them.

POPULATIONS OF THE FIVE RULES-OF-POWER CATEGORIES

For information regarding empowerment, it is important to have a general idea of the population ratios among the five foregoing categories.

Such ratios of course depend on a number of factors, such as which power structure is involved, its areas of influence, and its total populations either naturally present or acquired by aggressive expansionism of the power structure. But there are some logical general rules of thumb to go by.

For example, power-makers cannot really have too many primary executives, since increasing numbers of them would make overall control unpredictable.

Likewise, primary executives cannot afford to encourage the presence of numerous secondary executors, which, if allowed, would increase the numbers of possible competitors for the primary executive positions.

And something depends on whether the societal power structure is, for example, infused with democracy, monarchy, empire, declared authoritarianism, or open totalitarianism.

Although highly generalized, the following line up of the population ratios is hypothetically logical enough.

MAKERS: 1 to 5.

PRIMARY EXECUTIVES: perhaps 20 to 100.

SECONDARY EXECUTIVES: perhaps 5 to 50 for each primary executive.

YES-PEOPLE: including the power bureaucracy, and all who in some sense work or provide services for the power makers, this population set can number as much as one-third or more of the total populations involved and which have responded positively to social conditioning.

ZERO-PEOPLE: this population set constitutes the more or less remaining two-thirds, who have responded well to social depowerment processes, or have taken on aspects of powerlessness imprinted by their socio-environmental circumstances and influences.

ITEM TO EXPLORE

IN STEALTHY AND SILENT WAYS, TRY TO NOTICE THOSE WHO TRY TO SET UP RULES FOR POWER OVER OTHERS BUT WHICH RULES DO NOT APPLY TO THEMSELVES.

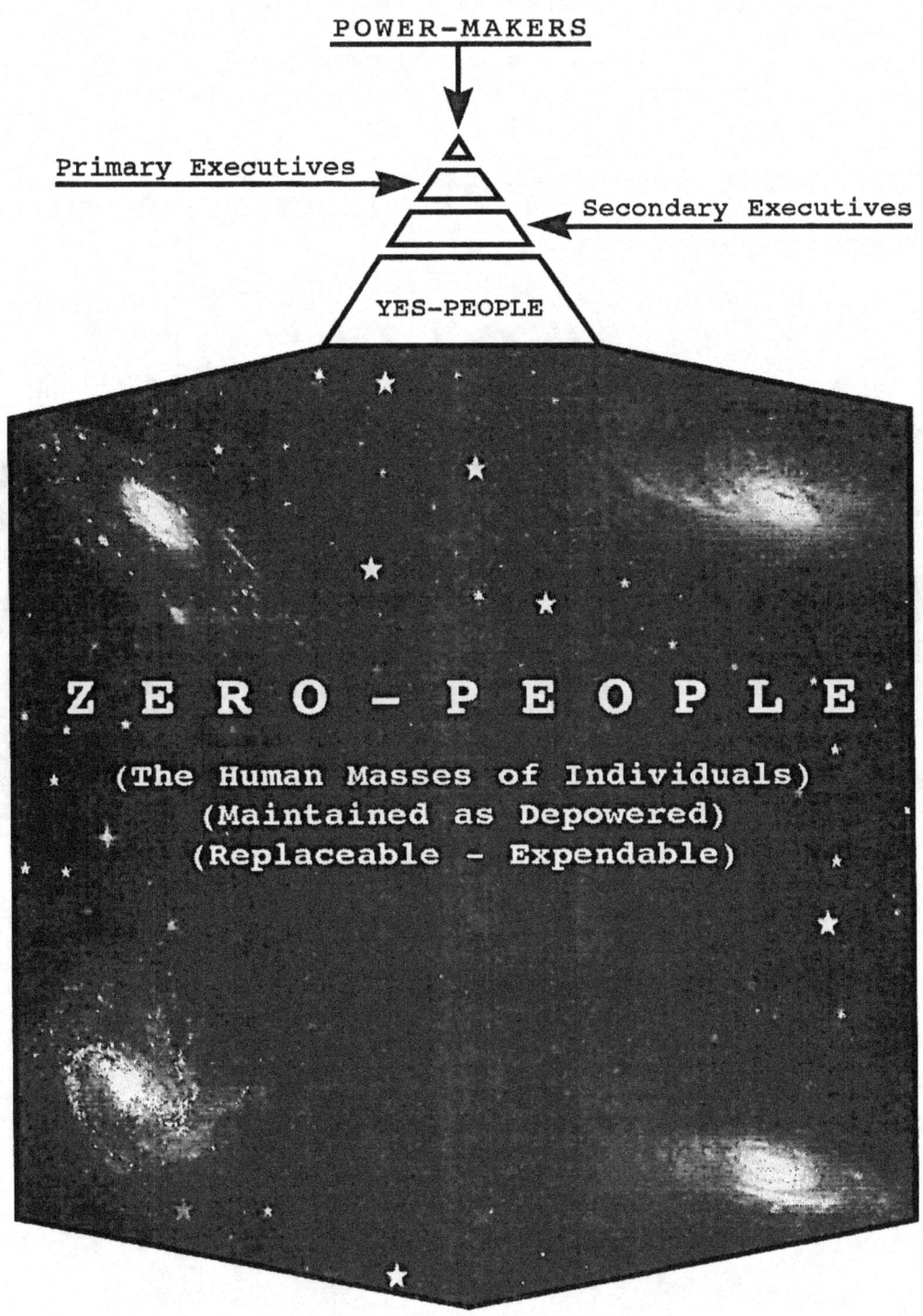

FIGURE 10.

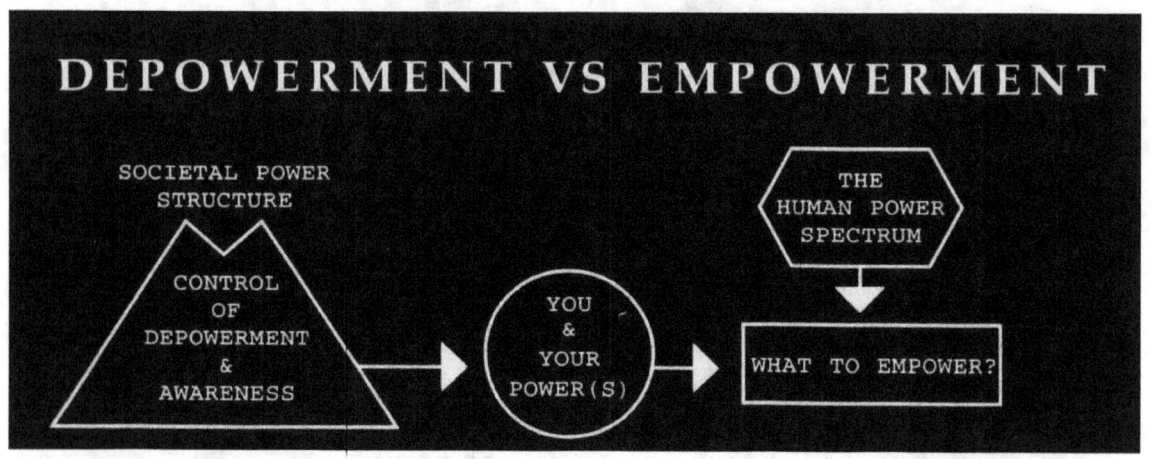

PART THREE
THE SITUATION OF POWER PERSONAL

Chapter 12

THE ON-GOING DICHOTOMY OF INDIVIDUAL AND SOCIETAL POWER

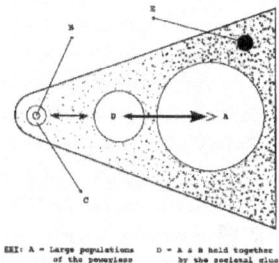

KEY: A = Large populations of the powerless
B = Tiny strata of the power elite
C = Societal power structure
D = A & B held together by the societal glue of ignorance, social conditioning and stupidity
E = Actual reservoirs of human powers

FIGURE 11: When human powers are thought of as a societal resource, the largest reservoirs are always found within the greatest number of individuals incorporated into the societal power structure, but beneath the tiny strata of the power elite. As a resource, even the so-called powerless are power sources in terms of labor, work, tax-paying "mega-slaves." The tiny power elite and the large reservoirs of the powerless form two mutually exclusive and contradictory groups. However, both are irrevocably BOUND together by the large reservoirs of power without which neither could survive, and WHICH is disproportionate balance by the accepted levels of ignorance, social conditioning, and stupidity shared by the elite and the powerless.

THOSE WHO are clairvoyant enough can "see" that most individuals have more power than they manifest or actively demonstrate. Something along these lines can also be groked by intuitives, empaths, and other kinds of sensitives.

There are probably numerous reasons why most individuals do not manifest or actively demonstrate their powers. Whatever the reason, and collectively speaking, their empowerment "switches" have somehow been turned off, or perhaps not turned on in the first place.

In general, most individuals somewhat sense this of themselves. Even if they can rationalize it away intellectually, there is always a residuum of frustration and internal after-effects that influence their behavior and their sense of themselves.

Indeed, such individuals can be thought of as suffering in some way not from lack of power but from empowerment deficiencies. With their empowerment switches turned off, the lights on their internal power control boards cannot be lit up.

For anyone interested in doing so, this kind of thing can be observed and studied within the ranks of zero-people, many of whom can be surprisingly frank and clear in discussing it.

Since there is nothing for zero-people to lose, most will admit to their personal deficiencies in various other categories. But most will finger society as the culprit that has somehow turned off not only THEIR power switches, but those of the entire zero-people populations as well.

Pointing the finger at society as the power-defeating culprit is an astute observation -- coming as it does from people who have not yet read this book.

From talks with the societally depowered, it can gradually be realized that although zero-people can accurately grok societal depowerment in general, they cannot identify the nature of the power switches that have been turned off.

This is a situation inversely shared with those seeking empowerment, who usually cannot figure out what power switches to turn on.

The missing factor that links this inversely shared situation has earlier been discussed in chapters 6 and 7: the total absence of an A-to-Z encyclopedia that identifies and discusses all known and suspected human powers and abilities.

This absence means that there is no organized source ANYONE can consult to find out about human powers in general, so as to be able to identify this or that power faculty in oneself and in others.

It also assures the ongoing societal presence of ignorance and illiteracy regarding power, empowerment, and depowerment.

This absence is therefore the important centerpiece of the power-knowledge vacuum.

THE SOCIETAL DIMINISHMENT OF THE IMPORTANCE OF PERSONAL POWER

In general, it is somewhat safe to say that two principal situations regarding power can be recognized.

The first has to do with the indwelling powers of the individual.

The second has to do with power within the larger societal panoramas.

It is seldom easy to discern the peripheries of the two principal situations in that the individual is always encapsulated within some kind of societal panorama.

By far and large, societal contexts are seen bigger, more compelling, and thus more powerful than the majority of the individuals encapsulated within them.

The larger societal system usually assumes importance as the first situation regarding power, while the power of the individual becomes demoted to some kind of secondary, and sometimes insignificant, status.

The individual can wonder about the nature or essence of power per se, and how it is to be energized or awakened in self.

However, within top power levels of societal panoramas, the chief concern usually has little or nothing to do with what power is per se.

The chief concern is rather focused on how power is to be distributed via a graded or class-like format. As has already been elaborated at length, the graded format is almost always pyramidal in shape and context, having a narrow top where most power is collected and a broad base where little power is permitted.

Thus, the societal concept or perspective regarding power has to do with who and what is and is not to have power within the societal pyramid.

It stands to reason and logic that if power is to be collected into the hands of the few, then it can neither be encouraged nor permitted to awaken too much at the individual level.

There are at least three principal fallouts from the two-part situation briefly outlined above.

1. Although elements and components of individual and societal power obviously interact and influence each other, any specific distinctions between them tend to be foggy at best.
2. Power is usually seen and thought of either as individual power OR as societal power, with the two options being seen as opposing, contradictory, or inconvenient to each other.
3. On average, societal power is more prevailing than individual power. And so individual power is usually seen as unimportant and worthless unless it functionally integrates with societal power patterns, or achieves some kind of visibility, place, esteem, or impact within the societal power set-ups.

THE DICHOTOMY OF IMPORTANT AND UNIMPORTANT POWER

The term DICHOTOMY is defined as "a division or the process of dividing into two mutually exclusive or contradictory groups or categories."

If human power per se is divided into two general categories as societal power and individual power, then they will naturally be seen as contradictory -- and a power dichotomy will quickly form.

There are a number of obvious and subtle reasons for this. One of them is that the management of societal power systems requires the control and containment of individual power within them.

A close examination of even benevolent societal power systems shows that power potentials of individuals must be shaped (or programmed) so as to fit thus and so within the societal contours.

This means that individual power, which is INTERNAL and indwelling within the individual, usually cannot activate and unfold of and as itself.

Rather, the activation and unfolding (if any) is shaped and limited by societal forces EXTERNAL to the individual.

The existence of the conflict between individual and societal power is amply recorded in history.

What is not pointed up is that the conflict itself arises largely because human power is seen only within the scope of the two viewpoints, and which form a dichotomy.

Thus, power is typically seen in an either/or kind of way -- either as individual or as societal -- and cognitive intelligence is thereby forced to pop back and forth between the limits of those two opposing and often contradictory options.

In the larger overview of all human activities, the on-going conflicts within dichotomies remain in place until it is realized that the dichotomy itself is nothing more than two rather artificial parts of one larger thing that has made the two parts possible.

In the case of the power dichotomy, the larger thing consists of human power per se, and from which both individual and societal power download.

In this context, it would be quite obvious that if human power per se did not exist, then neither would the power dichotomy that has formed within it.

So, a more fundamental way to think of power is not via the two-part dichotomy, but as a three-part triad diagrammed at the end of this chapter.

DICHOTOMY CANNOT EXIST EXCEPT AS SOCIETAL ARTIFICE

It now must be stipulated that two things that are downloading parts of a larger third thing CANNOT exist unless the third thing DOES exist. And discovering (or admitting) the existence of the third thing often has the effect of liberating one from the two limiting options.

It is thus that we can think that power per se does exist, and because it does exist it can be divided into the two dichotomy parts discussed above.

THE EXISTENCE OF PER SE HUMAN POWERS

The term PER SE is defined as "by, of, or in itself or oneself or themselves; intrinsic."

Modern philosophers, however, have generally preferred to use the term INTRINSIC, which is more glamorous. It can be taken as referring to some kind of obscure or inscrutable metaphysical situation whose essence cannot be discovered, and so is not available to physical measurement and quantifying.

None the less, INTRINSIC is a perfectly good term, and is defined as "inner, inwardly; belonging to the essential nature or constitution of a thing (as distinguished from its outward appearance)."

As to discovering the existence of the intrinsic third thing which enables individual and societal power to download and come into conflictive existence -- well, one is ultimately obliged to note two factors:

1. that if human powers did not exist per se, intrinsically, or outwardly, then
2. it stands to reason that neither individual nor collective societal power could come into existence in ANY format.

If power per se is not FIRST to be found within our species, then it will also not be found in the individual or within any societal power mishmashes.

Therefore, the idea of "our species" and its intrinsic power nature is worth quite a bit more than a mere bit of biological nomenclature.

ITEM FOR FIELD RESEARCH

INTERVIEW AT LEAST FIVE ZERO-PEOPLE WITH REGARD TO WHAT THEY THINK ABOUT POWER, EMPOWERMENT, AND DEPOWERMENT.

(Process Clue: For best results, you must first endeavor to get them to respect you.)

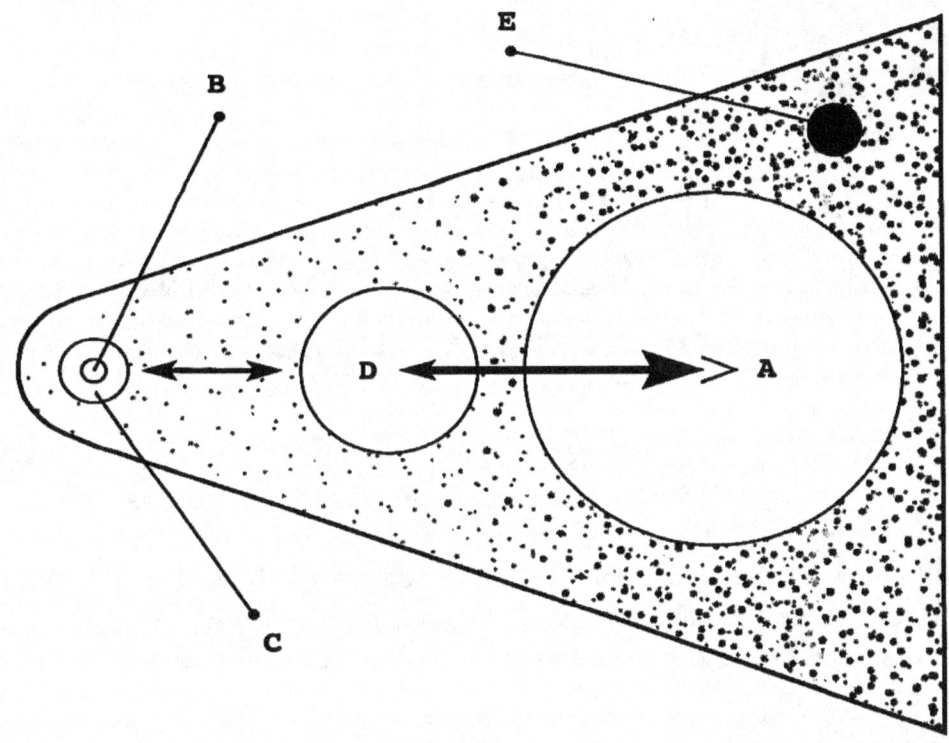

KEY: A = Large populations of the powerless
B = Tiny strata of the power elite
C = Societal power structure
D = A & B held together by the societal glue of ignorance, social conditioning and stupidity
E = Actual reservoirs of human powers

FIGURE 11. When human powers are thought of as a societal resource, the largest reservoirs are always found within the greatest number of individuals incorporated into the societal power structure, but beneath the tiny strata of the power elite. As a resource, even the so-called powerless are power sources in terms of labor, work, tax-paying "wage-slaves." The tiny power elite and the large reservoirs of the powerless form two mutually exclusive and contradictory groups. However, both are irrevocably BOUND together by the large reservoirs of power without which neither could survive, and HELD in disproportionate balance by the accepted levels of ignorance, social conditioning, and stupidity shared by the elite and the powerless.

Chapter 13

INDIGENOUS DEPOWERMENT AND PERSONAL EMPOWERMENT

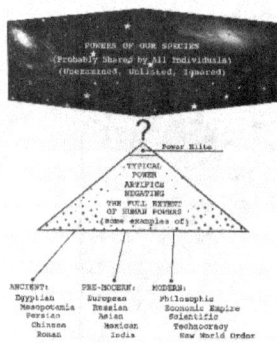

IF ONE attempts to discuss depowerment with zero-people, it can be found that THEY, in one way or another, understand, comprehend, and grok its nature quite well.

Other types of people who consider themselves above the zero-people class probably understand the implications of depowerment. But they are likely to shy away from discussing it because it is unfair, unethical, and indicative of practices characterized by cultivated deception.

Additionally, such practices are at least somewhat unhumanitarian, and, if openly admitted and discussed, the contexts and processes of depowerment promptly introduce difficulties with regard to the philosophy of egalitarianism.

Even more problematical, open and frank discourse on depowerment also sets the stage for thought-provoking discussions regarding empowerment and what THAT consists of.

So, any opening up of depowerment discussions signifies something of a dreaded horror within most societal power management systems.

The best way to keep this horror inactive and asleep in its subconscious cave is to bleep the very word from the language and dictionaries. The cognitive entrance to the cave is thus sealed over and made invisible via this intellectual contrivance.

And indeed, if there is not a word for something, then it can't be discussed, can it?

In any event, the concept of depowerment becomes very interesting when it is realized that if one really knows something about it, one will probably also know something about EMPOWERMENT and RE-EMPOWERMENT.

THE IMPORTANCE OF THE HIDDEN MAP OF APPLIED DEPOWERMENT

The importance of the hidden map of applied depowerment is that such map in reverse is also the hidden map of applied empowerment.

Furthermore, by contemplating the ramifications of depowerment, one might eventually realize that the applied processes of depowerment more constitute the "enemy" than does power itself.

If one is groking along nicely so far, then it is possible to realize that power over others largely depends on, and is certainly sustained by, clever and stealthy management of empowerment AND depowerment.

Without undergoing too much mental stress, it can be seen that depowerment is the enemy of empowerment.

There is a very old wisdom-adage advising that if one wants to outwit an enemy, one should first get to know the enemy quite well.

This adage, and its contained wisdom, is sometimes thought of as a mere platitude somewhat cliché in this or that intellectualism.

And this might be the case, if, for example, seen in the contexts of complete egalitarianism.

Egalitarianism is the theory of complete human equality, especially with respect to social, political, and economic rights and privileges. It is also the social philosophy advocating the removal of inequalities among everyone.

It is possible to think that egalitarianism just MIGHT be feasible with regard to just about everything -- excepting males, females, and most certainly power.

One merely needs to consider the real and ongoing existence of force power and stealth power to conclude that egalitarianism was engineered perhaps on Venus, but clearly not on Earth, and certainly not from within a serious consideration of Our Power Species.

In any event, if one seeks some kind of empowerment, one is foolish not to get to know its enemies quite well, and so the wisdom-adage, dating from very ancient times, is not too platitudinal.

In this sense, the hidden map of applied depowerment can be seen as something of meaningful importance. If more of the powerless and depowered had open and free access to such map, then power MIGHT become more egalitarian regarding empowerment.

But here again is the bad dream of societal power managers working on behalf of the powerful few.

EXPANDING THE KNOWLEDGE SCOPE OF DE-POWER

By placing the prefix DE in front of the term POWER, a particular subtle concept becomes intellectually available regarding the ways we might think of power, and of those who don't have any or much of it. Indeed, the prefix DE is very serviceable in many important ways.

It means "from, down, away," or "do the opposite of in some negative rather than positive sense." It also implies detracting and repelling, as contrasted to attracting -- as in pushing away as contrasted to pulling toward.

"DO the opposite of" also implies volitional activity on the part of those who are doing it. Causing others to do the opposite of power and empowerment is one format of this kind of volitional activity.

Thus, there would be a subtle distinction between merely depriving someone of power and depowering them.

To deprive one of power would mean simply taking something away. But depower would imply a change of state, a change of condition DOWN from some kind of original or innate power format.

And then, EM-POWER would also involve a change of state or condition UP from its original format. The prefixes EM (and EN) are utilized to mean: to cause to be, to cause to have, to come to be, to come to have, to provide with.

If we think that everyone has a potential median state or condition of power, then to depower the median state would mean utilizing active measures to drive it downward to a lower condition of functioning -- while empower would mean driving the median state upward to a higher state of functioning.

Thus, we can arrive at the concept of DEPOWERMENT as a slowing down or devitalizing of someone's median state of natural power potential. The ideas of low and high volume of power are also serviceable.

In this opposite sense, empowerment would consist of turning up power volumes, of a speeding up or revitalizing someone's median state of natural power potential to a higher state of functioning.

These subtle distinctions are important, because ahead will be presented evidence that has to do with turning up or turning down power thresholds in terms of energy and force.

To energize something would of course mean pumping up its power. De-energize would mean pumping down its power.

Since the term DEPOWER does not officially exist, most people seek to utilize the term DEPRIVE in its stead. However, the two terms are not synonymous because we usually know what people are being deprived of.

DEPRIVE usually involves rude and crude force to take away something, either by lawful or illegal measures, by moral or immoral force, or by ethical or unethical activity. Few can mistake what deprivation consists of.

But depowerment, if it is to be successful, requires more subtle, less visible factors. Few of our species like to be depowered, and most will usually resist it if they can understand what it is and what is happening to them.

Thus, depowerment tactics and strategies must be quite subtle, at least when used on reasonably intelligent people -- so subtle that they will not realize they have become the products of depowerment efforts.

COMPETITION AS INDIGENOUS WITHIN OUR POWER SPECIES

The term INDIGENOUS is taken into English from the Latin DE + GIGNERE, which meant TO BEGET.

In English, however, the definition is rendered as "produced, growing, or living naturally in a particular region or environment." A synonym is NATIVE.

Although not conventionally done, it is entirely proper to consider that power is an environment that one can step in and out of, be accepted into, pushed outside of, or conquered or killed within.

One of the chief characteristics indigenous to this environment is competition, and usually not of the amusing sort governed by knowledge of the rules, and by fair play.

Our species is all too obviously exceedingly competitive. This has not gone unnoticed during the ages gone by. And so a rather generalized historical solution has been developed, one which is quite dependable.

That solution is this: Competitors can of course be dealt with via force power. But the best way of dealing with ostensible competitors is to prevent them, via stealth power, from becoming competitors in the first place.

By general rules of thumb, competitors need to accumulate various kinds of power in order to succeed and prevail.

It is therefore quite sensible to arrange power matters and power schematics so that the potentially up-coming populations of competitors are depowered before they can format themselves into successful competitors. This warding-off, prophylactic solution is widespread throughout our species, so much so that it is indigenous. And so if we can speak of indigenous power within our species, we are also obliged to think in terms of indigenous competitiveness, and then in terms of indigenous depowerment.

Indigenous depowerment is of course utilized not only to down-power competitors, but also to narrow and limit the open field of competitors -- so that the few can obtain to power.

THE DEPOWERED ARE STILL "CARRIERS" OF POWER

Hypothetically speaking, if via depowerment measures one's power volume has been turned down too low, one will be unable to sense power, or at least not very well.

Further, if the power energy level has been turned down, or reduced in important ways, one might no longer even have the smallest hint of power-energy reserves.

As a collective, these then would constitute those who FEEL they are powerless, because even if they can still sense the powers within them, they can neither hear, feel, nor sense what those powers are.

They cannot know that they, as living, animated and animating humans, are still CARRIERS of power.

The super ultimate depowerment tactic, of course, is to kill the carriers of power.

If this is achieved on a large scale, then power systems, power pyramids, and playing-for-power games are soon deprived of workers whose collective labor and products support those systems.

After all, and as already emphasized, if power means to have control, authority, and influence OVER others, then OTHERS must exist in order to have these. No one can have power over the absent.

Thus, the masses of humans, all of which are carriers of power, cannot be terminated or completely done away with.

So they somehow have to be rendered into stepped-down power conditions and states, the methods of which are indigenously understood.

If this stepping-down is successful, then there will be plenty of the depowered to have control and authority over.

And the systems' profitable wealth for the few will get manifested, too.

ITEMS TO DEDUCE

DISCOVER AT LEAST THREE IMPORTANT SPECIES INNATE POWERS WHICH MUST BE DEPOWERED IN ORDER TO REDUCE THE POPULATIONS OF POWER COMPETITORS.

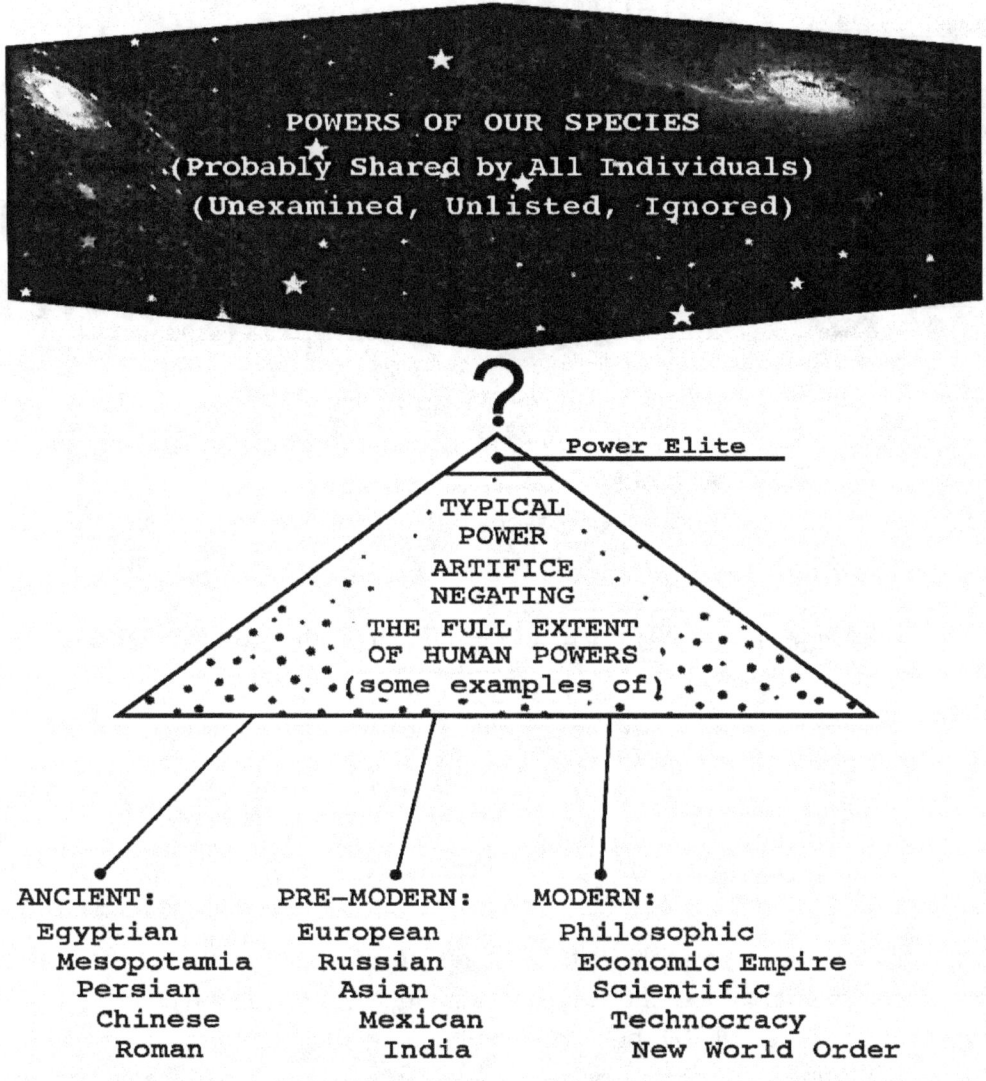

FIGURE 12. All human individuals are manifestations of the same species, and are thus "carriers" of its innate qualities, including the spectrum powers of awareness, intelligence, creativity, language-making, memory storage, insight, invention, foresight, intuition, and extensive forms of "sensing." Individuals are also "carriers" of our species innate powers for erecting physical, mental, and societal artifices. Each pyramidal system is habitually formatted as the power of the few and built on top of the many who are kept massively illiterate about innate human powers. Only what can be used by the powerful is permitted. No known societal system has endorsed real discovery of the full extent of human powers and all have established penalties against doing so.

Chapter 14

POWER ENERGIES MAGNIFIED vis a vis THOSE WHO DON'T HAVE POWER

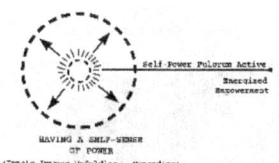

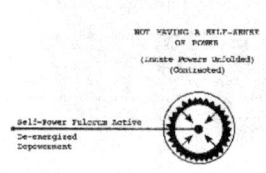

FIGURE 11. Many who don't have a constructive self-sense of power are probably victims of socio-cultural power artifice favoring the powerful few by actively diminishing the knowledgeable powers of the many. Direct observation of such societal situations will confirm that the few powerful don't want squads of the empowered-many set loose and having freedom of power movement within THEIR power systems. Conditioned ignorance about human powers in general is the best historically proven way to prevent this.

THOSE WHO are interested in power exclusively tend to study those who manifest it and devote no attention to those who don't.

There are probably a number of reasons behind this. The most obvious is the belief that if one imitates those having power, then one stands a better chance of having it oneself.

This seems logical on the surface, and it may even be true in some part. But there is a significant flaw involved.

IMITATIVE POWER

The flaw consists of this: one seldom ever sees power itself. What is actually seen is the RESULT of power being produced by someone within whom power is active and manifesting.

It is possible to convincingly imitate the results of power and have the appearance of being powerful. But in the end this type of activity is a charade which others can easily identify as such -- especially by those who do have power.

Being identified as a power-pretender or a power-faker is usually not good for one's career, and sometimes not even for one's life.

There is, of course, the old axiom of "fake it until you make it" which nervously implies that one MIGHT make it ultimately. In some cases, this procedure might be temporarily useful.

But power structures are usually awash with both power-pretenders and power-contenders, and so one must assume that those having the real thing can spot the fake thing. And, after all, pretending to have power is one of the oldest and most superficial of the power games. It is likely to fool only the most gullible.

Different realms of human activity can be thickly populated with those who are faking it with the prospect of eventually really achieving it.

And it is important to realize that many of the most bitter disputes and conflicts regarding power take place among those who are imitating or are faking it.

This imitate-fake-it issue can better be understood if it is considered that valid power people comprehend that the frequency and proliferation of power conflicts must be REDUCED.

For one thing, the proliferation of power conflicts might just as easily consume them as it does the pretenders. It is exceedingly difficult to maintain an effective and continuing power presence when all else around it is aflame with power conflicts.

One of the first mandates of those who do gain power over others is to establish and maintain social ORDER, without which the powerful probably cannot survive very long. (It should be mentioned that establishing order should not automatically be confused with establishing justice.)

A study of the distribution of active power among, for example, gangs and criminal overlords easily reveals that even those social sub-sets eventually come to realize that power conflicts have to be kept to a minimum.

Indeed, the on-going maintenance of active power can only be achieved in an atmosphere of relative peace and amicable agreements. For it is via AGREEMENTS that active power can become constituted and maintained.

Likewise, a study of the appearance and distribution of active power among socially approved political parties and religious groups reveals much the same thing. All power structures can be torn apart by internal power games and power strife.

In any event, as this book proceeds it will become more visible why power can't be faked and that attempts to imitate it are seldom successful.

THOSE WHO DON'T HAVE POWER SHOULD BE OBSERVED

If one would like to have more power, to become empowered or re-empowered, then, as a first level of interest, it is not important why others have it.

The principal reason is that one cannot cure or fix something until one identifies what needs to be cured or fixed. And so WHY those who don't have power DO NOT have it becomes interesting.

To be precise, one must fix and cure the reasons why one does not have power in order to have much hope of really activating it in oneself.

As long as those conditions or situations contributing to a lack of activating power remain unidentified, then no amount of trying to imitate the valid or the fake powerful will do much good.

If those conditions or situations ARE cured or fixed, then it will not really be necessary to imitate anyone else.

THE DIFFICULTY OF SEEING ONE'S OWN LACKS REGARDING NOT HAVING POWER

If adequate formal studies regarding power existed, they would include guidelines not only regarding empowerment, but also reasons that result in a lack of it. As already established, such studies do not exist, and so there are no guidelines to refer to.

Self-examination is quite difficult, largely because people live within their frames of references and cannot easily see beyond them.

It is easier to examine others who don't have power, and to discover the most apparent reasons why they do not. The reasons might set ticking some new thoughts and increased observations that are not available within one's own frames of references.

OBSERVING THE "POWERLESS" AND THE DEPOWERED

Those who don't have power are commonly referred to as "the powerless." And so those who want more power usually ignore and avoid them because of the culturally fixed idea that since the powerless ARE powerless, there is nothing to be learned from them.

This is not altogether true -- because the powerless are a very rich resource in identifying and understanding the reasons why ONESELF might not have power.

But this rich resource cannot be utilized unless we begin to shift some ideas around. As already mentioned, those who don't have power are commonly be referred to as "the powerless."

This designation cannot be completely accurate if it is considered that the biological and mental human is actually composed of animating power.

If it is accepted, as it should be, that each human is also essentially a born power dynamo, then we can NOT say or think that those who don't have power are POWERLESS.

We can say that they have been DEPOWERED in some fashion, so that as natural and inherent power dynamos they have become dysfunctional regarding extending their animating forces and energies into the environments around them.

The powerless are almost universally considered as deficient of power. But if it is possible to assume that powers are innate in our species, then, strictly speaking, powerlessness is the result of powers:

1. That have not been activated and nurtured either for environmental or social reasons;

or

2. Have been deliberately suppressed for the same reasons.

THE ADMITTED EXISTENCE OF POWER "POTENTIALS"

In all sociological strata, at least in modern times, it is generally admitted that all individual humans possess "potentials" regarding powers of all kinds.

Indeed, during the early decades of the twentieth century and through the 1950s, various movements were set up to consider, study, and to creatively philosophize regarding human potentials.

In a chapter ahead, human potentials will be elaborated more extensively. But here it can be indicated that the term POTENTIAL has two meanings with regard to power and empowerment.

THE FIRST DEFINITION OF "POTENTIAL"

The first meaning is given as something "existing in possibility, and capable of becoming and actual."

In keeping with the definition above, the realm of human potential studies would of course be an arm of a larger issue of power studies, and power schools as well.

But as has already been elaborately discussed, power studies are absent, meaning that there are no truly informed frames of reference for them.

So, of course, the field of human potential studies dwindled after the 1950s and has since remained cocooned in defeating ambiguity.

Our species likes to make visible and active everything that can be thought of. So the lack of this kind of effort regarding power potentials clearly amounts to dis- or counter-engineering -- the goal of which can only be the deliberate perpetuation of the conditions and situations of powerlessness.

This depowerment has significant implications at both the social and individual levels.

THE SECOND DEFINITION OF "POTENTIAL"

There is a second definition of POTENTIAL that is not generally applied to the contexts of human powers and potentials in general.

It has nuances with regard to real power, but it may be difficult to completely grok it until several of the chapters to follow can be taken into account.

The second definition is: "Any of various functions from which the intensity or the velocity at any point in a field may readily be calculated."

This definition brings an energetic element into the first definition of human potentials: if they do not somehow become energized, they cannot become developed into actuality.

It is this second definition of potential that has great ramifications with regard to empowerment (energize) and depowerment (de-energize).

As it stands in dictionaries, the second definition seems only to be technical. But if we change the phrase "may readily be calculated" to "may readily be sensed," then the definition can more easily be applied to human powers, the powerful, and the powerless.

Certainly, the idea of energy magnified can be associated with the concept of power energized -- so much so that power energized can be sensed as such.

Here is one of the crucial demarcations between the powerful and the powerless.

AN OBSERVATION TO ATTEMPT

OBSERVE A SELECTION OF THE "POWERLESS" AND ATTEMPT TO SENSE WHAT ACCOUNTS FOR THEIR CONDITION AND WHAT POTENTIALS HAVE BEEN DE-ENERGIZED.

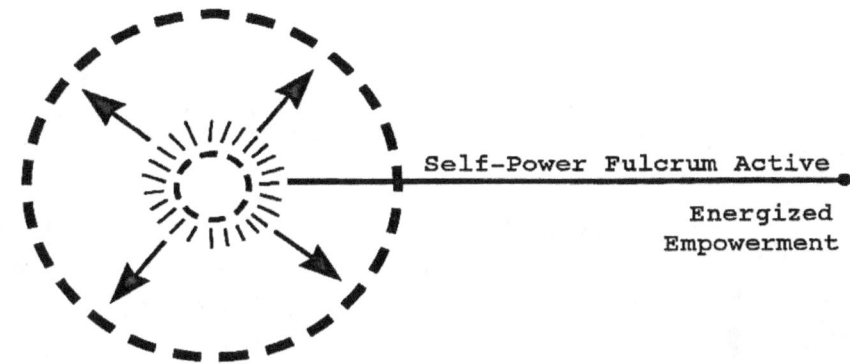

**HAVING A SELF-SENSE
OF POWER**

(Innate Powers Unfolding - Expanding)

NOT HAVING A SELF-SENSE
OF POWER

(Innate Powers Unfolded)
(Contracted)

FIGURE 13. Many who don't have a constructive self-sense of power are probably victims of socio-cultural power artifice favoring the powerful few by actively diminishing the knowledgeable powers of the many. Direct observation of such societal situations will confirm that the few powerful don't want squads of the empowered-many set loose and having freedom of power movement within THEIR power systems. Conditioned ignorance about human powers in general is the best historically proven way to prevent this.

Chapter 15

YOU - AND YOUR POWER

VIA THE fourteen preceding chapters, an attempt has been made to sketch out some of the aspects that constitute the bigger picture of power and empowerment.

There are two principal purposes for having done so, the first of which is to give some idea of what the individual is up against if wanting to embark on any empowerment trek.

In this sense, it is not all that unreal to establish that most societal power systems are, in some full part, rigged AGAINST empowerment and rigged FOR depowerment.

This double rigging makes it very difficult for the individual to achieve very much empowerment -- except via self-discovered loopholes in the rigging, and by cunning and stealth sufficient to outwit empowerment preventives.

THE USELESSNESS OF SWEETNESS-AND-LIGHT EMPOWERMENT RECIPES

Most books dealing with empowerment focus on the individual, and usually exclusively so. These are the "powers within you" type of book.

Some of them have been quite popular in their time, but none have ever been endorsed by any conventional societal mainstreams, and none of them has ever been added into in any academic agendas or curriculums.

There are two central themes these books share.

The first, and very attracting, theme is that if individuals can awaken the powers within them, then there is something like automatic clear sailing ahead.

In the sweetness and light of this promising expectation, there is no real need to inform the individual of societal empowerment preventives that will soon be encountered in spite of the awakening.

The second theme, a rather sugar-coated one, has to do with making the individual feel good, important, and of bigger stature than whatever might inhibit the awakening -- and so there is no real need to elaborate upon social-conditioning inhibitors.

IDENTIFYING THE SMALLEST POWER "UNIT"

However, via the combined discussions in the preceding fourteen chapters, it can be deduced, without much equivocation, that the individual is the smallest power "unit" in any societal power schemata.

And to establish this has been the second reason for presenting those chapters BEFORE beginning to discuss power and empowerment at the individual level.

If the fuller panorama of societal powers is considered, there is nothing to suggest that sweetness-and-light expectations and sugar-coated clichés can be workable in the open field of power machinations of every possible kind. That field is thickly populated with lean, mean, fighting machines.

None the less, this book has now arrived in the vicinity of the individual, and this chapter begins the discussion of the individual versus the societal panorama of power.

THE LIFE FORCE EQUALS POWER AND EMPOWERMENT

If you are among those who feel they have little or no power, you can be assured, with quite some certainty, that you do have implicit power.

After all, individuals of our species are basically comprised of a Life Force, or Life Energy. And where there is Life Energy there is power, because that is what it takes to be alive, and in motion and in activity.

That this is so is not a mere sugar-coated palliative. Rather, it is a logical extension of the notable fact that whatever else our species consists of, it is a power species possessing tremendous known powers, and probably many more that are unknown.

Something may have happened to prevent, deactivate, or dwindle your powers, to break your intellectual and energetic contacts with them, to make you confused about them. But they are still innately there, awaiting a renewed activation.

If you are among the living, then no matter what other conditions might be prevailing within and around you, you do have power(s).

You see, life does not exist unless it is both an expression and a function of the power that makes for life in the first place. Life itself is power, is maintained by power, is enhanced and expanded by power.

The considerations above do not represent merely some philosophical, metaphysical, or let's-feel-good sermonizing. They represent facts regarding power -- facts most pay no attention to -- facts which have become belittled, avoided, marginalized -- facts which today are thought (and taught) as being insignificant in the greater vista of what is thought to be power, and what is thought to be life as well.

A BASIC IDEA OF POWER

A little over three hundred years ago, the tremendously influential English empiricist and political philosopher, John Locke (1632-1704), published the following concept in AN ESSAY CONCERNING HUMAN UNDERSTANDING, Vol. II, p. vii, 1690):

> "Power is another of those simple Ideas which we receive from Sensation and Reflection. For observing within ourselves -- that we do and can think, and that we can, at pleasure, move several parts of our Bodies which were at rest; the effects also, that natural bodies are able to produce in one another, occurring every moment to our Senses -- we both these ways get the Idea of Power."

Locke's statement is probably one of the very few of the most fundamental statements regarding BASIC powers.

Locke was saying that when you move your legs, arms, eyes, head, and so forth, that it takes power to do so.

He was also saying that when you think something, again it takes power to do so.

When you experience a sensation or pause to reflect upon something you perhaps have not understood before, again it takes some kind of power to do so.

And what he was also saying, but between the lines, was that it takes bio-kinetic and mental-kinetic energy to produce motion of any kind, and that the source of the energy-motion is power of some kind.

Another way to look at this, one which Locke intended, was to consider that if you could not produce motion of limbs or thoughts, then you would be dead -- which is to say, be energy-less, power-less.

Locke's statement about power, and about getting the Idea of power, was in fact quite widespread during his times, and until some point during the late eighteenth century.

People seemed to understand, or grasp, the Idea that humans, in some essential, innate, and direct sense were power entities or mechanisms, energy-driven mechanisms with the energy/power inherent in the life force which endowed them with the processes of life, breath, physical prowess and mental activity.

Furthermore, and although it is difficult to find comment on it today, this life force was granted a great deal of respect no matter where it was encountered. It was also feared -- if it was seen not to be on one's side, so to speak.

THE LOSS OF THE LIFE FORCE IDEA

One of the contemporary problems regarding knowing what power consists of is that touch has been lost not only with the Idea and meaning of the indwelling life force which powers our bio-mind systems, but with concepts which would draw it to our attention.

In fact, since the 1890s, the reality of the life power which fuels kinetic physical and mental motion has become so submerged that even highly educated scientists and philosophers seem to be unaware that it takes power to activate and drive them.

We walk, talk, digest, excrete, think, and experience sensations all the time -- without the least idea that somewhere within each of us dwells the inherent life power which makes those functions possible AS POWERS.

And since there is hardly any Idea at all of the existing power within individuals, attention is turned to phenomena and activity outside of our Selves to give us our ideas of what power consists of.

Since we have no notion, no Idea of our own indwelling life power(s), to get and gain power we try to emulate what we perceive to be power factors outside of us.

But this represents a REVERSAL of over four thousand years of thinking regarding what power consists of. Indeed, Locke's idea regarding basic, or essential, power was not really original to him.

If one studies history with an eye to discovering what past cultures thought about power, it will be found that the life force was always considered the fundamental source of all human power. All other factors which might come to represent power were thought of as extensions of the central life force power.

The living biological body was considered the container, the vehicle, of the power of life force -- which was why life (of any kind) was considered sacred. The only exceptions were those power-life vehicles which were enemies, and those life forms which needed to be eaten in order that the human power-energy mechanism might survive.

But during the last two centuries, a gradual, but tremendous reversal of those concepts has taken place -- several reasons for which will be discussed ahead.

When you, today, wish to know about power and what it consists of and how to enhance it, consider the following very carefully.

TWO OPTIONAL AND CONFLICTING BASIC IDEAS ABOUT POWER

Do you have the following two Ideas? Do you consider that power pre-exists within you? That there is a power blueprint, a power pattern, pre-coded within you?

Or do you have the following idea? Do you consider that power exists in phenomena and activities outside of you, and that you have to get into them, participate in them, perhaps take them over, in order to graft that power to yourself?

Consider the two options above very carefully. Both are actually feasible, but between them is the first glimmering that can result in power recovery, power enhancement, re-empowerment, or the blossoming or unfoldment of your power, or whatever you want to call it.

Real power has no names, no descriptors, except what you want to call it. You can call it Power-X, if you want to. Whatever you might like to call it, it is you, and your power. Name it what you want.

To help get the Idea a little better, slowly lift you hand and arm up and down. Do this several times and increase your focus on the kinetic motion it takes to do so.

Do not focus on the fact that you CAN do it. That we CAN do it is what we mindlessly take for granted.

Instead, focus on the fact that it takes some kind of activating power to do it. Focus on the power BEHIND the motion, the power that makes the motion possible.

Where does this kinetic power come from?

Now, pretend your bio-mind body is dead. Then see if it is as easy to lift your hand and arm.

Try to get the Idea that energy is directed power of some kind.

You may see that it takes directed energy to lift and lower your hand and arm. One can be very familiar with directed energy. But one should become just as familiar with the power in us which can be directed into any energy we want.

And you might want to remember something many forget all too often: all power things begin small, grow and get larger. Hardly any power manifestations begin as BIG things.

The beginning of an individual's power starts with the frank admission that one DOES have it somewhere within. Power should not be considered as potentially existing, because it is actual.

The power(s) of individuals may be blocked, hampered, confused, ineffective, defeated, distorted, mind-programmed into depowerment conditions. The power(s) may have been educated to non-effective levels, adulterated, intimidated, willingly or unwillingly suppressed by yourself or by others, polluted with anti-power considerations. But the power(s) exist even so.

One's sense of power may even be intellectually and emotionally confused. Or it may simply be that others don't want you to manifest your power, and have taken active, preventive measures to prevent its consolidation within you.

It is far more likely that most are merely mis-educated or mis-experienced regarding not only their power, but power in the circumstances and the world around them.

A PERSONAL ANECDOTE

Many years ago, when I was in college, I had to study German, which back then was thought of as one of the three "scientific" languages. I had decided to major in biology, and so as an English speaker, I had to minor either in French or German.

My German teacher was a certain Frau Doctor May Mabel Schwender, the youngest child having twelve brothers before her. She was powerful, a wizard, and the most direct and aggressive ball-breaker I've ever encountered down until today.

After some harrowing experiences with her, I made the mistake of saying that I felt powerless, at least with special reference to her ball-breaking presence.

"Oh, Bosh!" she sneered. "You Americans wail and pamper yourselves too much. No one will ever GIVE you power. Take paper and pencil and list ten of the times during your miserable life you DID feel powerful.

"As you remember and write down each item, beside it make a note of what happened because you were powerful at that time. When you have finished that list study it well several times. And then YOU dare to come here again and say you ARE powerless."

I was by then almost in tears. I made as if to say something, but the Frau Doctor waved her hand. "Nein, nein, nein (in German 'No," or 'enough of that shit'.)"

So, I HAD to make that list. Yes, I could remember ten times in my youth that I had felt relatively power-full. And I could remember that the precious feeling was sunk, not by myself, but because of others or because of some kind of situation which was inimical to ME having MY powers.

Since then, possibly because of the shock-value of the Frau Doctor's challenge, I have never once FELT powerless. I have felt confused about power and all its many complexities. But never power-LESS. There were to be many occasions in which I did not have power relative to others and to other situations. But power-LESS. Nein, nein, nein.

And since then, among other reasons to perpetually adore her, I have been eternally grateful to that Frau Doctor Ball-Breaker. You see, she didn't recommend reading a book on empowerment. She made me consult myself.

YOUR life force, or life energy power loves to have you remember that it is there. When you forget it, become out of touch with it, various kinds of depowerment can proceed accordingly.

AN EXERCISE TO CONSIDER

MAKE YOUR OWN LIST OF TEN INCLUDING WHAT HAPPENED BECAUSE OF THEM.

Chapter 16

ON HAVING A SENSE OF POWER

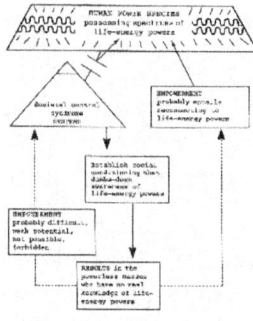

FIGURE 16. [caption illegible]

IT IS fair to say that the topics discussed in this chapter might at first be a little difficult to take on board.

It is only after they have been studied and more fully realized that they can be seen as easy to deal with.

There are at least two principal reasons for this.

The first is that power is usually associated with actions rather than with the processes of thinking or sensing.

This is especially the case regarding force power situations in which one needs guns or armaments but not necessarily a mind. It can also be the case regarding artificial power where one needs the status, but not necessarily a mind that is commensurate with it.

The second reason for the difficulty is that education in general teaches WHAT to think in terms of topics, subjects, assumptions, standards, and beliefs, but not HOW to examine and constructively manage and expand one's own thinking parameters.

THE TERM "SENSE" WITH REGARD TO POWER AND EMPOWERMENT

There are several definitions for SENSE as a noun and verb. But with regard to having a sense of power, the term SENSE is used within the following meanings:

1. To be or become conscious of;
2. To grasp or comprehend, or to grok;
3. To detect automatically.

Having (or not having) a sense of power is important when it comes to understanding many things -- such as the world of human affairs -- but it is also important regarding desires for empowerment and increases of power.

As it is, having or not having a sense of power is always an individual thing. So it is very hard to articulate what may be involved in general.

The central difficulty needs to be openly and fairly pointed up. If individuals do have a sense of power, it is probably formulated within the contexts of their personal frames of reference.

Those frames of reference not only formulate an individual's sense of power, but also are quite likely by that individual to be projected onto others in order to influence them.

After all, the definition of power as "power over others" clearly and literally implies power over the power of others.

The idea that power over others consists merely of having power over their bodies, minds, possessions, behavior, and activities is actually quite misleading.

Indeed, if one achieves power over those factors, but not over the innate and potential powers of the same others, then power could change hands with some rapidity.

Thus, the conventional dictionary definition of power as control, authority, and influence over others really does need to be amended so as to bring this hidden aspect into visibility.

POWER: control, authority, and influence over the powers of others, including their sense of power.

But if one is to obtain power over the powers of others, including their sense of power, then logically one must also obtain power over their frames of reference.

If societal and lesser formats of power structures are examined in enough detail, it become possible to discern that managers of those structures work overtime to provide and manipulate the frames of reference that others are required to adapt to.

Thereafter, individuals do not really know if their frames of reference are actually their own in a self-creative sense.

What they might think of as their personal frames of reference regarding power might have been imbibed and adapted from some external source which will not tolerate too much self-creative and self-sustaining expressions of individual power.

The reason this discussion is relevant to individual empowerment is two-fold and:

1. Individual empowerment most certainly involves discovering WHAT to empower within self; and
2. If one attempts to empower oneself only in the light of frames of reference one has been conditioned to adapt to, then the attempt probably will not bear much fruit. The reason is that such attempts automatically give back control of one's sense of power to the originators and managers of those frames of reference.

The foregoing two factors might at first be somewhat difficult to completely grok because of a lack of understanding about what frames of reference actually are.

FRAMES OF REFERENCE

The most commonly shared understanding of FRAMES OF REFERENCE has to do with "the standards by which a person compares something in order to form an attitude or make a judgment or analysis."

This idea seems perfectly efficient. But when applied to power and to empowerment it doesn't quite do the job.

One part of the difficulty has to do with the use of the words FRAME and FRAMEWORK, and both of which have several definitions.

In general, a FRAME is usually thought of as something that encloses something else, such as a picture or painting, or an enclosing border. But as a verb the term also means "to formulate, shape, or construct."

As a noun, the principal definition refers to "something composed of parts fitted together and united."

FRAMEWORK refers to "a skeletal, openwork, or structural unit made for admitting, enclosing, or supporting something."

FRAME OF REFERENCE is also defined as "a set or system (as of factors or ideas) serving to orient or give particular meaning."

In the context of that definition, then, frames of reference are sets or systems of frameworks serving to orient or give particular meaning.

But there is another definition for FRAME OF REFERENCE: "an arbitrary set of axes with reference to which the position or motion of something is described." An AXIS is defined as:

1. A straight line about which a body or a geometric figure rotates or may be supposed to rotate; and
2. A main line of direction, motion, growth, or extension.

The foregoing definitions might at first seem unduly complicated.

But digging through them is necessary in order to point up that there are TWO kinds of frames of reference: the framework kind, and the axis kind. And both have monumental importance with regard to power and empowerment.

It is now possible to point up that the framework kind refers to "a set or system of facts or ideas serving to orient or give particular meaning."

The axis kind refers to "a main line of direction, motion, growth, or extension."

By comparing the two, the framework kind is implicitly more static than fluid, while the axis kind is explicitly fluid and thus vital and vitalizing.

The important distinctions between them can now be elaborated as follows: FRAMEWORKS OF REFERENCES refer to sets or systems of facts or ideas serving to orient or give particular meaning WITHIN the contexts of the set or system.

Such frameworks would therefore tend to be involutional, i.e., infolding or entangling back into the static sets or systems of reference.

AXES OF REFERENCES refer not to already proscribed and predesigned sets or systems, but to evolutionary main lines of direction, motion, growth, or extension.

Such axes of references would therefore tend toward unfolding or untangling from proscribed and predesigned sets or systems.

Of course, the two kinds of references are not mutually exclusive, and can, as they should, be interactive.

But pertinent to empowerment, the central problem would be one of emphasis, particularly with regard to having, or developing, a sense of unfolding power at the individual level.

If the foregoing is considered patiently and deeply enough, then it becomes possible to grok that established societal power structures would design and promulgate sets or systems of references for power that refer BACK only to those power structures.

Earlier in this book it was mentioned that all books attempting to identify and describe the anatomy of power ALWAYS focus on the powerful, not upon the nature of the so-called powerless.

The involutionary result of this is that the only framework references for power we have reflect ideas about power only regarding the powerful and their societal power structures.

This gives the almost universal idea that the powerful and their societal power systems ARE what power IS.

This, of course, is cleverly manipulated nonsense, for the powerful are merely manifesting certain uses of power, while the elements for power itself are innate in our species and are therefore technically available to everyone.

The central problem here is that there are no frames or axes of reference for power that are available to everyone. As discussed in chapter 6, there are no power schools or power studies that everyone might consult in order to develop adequate frames and axes of references regarding power.

Most pointedly, there is no encyclopedia itemizing all known or suspected human powers and abilities that would help everyone to identify their own powers and abilities.

Such an encyclopedia would of course serve as extensive frames of references, and also help orient the individual regarding WHAT powers might be developed in self.

Such an encyclopedia would also have to contain discussions regarding USES for the various kinds or types of powers and abilities.

Dominion over others is one of the more obvious and simplistic uses of power. But there are many other uses as well, and so the idea that dominion over others IS power, IS the only form of power, is so retro as to be Dark Age.

ON HAVING A SENSE OF POWERLESSNESS

Having, or gaining, a sense of power must be contrasted with its opposite -- having, or adapting to, a sense of powerlessness.

It is worth considering that if one feels powerless, or does not have enough active power, then the fault is not with the individual as a life force, life energy being, but with the frames of reference that being is utilizing or has become stuck with.

If one is seeking empowerment, it is also worth admitting that frames of reference can be very limiting, especially if based on some kind of illusion in the first place.

It can easily be observed that most people will cling to their frames of reference through thick and thin, and perhaps do so even without having a complete understanding of what their frames of reference actually consist of.

However, no one in the alive, living state can be powerless, at least in any complete or total sense.

But all the evidence shows that they can be depowered, with the result that they can FEEL powerless. Depending on the circumstances in which individuals find themselves, depowerment can be partial or seemingly complete.

But the FEELING of powerlessness and the ACTUALITY of it are two different matters.

FEELING versus ACTUALITY OF POWERLESSNESS

Feelings are an internal matter and as such they have considerable impact within the working "mechanisms" of the individual -- such as the ability-mechanisms of perception, intelligence, putting things together so as to grok their whole. Thus, feelings are more intimately and immediately experienced than is perception of actuality outside of one's self.

Feelings also tend to cause one, as it is commonly said, to introvert into oneself -- to introvert and exist within one's local realities, the perceived scope of which is governed by one's limited frames of reference.

In the early days of modern psychological discovery, it was determined that introverts usually did not manifest much that could be called power recognizable to themselves or to anyone else either.

Introverts did not usually attempt to impress or imprint themselves into whatever happenings were going on outside themselves, and mostly tended to withdraw from them.

On the other hand, extroverts tended to feel more powerful because they sought to impress themselves into happenings external to themselves, and as such were more easily recognizable to others.

In a certain sense, then, the psychological as well as the energetic dynamics of introversion and extroversion were thought to be opposites of some kind, the one imploding and the other exploding.

Applied depowerment tactics are apparently designed to induce power implosion -- which is to say, to reverse the externalizing and exploding manifestations of power and empowerment which might occur if methods of depowerment were not applied.

Put this way, applied depowerment seems silly and unworkable -- because on the surface of things it is understood that most humans cannot really be controlled in such a manner, or at least for very long.

For one thing, the urges and drives to life are very strong, and it would be difficult to defeat and contain them if this was all there was to the picture of depowerment.

After all, empowerment at least partially consists of self-acknowledging one's urges and drives to life, and the living of it to the fullest.

So additional factors regarding depowerment must be involved, and in such a way that they are subtle and not easily linked to depowerment environments and situations.

REACTIVATING A SENSE OF LIFE ENERGIES

One of the problematical factors here is that we can understand things outside of us quite well and do so whether we are depowered or empowered. But we understand our energy-life-consciousness qualities very little.

As it can be shown, the frames of reference regarding ourselves as energy-life-conscious entities are usually set up within our local environments and circumstances. And so a discussion of these is the central topic of the next chapter.

ITEM TO IMAGINE

IMAGINE AT LEAST TEN FRAMES OF REFERENCE THAT INDUCE A SENSE OF POWERLESSNESS LIST THESE ON PAPER AND CONSIDER HOW THEY FIT TOGETHER TO IMPLODE A SENSE OF POWER.

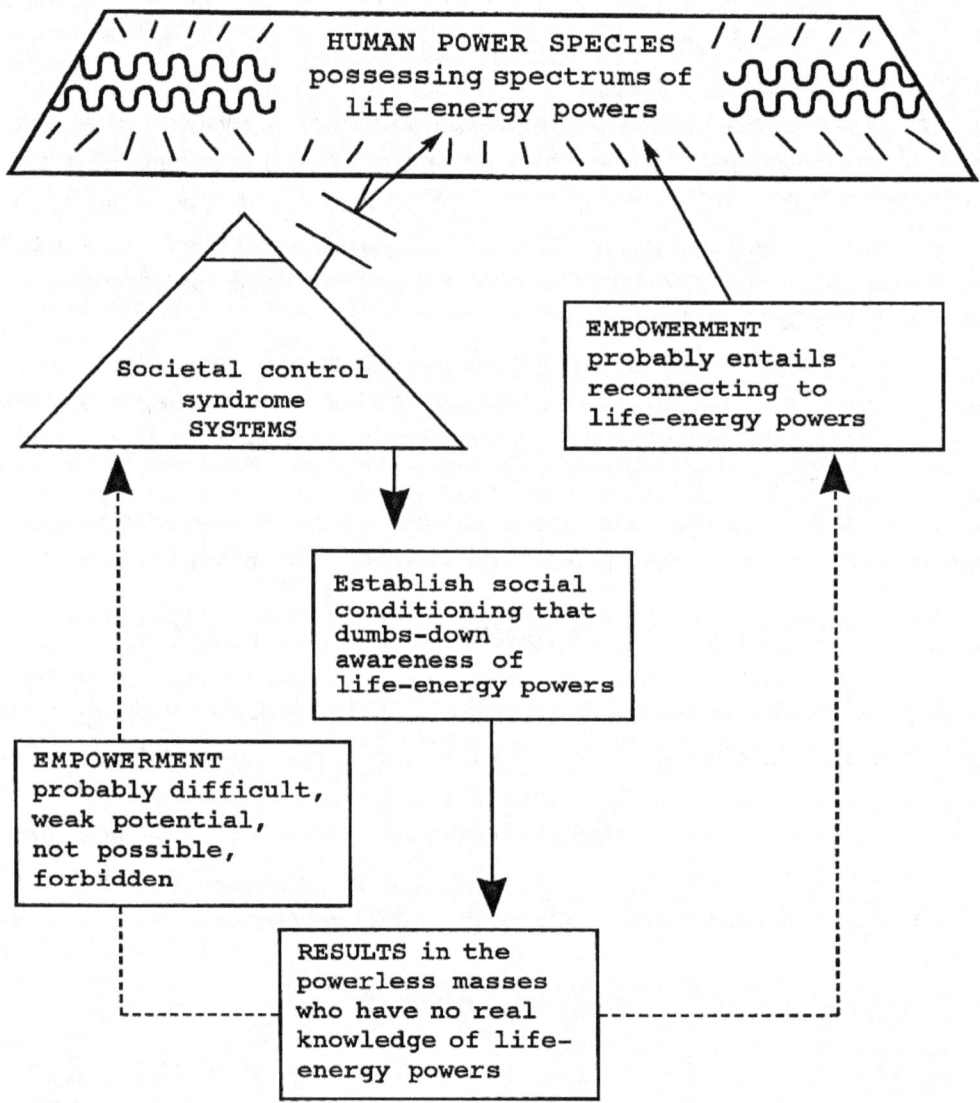

FIGURE 14. Systematized societal power of the few over others cannot really exist unless there is a broad base of the powerless who, via social conditioning, are dumbed-down about the nature of any kind of power(s). Because any given societal power System is always a particular, but temporary, socially engineered artifice, control of the powerless within it can exist only as long as the System itself does. It is thus possible to distinguish between temporary SOCIETAL power syndromes and the real existence of HUMAN life-energy powers in general. At the individual level, a sense of powerlessness can result from (1) feelings of inadequacy within the societal power syndrome, and/or (2) socially-conditioned dumbed-down awareness of human life-energy powers over all.

Chapter 17

PERSONAL POWER versus LOCAL CIRCUMSTANCES AND FRAMES OF REFERENCE

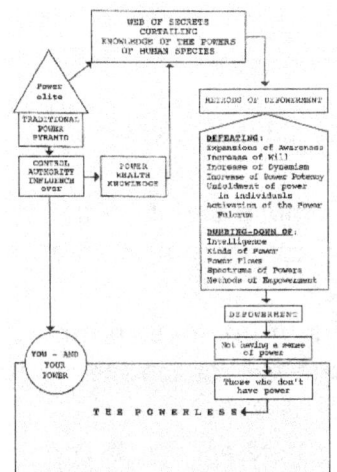

THE PHRASE "frames of reference" is important enough to be included in many dictionaries.

Yet it is surprising how many people have no knowledge of it -- or, if they know of the phrase, consider that it applies to others, not to themselves. Some even consider that it has no applicable meaning at all.

One of the usual results of this is that many never attempt to examine their frames of reference. And to be sure, this failure clearly has many negative and rather dismal outcomes. It is especially deadly when it comes to ideas of power and empowerment.

FAILURE OF FRAMES OF REFERENCE REGARDING POWER AND EMPOWERMENT

There are several societal reasons behind this failure. For example, the concepts of information, knowledge, facts, and realities usually take precedence over frames of reference, and so most will think in terms of those concepts.

However, it can be shown that information, knowledge, facts, and realities are built up out of accumulated frames of reference that are stuck together to form a basic framework of some kind -- and which thereafter has much to do with how things are perceived and understood.

It can also be shown that after the initial framework has been constructed and formatted, it equates to a mind-set through which any additional information, knowledge, facts, and realities are processed in a kind of closed-loop way.

It is thus that frames of reference at the personal level emerge as enormously important regarding perceptions of power, personal empowerment, and any desire having to do with becoming power-active in any sphere of activity.

This becomes more vividly understandable if one considers the total absence of power schools and in-depth power studies. This absence means that frames of reference that are more exact and appropriate regarding empowerment have been deleted from broad common awareness of them.

CONSTRUCTING AND DECONSTRUCTING FRAMES OF REFERENCE

It may, by now, seem needlessly repetitive to go on so much about frames of reference. But it is quite likely that a good deal of what we can become aware or conscious of depends on having appropriate frames of reference.

This can be computed from the easily observable fact that if one does not have frames of reference regarding certain things, then on average one will not achieve much exact, or even any, awareness or consciousness of them.

If one very carefully considers the existence of frames of reference, it becomes entirely possible to think that our species has the generic faculties for constructing frames of reference, in much the same way as we have generic faculties for making and speaking thousands of different languages.

But if our species possesses the innate faculties to construct frames of reference, the same faculties, when applied in the reverse, can be utilized to deconstruct them.

And, to be quite sure, the deconstruction of frames of reference is not only one of the tools of power, but is a tool that has quite a number of uses.

For example, openly or covertly deconstructing the frames of reference of others is often a very workable way of achieving control, authority, and influence over them -- at least in a general perspective.

However, and as already discussed, the very best way is to deprive others of frames of reference in the first place. This deprivation is the equivalent of deliberately engineering different kinds of stupidity in others.

And this process not only makes it easier to establish and maintain power over the victims of the engineering, but also is helpful in keeping them stupid about the processes of empowerment.

THE RELATIONSHIP OF FRAMES OF REFERENCE TO BASIC PREMISES

The term PREMISE is taken from the Latin term PRAEMITTERE which means "to place something ahead of something else."

The English definition of PREMISE is given as "a proposition antecedently supposed or proved as a basis of inference or argument."

The several meanings of ANTECEDENT are:

1. To precede;

2. To be or place in front of;
3. To have occurred earlier;
4. The significant events, conditions, and traits of one's earlier life;
5. A model or stimulus for later developments.

While it is true that a basic premise can be based on facts, it is also the case that it can be based on smoke or columns of air.

Even so, frames of reference can be built up around a premise thought to be basic, and which framework thereafter is assumed as giving authenticity and actual reality to the premise itself.

These frames of reference might be confused or confusing, but their general authenticity is seldom inspected, while the assumed authenticity of the basic premise is hardly ever questioned.

As but two examples of this kind of thing, in male-dominant societies, the basic social-conditioning premise for power was seen as an exclusively male thing, and the frames of reference built up around this premise achieved a rather enormous and fantastic architecture.

But the same can be said of the ancient female-dominant societies, where power was exclusively a female thing -- and in which, as of this date, the exact functions of males has never been intimately identified.

In actuality, however, it is quite obvious that power falls into the hands and minds of those who have achieved excellent knowledge of the workings of stealth power.

This is a sort of hidden equal-opportunity kind of thing which of course applies to males and females and could even be relevant to extraterrestrial societies elsewhere in the cosmos.

FRAMES OF REFERENCE REGARDING PERSONAL POWER

The fourth definition of ANTECEDENT given above refers to significant events, conditions, and traits of one's earlier life.

For the purposes of this book, this refers to antecedent premises and frames of reference having to do with depowerment, empowerment, and power.

"Earlier life" presumably refers not only to childhood, but to anything before "now" that was significant about power, conditions around it, and traits that formed because of those, the sum of which has somehow been formatted into basic premises and frames of reference.

What comprises earlier life of each individual presents a massive and ultra-complicated scenario of different events and traits whose significance is clearly related to the local circumstances in which each individual has lived or is living.

It is thus up to the individual to assess the frames of reference acquired within or because of those local circumstance.

However, it is worth taking time to examine what is meant by "local circumstances."

LOCAL CIRCUMSTANCES WITH REGARD TO POWER AND EMPOWERMENT

It is now understood quite well in various psychologies that infants and children do observe very carefully the power dynamics prevalent in their local circumstances and societies.

Such observations are clearly significant and dynamic, and regardless of what they consist of, they are probably permanently imprinted, the imprints tending to automatically format frames of reference regarding power.

It is true that some individuals appear to have a broad sense of power that transcends local circumstances.

But most people conceptualize power principally within the terms of their local circumstances -- those circumstances into which they have been born, which persist around them, and within which they live out their lives.

The realities people do have or acquire are initially derived from those circumstances, although the realities can be altered by education and experience of different locales and their circumstances.

A good deal of rather basic mind-set programming is also derived from local circumstances one has adapted to. And so one tends to think about power as it was generally thought of by others participating and sharing in the same local circumstances.

The various elements which go into the formatting of local circumstances are absorbed early in one's life, and as one grows up they more or less sink beneath the levels of active consciousness.

The foregoing comments are good enough for superficial thinking. But in order to get beyond or beneath the superficial, it is necessary to examine the meanings of three terms having relevance to power and empowerment.

The term LOCAL has four slightly different definitions, but each of which has relationship to empowerment:

1. Characterized by, relating, to, or occupying a particular place;
2. Primarily serving the needs of a particular limited district;
3. Characterized by or relating to a position in space; and
4. Not broad or general.

For the purposes of this discussion, definitions (2) and (4) above can be slightly altered and combined as: Primarily serving the needs of a particular limited reality, which is not broad or general. Of course, something that is limited cannot be broad or general, but the slight redundancy here is utilized to increase emphasis.

What is not limited, and is broad and general, is thought of as being UNIVERSAL. This term also has four useful definitions:

1. Including or covering all of a whole collectively or distributively without limit or exception.
2. Present or occurring everywhere;
3. Comprehensively broad and versatile; and
4. Denoting every member of a class [or a species].

UNIVERSAL, GENERAL, and GENERIC are given as synonyms:
GENERAL - Implies reference to all or nearly all;
GENERIC - Implies reference to every member of a class or species.
UNIVERSAL - Implies reference to everyone without exception in the class, category, or genus considered.

The third term to be considered is UNIVERSALITY, which has three meaningful definitions:

1. The quality or state of being universal;
2. Universal comprehensiveness in range; and
3. Unrestricted versatility or power of adaptation or [power of] comprehension.

Please note that the use of the term "power" in the third definition above IS found in most dictionaries and is therefore not merely a convenient additive interjected by this author. (Please note that the third definition refers to "essential" powers of our species, which were defined and discussed in chapter 2.)

The reason for reviewing these definitions is to point up two factors that people usually don't think about, but which are significant to power and empowerment:

1. That members of our species universally possess the generic power of adapting to local circumstances; and
2. Also have the generic power of contracting and confining their powers of comprehension to the needs of those local circumstances.

The foregoing is needed in order to point up something about local circumstances that has direct importance not only to one's notions about power, but with regard to any hope for vivid empowerment.

The term LOCAL CIRCUMSTANCES seems automatically to be interpreted as referring exclusively to a position in physical place, or to factors that belong in or are part of it.

Thus, one may physically move to this or that different locale and therein experience circumstances local to it. These circumstances may provide one with additional significant events and traits regarding power and empowerment.

But there is one local circumstance that remains permanently local no matter where one goes in physical terms.

Wherever one goes, one takes one's "head" with them, and it contains the premises and frames of reference one has regarding power, empowerment, and even depowerment.

Because of this, it is possible to think that one's head is the most permanent of all local circumstances.

LOCAL VERSUS UNIVERSAL CONCEPTS OF POWER

From the foregoing, it is possible to intuit that as long as individuals consider power and empowerment in some kind of local way or format, including the frameworks in one's local head, their overviews of power will remain local in one way or another.

Perhaps this is as it should be -- if one wishes to permanently dwell within power constructs that are applicable only within local circumstances, including the local circumstances of one's own head.

But as mentioned earlier, to some large degree individuals can become aware of or perceive only what they have frames of reference for.

But if it can be thought that local stuff is only good within the contexts of local stuff, it could also be thought that universal stuff is good within the contexts of universal stuff.

In this sense, one can bet with some certainty that even working overtime trying to itemize one's local frames of reference regarding power and empowerment, one might never recognize the absence of more universal frames of reference.

UNIVERSAL FORMATS OF POWER AND EMPOWERMENT

Hypothetically speaking, then, one could achieve local power over those dwelling in the same locality or within the same localisms.

However, acquiring more universal frames of reference regarding power could result in achieving more universal kinds of empowerment.

A significant empowerment objective, or method, therefore, is not only to focus on and examine local frames of reference (with the hopes of improving upon them), but also ADD other frames of reference that are more universal in nature.

It might take some time to grok this, but then there is nothing about power that is easy.

ITEMS TO MEDITATE UPON

CONCEPTUALIZE FOUR ELEMENTS OF POWER THAT ARE MORE UNIVERSAL THAN MERELY LOCAL.

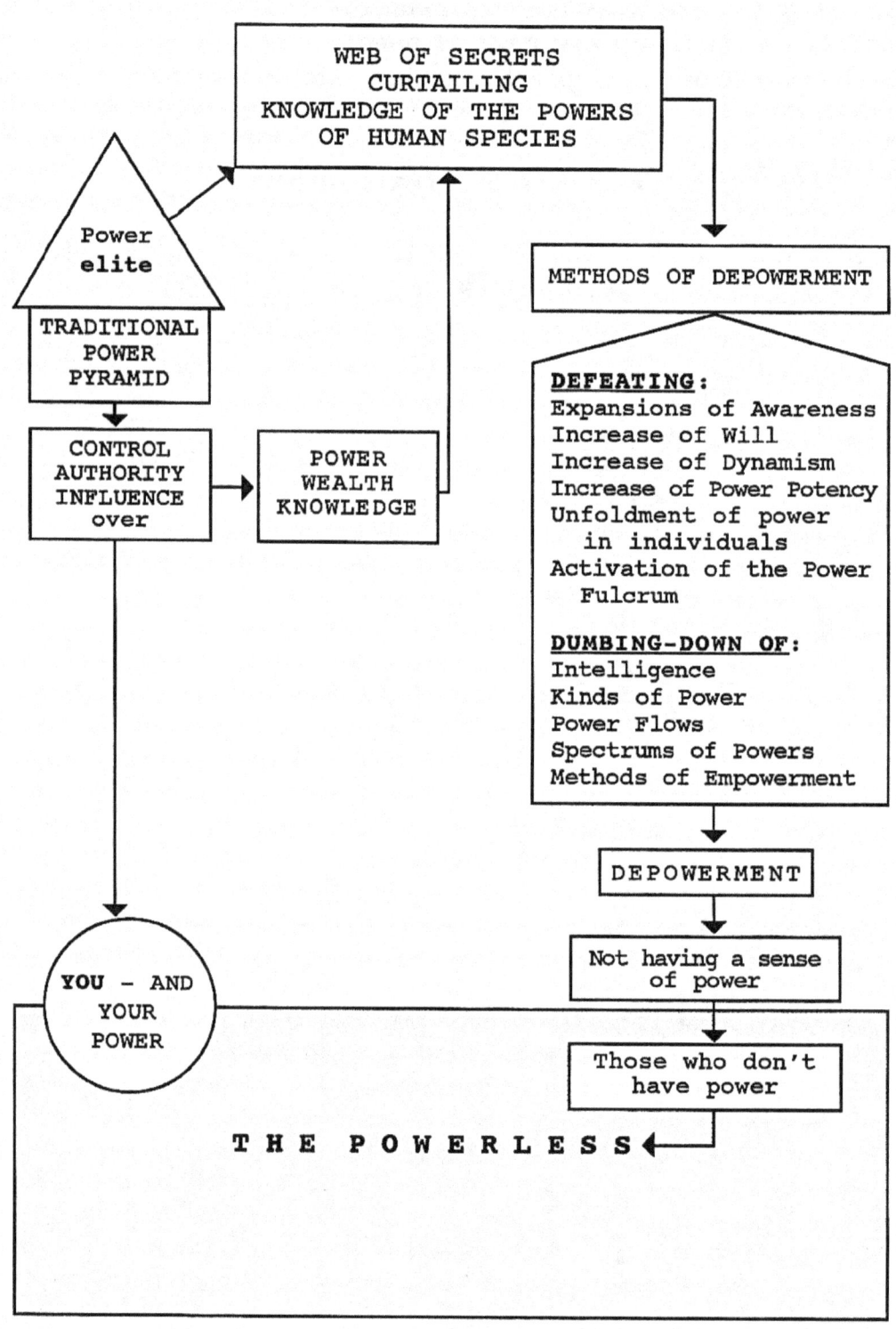

PART FOUR
GETTING BEYOND SOCIETAL, GROUP, AND INDIVIDUAL VERSIONS OF POWER

Chapter 18

CLOSED-LOOP VERSIONS OF POWER

IT IS quite natural to become interested in examples of power that are manifest within smaller or larger areas of activity one has access to. Various formats of power can be examined in this way, the endpoint being that one will think that one then knows something about power.

There is no reason not to examine various formats of power in this way. ANY knowledge acquired about power is better than not acquiring any at all. And it is certainly possible to study power manifestations within the contexts of societal, group, and individual power formats.

It is quite logical to do this. After all, it is within the contexts of those formats and frames of reference that individuals will seek empowerment if they can figure out how to do so.

Even if people fail in their empowerment objectives, they nevertheless will have added frames of reference to their knowledge pools.

Indeed, the most fundamental basis for empowerment is to continuously add frames of reference. Otherwise ignorance of power and empowerment will never be ameliorated and upgrading toward empowerment will remain stultified. But there are subtle issues involved with this kind of study that are important to achieving a larger understanding about power.

One of the issues is connected to the fact that when people aim for empowerment, they do so within the contexts of the power environments in which they wish to achieve it.

The contexts of those power environments are based upon specific frames of reference, and which imply "rules" regarding power and empowerment. The direct implication is that if one obeys the rules implicit in the frames of reference, there is at least hope for empowerment.

But this is a situation in which the power activities within the environments more or less feedback the authenticity of the frames of reference and their working contexts.

This is clearly a closed-loop kind of thing, in that success or failure is governed by acting in ways that are consistent with the local frames of reference. This can be stated another way.

It is possible to achieve power within certain frames of reference and doing so in turn confirms the authenticity of those frames of reference.

The closed-loop power environment can easily be thought of as the model of what power is in general. But the model may not effectively transfer to other power environments based in other frames of reference.

There is a blunt way of clarifying this. Small-time power can be achieved within small-time frames of reference. But that power might not work when, for example, it comes it comes to big-time frames of reference or other kinds of frames of reference.

As it is usually perceived, the principal goal of empowerment is to succeed within a specific area of activity one is interested in.

For example, consider the "worlds" of politics, sociology, business, criminality, education science, philosophy, and even of art, literature, and music. Each have their own manifesting power systems based in their own closed-loop frames of reference, as well as their own hidden mechanisms and situations.

So an individual achieving power within science can easily be power defunct in the worlds of politics, art, and philosophy because the frames of reference are different.

VICISSITUDES OF POWER AND EMPOWERMENT

It is quite usual to construct a model-for-empowerment for the different "worlds" of activity based on what can easily be seen in some objective way.

However, most power systems are also encapsulated within hidden situations, and which themselves are based on hidden frames of reference.

The first of the hidden situations involved with those "worlds" is the fact that not only are they largely transitory in nature, but the personnel achieving or manifesting power within them are decidedly transitory.

Even the modalities of power within them can change at any given time. Some of the modalities can suddenly become inefficient, politically incorrect, retro, moribund, undesirable, even incomprehensible.

Indeed, one of the working characteristics of Machiavellian stealth-power techniques is to deliberately CAUSE power modalities to change so that the existing power people can be dethroned, and new up-coming ones can claim installation in their place.

There are some recognizable fallouts of this. If, for example, one is utilizing the empowerment criteria and frames of reference of one of the transient power worlds, one can easily be not very knowledgeable with regard to other power worlds.

One can even wind up being not very knowledgeable about a selected world of power and empowerment if that world undergoes change -- which it eventually will.

The foregoing observations apply to societal, group, and individual power and empowerment formats -- all of which are temporary and transient to one degree or another.

It is this kind of thing that obviously inspired the old axiom that "power is fickle" and also brought about the expression regarding "the vicissitudes of power."

VICISSITUDE refers to "the quality or state of being changeable; natural change or mutation visible in nature or in human affairs."

STAYING POWER

STAYING POWER can be conceptualized as "surviving power changes in an ever-changing power world."

If one is utilizing power models based on any given societal, group, or individual power frames of reference, then whether one will also achieve staying power over time is at least somewhat questionable. The principal reason is that power systems are always composed human affairs, and those affairs are always undergoing change.

Even the well-used format of force power does not automatically bestow staying power.

And of course, those who manage to occupy positions of artificial power often fall like lined-up dominos when strategic power changes come about.

Stealth power can be thought of as more staying, especially if it is invisible behind the scenes of changing power.

But stealth power devotees and functionaries are always at staying power risk because of the equally stealth power machinations of other opportunistic devotees and functionaries. Indeed, stealth power wars are usually quite nerve-racking in that regard.

But it is from an in-depth examination of stealth power wars that a clue emerges regarding the nature of staying power.

That clue is this: anyone who does become at least somewhat proficient in stealth power CANNOT possibly think only in terms of existing formats and models set up at the societal, group, or individual power levels.

The reason is that those formats and models are based in limited frames of reference that feedback upon themselves in closed-loop kinds of ways.

In high contrast, proficient stealth power activity must be based on factors that transcend the limits of closed-loop power activities in order to survive the changes that go on within them.

It is therefore obvious that staying power is closely related NOT to limited frames of reference, but to other power factors that transcend them.

One of the meanings here is that those other power factors do not need to be discussed by continuously referring back to closed-loop power situations at the societal, group, or individual.

It is the case, however, that those other power factors can be applied to closed-loop power situations or can at least trickle down into them. The closed-loop frames of reference, however, do not serve as the basic premises for power contexts that transcend all of them.

The import of this chapter might be a little hard to grok at first reading. It may be helpful to be reminded that all visible societal power structures do not represent power itself but are merely societal artifices via which power is distributed to the few and withheld from the many.

ITEM TO EXPLORE

IDENTIFY AT LEAST FIVE SOCIETAL POWER STRUCTURES THAT HAVE CLOSED-LOOP FRAMES OF REFERENCE DO NOT INCLUDE "THE WEALTHY" BECAUSE THEIR SOCIETAL POWER STRUCTURES ARE ALL TOO OBVIOUS AND THEREFORE DON'T CONSTITUTE A COGNITIVE CHALLENGE.

Chapter 19

POWER - INTELLIGENCE - SMARTS

A SUBTLE aspect that is embedded in social conditioning gives the teaching that the top echelons of the typical power pyramid personify power itself.

This teaching is easily converted into the idea that the personification of power actually IS power itself.

It then follows that there are no other modes of understanding regarding what power actually is beyond this teaching. The top echelons have control, authority, and influence over others, and so that is what power is.

If this is accepted as the fundamental and absolutely indispensable and essential definition of power, then it becomes difficult to conceptualize anything that can transcend this unilateral teaching. There are three functional definitions of UNILATERAL:

1. One-sided;
2. Of, or relating to, one side of a subject; and
3. Whatever is produced or arranged so as to be directed to one side, to the exclusion of other sides.

The concept that power IS control, authority, and influence over others is actually only one side of the subject of power.

But if that single-side is to be effective and efficient in social conditioning, then the idea that power might have other sides must be concealed, or at least not emphasized.

That power unilaterally IS only control, authority, and influence over others is, of course, a closed-loop frame of reference, and which, via social conditioning, inspires all to think of power in no other way.

It thus follows that if THAT is what power IS, then it is difficult to conceptualize anything that might transcend that unilateral, closed-loop frame of reference.

All societal and social matters considered, this closed-loop framework can be made so airtight that it will escape notice that control, authority, and influence over others are merely USES of power, but not power itself.

This is to say that the anatomy of control, authority, and influence over others is NOT the anatomy of power itself, but merely the anatomy of uses of power.

Indeed, if the USES, as contrasted to the anatomy, of human-designed power structures are examined closely, it can be seen that they easily break apart into TWO purposes having the following priority.

The FIRST purpose has to do with distributing the uses, functions, and rewards of power among those who become part of the structure.

This usually means that more uses, and the dominion that goes with them, will go to those few who establish the dominion. Those few are often referred to as the power elite, either visible within or invisible behind the scenes of the structure.

Lesser uses of power will go to those who agree to the dominion of the few, who will also agree to work within and on behalf of the dominion of the few.

It is now important to point up that UNLESS the distribution of the uses of power is first sorted out among the powerful, then the second purpose cannot really come into being.

The SECOND purpose, of course, IS the infamous control, authority, and influence over others within the power structure entire. This includes the relatively powerless, and the functionally powerless.

But it must be carried in mind that human-designed power structures are seldom called as such. Rather they tend to be referred to as "social structures," while those incorporated in them from the top to the bottom are referred to as "society."

TRANSCENDING SOCIALLY CONDITIONED CONCEPTS OF POWER

As has been discussed in earlier chapters, the general public is denied access to power knowledge, not only via social conditioning, but as a result of actually making such knowledge permanently unavailable.

Beyond that, one of the prevailing aspect-problems is why power seems to flow to or collect within some humans and not others.

The English language does not have an exact term for this kind of person, but German does: MACHTMENSCH.

This could be translated into English as "power-maker." But in German it's closer to "power-human," examples of which, in a fundamental essence, have some kind of intuitive contact with kinds of "power energies."

So, in English, perhaps the closest meaning to the German might be something like power-energy-human -- as contrasted to power-de-energized-human.

In societal terms, it might first be thought that simply denying access to power to the members of those echelons might be a most efficient goal.

But as it could turn out, unless the power potentials among those members were de-energized in some fundamental way, then merely denying access to power could become quite a contest and burden.

In other words, the powerless must somehow be made to FEEL powerless in some kind of way that seems logical and authentic to them, and in a way that will neutralize, and/or de-energize, any feelings of being powerful.

Some examples of this might include: being born into a naturally powerless class; being socially conditioned to think of oneself as stupid and illiterate; not having enough education; not being too intelligent; not being acceptable to one's betters; being taught to respect the powerful; and so forth.

Above all, the powerless must not be permitted to have any idea of what can transcend human-designed power structures -- those societal artifices mistaken as power itself.

In the sense of the foregoing, the ideas of power energization and de-energization begin to take on meaning, at least with regard to starting up empowerment processes within self.

And indeed, it would be logical to suppose that power energization attracts power, while power de-energization would not do so, and might even repel power.

So, a MACHTMENSCH would, in a fundamental way, be power-energized -- if only because a machtmensch could not be considered as being power de-energized.

Among many other possible power-energy factors, there are at least three that can be energized or de-energized. All three of them can be distinguished as characteristic of power-energized-humans, and as qualities that transcend the uses of power for purposes of control, authority, and influencing.

These three factors can be identified as essential power itself, intelligence, and smarts. These three factors might also be thought of as:

1. Empowering-powers over power manifestations and uses;
2. Empowering formats of intelligence; and
3. Empowering smarts.

It should already be obvious that these three factors can transcend the usual definitions of power uses, and that they have something to do with staying power.

But it should also be immediately obvious that there are few frames of reference that are applicable to them.

And, by hypothesis at least, it could be obvious that the three factors would attract power to those in which they become energized.

In chapter 9, four generic and more easily recognized kinds of power were identified. The concept of STAYING POWER was added in chapter 18. These were:

FORCE POWER
ARTIFICIAL POWER
REAL POWER

STEALTH POWER
STAYING POWER
To those five can be added:

EMPOWERING-POWERS OVER POWER
MANIFESTATIONS AND USES
EMPOWERING FORMATS OF DIFFERENT KINDS OF INTELLIGENCE
EMPOWERING FORMATS OF SMARTS

ITEM TO FOOL AROUND WITH

IN A POWER-GAMES KIND OF WAY CONSIDER WHICH OF THE EIGHT KINDS OF POWER COULD TRANSCEND OTHERS.

Chapter 20

EVOCATIVE POWER, INTELLIGENCE, AND SMARTS

IN ORDER to discuss the nature of evocative power, intelligence, and smarts, it is necessary to review a number of terms and the background basis for Intelligence Quotient (IQ) testing.

The reason for examining the terms will become apparent. But there are two notable reasons to be taken into account regarding IQ testing.

The first is that during the twentieth century, the concepts of IQ and Intelligence came to be thought of as the same thing, in that they were interpreted as reflecting the status of each other in individuals.

It is thus necessary to examine the background of IQ testing. This leads to a discovery not only regarding what aspects of intelligence have been integrated into IQ testing, but, more importantly, what aspects have never achieved integration.

The second reason is that although human power and human intelligence have different contexts, intelligence undeniably does have something to do with power and empowerment. In that inescapable case, it is necessary to make some kind of studious attempt to expand frames of reference regarding intelligence.

Rather than fly off into imagination exercises, there is a most efficient and productive way of achieving this, at least in some full part.

This involves a patient examination of dictionary words and terms whose meanings are somehow directly connected with basic concepts that are evocative of intelligence.

EVOCATIVE POWER

Words can, of course, be understood, but sometimes only in passive or dead-head kinds of ways. The terms INTELLECT and INTELLIGENCE are used all the time, but frequently in the absence of knowing their precise definitions. And their definitions bring to light other important terms.

EVOCATIVE means "to call forth or up; to summon up," in ways that go beyond merely passive or so-called "intellectual" understanding.

With respect to power and empowerment, it is technically possible to merely understand many things that are involved.

But if the understanding does not also trigger, stimulate, activate, or initiate vitalizing empowerment processes, then whatever is involved will not become enabled.

And as an aside, here is a clue with regard to depowerment. If one wants to keep others depowered, then one must ensure that they do not experience anything that would be evocative. Thus, control, authority, and influence over others more or less suggest control over the evocative powers of those others.

More to the point of this chapter, whatever is evocative has something to do with whatever individuals find interesting.

One should therefore read this slightly complicated chapter not only toward understanding and groking, but with some attention to what the various topics evoke.

SMARTS AND SMART POWER

Any discussion about the nature of intelligence and its many confusing factors is surrounded by many complicated and misleading frames of reference.

Of course, this is to be expected if power is defined as the control, authority, and influence of others.

In this case, it is logical that the powerful must have control, authority, and influence not only over the intelligence of the others, but over how misunderstandings about intelligence should be engineered.

In this sense, the engineered misunderstandings would act like prophylactic preventives against the emergence of evocative understandings that might trigger and activate empowerment and power.

Indeed, induced misunderstanding is always a powerful prophylactic to prevent evocative understanding of almost everything.

In societal terms, the exact nature of intelligence has always undergone massive social attention, one of the results being that it is NOT understood very well.

Even so, that great lack of understanding has always been surrounded by extensive confusions simply because of the inordinate interest in the topic involved.

Thus, in order to temporarily side-step the possible confusions surrounding intelligence, it is the better part of valor to first discuss a topic closely related to it.

This is the topic of SMARTS, and it is one that is not encumbered by confusions -- and most realize it is entirely relevant to achieving power.

THE EVOCATIVE NATURE OF SMARTS

In its first official definition as a verb, TO SMART generally has to do with "pain, grief or remorse."

As a noun, SMART can also officially refer to "an affectedly witty or fashionable person."

The definition of SMART as an adjective, however, is given as: "marked by often sharp forceful activity or vigorous strength."

With this, we again find ourselves in the vicinity of power, whose many manifestations and uses can be marked by forceful activity or vigorous strength.

Most dictionaries will go on to define, for example, SMART MONEY -- this kind of money having an association with inside information or experience.

Indeed, today one can talk of various kinds of smarts -- smart economics, smart politics, smart industry, smart technology, smart art, and other smart whatnot -- including, of course, smart power.

It seems that the essence of SMARTS being used in those ways has to do with knowing, taking advantage of, or becoming affiliated to something BEFORE it becomes more broadly known.

In that sense, smart power, for example, is at least somewhat related to stealth power.

As a term used in the sense of the above, SMARTS is at least partially slang. Dictionaries of slang establish something that official dictionaries do not: that SMARTS is some kind of combination of "intelligence, cleverness, and acumen."

ACUMEN POWER

One can immediately recognize that cleverness has something to do with power and empowerment. But it is via the word ACUMEN that one hits deeper pay dirt.

ACUMEN usually has only one definition which is given as "keenness of perception, discernment, or discrimination, especially in practical matters."

Given as a synonym for acumen is DISCERNMENT and which is defined as:

1. An act of discerning;
2. Skill in discerning or discriminating among different things; and
3. KEENNESS OF INSIGHT [emphasis added.]

Voila! SMARTS is something like keenness of insight, based on the extent of one's active perception faculties, combined with intelligence, cleverness, and acumen. (Please note that the foregoing is a good example of the advisability of tracking down the meaning of words.)

STREET SMARTS

One of the reasons for having made the above trek into the definitions of smarts is to bring into view two factors that are relevant to the topics of this chapter:

1. It can be observed that many who have low IQ status have some and even high functions of smarts;
2. It can also be observed that many who have high IQ status have low or no functions of smarts.

An observable distinction here is that smarts is not measured by IQ testing, and that IQ testing that measures intelligence probably does not measure SQ (smarts quotient).

Since smarts and IQ can be identified by any number of contrasting variables, they are probably not the same thing, and therefore do not fall into the same category of evocative human activity especially when it comes to power and empowerment.

KEENNESS-OF-INSIGHT POWERS

A problem with groking the nature of smarts has to do with comprehending the meaning of keenness of insight.

The official definitions of INSIGHT are amazing. They are given as (get this):

1. The POWER [emphasis added] or act of seeing into a situation;
2. Penetration [via some kind of mental powers];
3. The act of apprehending the inner nature of things or of seeing intuitively.

As one of its definitions, APPREHEND means "to recognize the meaning of." I.e., NOT the facts of, but the meaning of them.

The definitions of KEEN (as in "keen insight") refer to:

1. Extremely sensitive in perception;
2. Acute, astute;
3. Showing a quick and ardent responsiveness;
4. Sharp, to the point.

As an aside, it is worthwhile at this keen point to suggest that all one has to do to depower others is to reduce the scope of their perceptions.

SMART INTELLECT, SMART INTELLIGENCE

With the foregoing definitions in hand, one is now prepared to examine not just intelligence per se, but smart intelligence and smart intellect.

Here one has to consider the possibility that there is a difference between intellect and smart intellect, or between intelligence and smart intelligence.

And about the only frame of reference we have to refer to those considerations is what is commonly known as STREET SMARTS.

If one thinks about it, cleverness, alertness, quick-wittedness, keenness, and special knowing or special awareness are all elements of street smarts, and in almost the same way that they are elements of smart money, smart technology, smart power, etc.

If one considers the nature of street smarts carefully enough, it can be seen that there is a considerable difference between intellect and smart intellect.

Intellect would be, well, just intellect. Street smarts intellect would have the attributes of sharp, forceful activity or vigorous strength.

And as already mentioned, sharp, forceful activity or vigorous strength can easily be accepted as one of the essential definitions of power that can download into numerous manifestations and uses.

It therefore stands to reason that the downsizing or lack of forceful activity or vigorous strength can just as easily be seen as a condition of depowerment or

powerlessness.

And indeed, the up-grading or down-sizing of perceptions, awareness, insight, acumen, intelligence, and smarts, etc., have direct reference to empowerment and depowerment.

CONFUSIONS SURROUNDING THE NATURE OF HUMAN INTELLIGENCE AND INTELLECT

If it can be thought that intelligence has some important connection to power and empowerment, then exact knowledge regarding the nature of intelligence must be denied to the powerless masses.

If that is not completely possible, then the topic of intelligence must somehow become surrounded with dense, smoke-like layers of confusion.

The ancient Romans had a great metaphor for those who spread beguiling confusions: they were called smoke vendors who "sold" smoke to innocent and not-so-innocent intellects.

That smoke-like confusions can be brought into existence about intelligence can be deduced from the fact that one can study what is known about intelligence -- but hardly ever find it linked to the topics of power and empowerment.

Of course, the almost total absence of accessible knowledge about power and empowerment makes it quite easy to detach information about intelligence from knowledge about power.

One can hardly comprehend links between two sets of knowledge if one of the sets is concealed.

As everyone knows, at least in part, research on the topic of intelligence received enormous visibility during the nineteenth and twentieth centuries.

Based on the sum of that research (which, all things considered, is impressive), it would seem that intelligence could be energetically nurtured on a broad societal basis, and in growth-oriented ways.

After all, if knowledge about something is increased and accumulated, then it is at least theoretically possible to manage it in increasingly productive ways.

As it has turned out, though, and as other writers have pointed up, extremely little along such lines has come to be.

This is a vast discrepancy of no mean importance. It is completely amazing, even wondrous -- for a species that identifies the possession of intelligence as perhaps its most glorious virtue.

If one can get past the astonishment, there is at least one feasible reason for the discrepancy.

Intelligence, like power, wealth, control, and dominion, is a precious thing-commodity-possession.

If the masses were to have up-graded intelligence, and access to ways and means of empowering it, then the boundaries of the needed status quo between the few powerful and the powerless herds of the labor-oriented masses would quickly become wobbly, uncertain, and unpredictable.

A study of most past societal power structures reveals that all of them have somehow had to deal with this pregnant situation -- in that the existence of intelligence cannot be kept perpetually hidden within an intelligent species.

The most infamous societal way to manage this was simply to keep the masses illiterate -- the acquisition of literacy being, of course, the enormously powerful growth hormone that evokes and activates increasingly greater levels of intelligence.

The other most infamous way was to establish class systems in which only the intelligence among high power orders was of importance. This method is still being utilized, but in neo-formats based in desensitizing the powerless masses to the evocative nature of knowing TO MUCH about intelligence.

THE STRANGE STORY OF IQ TESTING

The advent of the modernist scientific-technological age brought about the need for general literacy among the masses in order to open up a rather extensive resource of competent workers. This required a limited activation of intelligence among those workers.

Thus arose the problem of how to activate intelligence but to keep it limited so as not to empower too much.

One feasible way of accomplishing this admittedly delicate matter was to openly admit that all humans had intelligence, but most of them did not have ENOUGH of it to matter.

It is now necessary to labor through the history of IQ testing, short and concise versions of which can be found in most competent encyclopedias.

The one leaned upon for the following is taken from the entry regarding INTELLIGENCE found in THE NEW COLUMBIA ENCYCLOPEDIA, published in 1975, and is herewith quoted in part.

For starters, the encyclopedia establishes a general information set for intelligence.

> "INTELLIGENCE, in psychology, the general mental ability involved in calculating, reasoning, perceiving relationships and analogies, learning quickly, storing and retrieving information, using language fluently, classifying, generalizing, and adjusting to new situations. (NOTE: THIS definition will be dissected ahead.)
>
> "Alfred Binet, the French psychologist, defined intelligence as the totality of mental processes involved in adapting to the environment.
> "Although there remains a strong tendency to view intelligence as a purely intellectual or cognitive function, considerable evidence suggests that intelligence is an attribute of the entire personality that cannot be measured adequately in isolation.
>
> "It is generally accepted that potential intelligence is related to heredity and that environment is a critical factor in determining the extent of its expression."

Please note the references to "potential intelligence" and what may or may not be involved "in determining the extent of its expression." Also note the omission of the idea of nurturing potential intelligence.

> "The concept of intelligence has proved to be so elusive that psychologists often prefer to define it as that which is measured by intelligence tests.
>
> "While no consensus of opinion prevails about what such tests actually measure, their use in education has had great practical value in assigning

children to suitable class groups and in predicting academic performance. [Note that there are grounds for questioning the efficiency implied by this last, rather slick statement.]

The encyclopedia now continues with a synopsis of the history of IQ testing, beginning when Binet and Theodore Simon pioneered the first modern intelligence test in 1905, which was used to identify retarded children in the French school system.

Subsequent developments in such testing are noted, such as the Otis Group Intelligence Scale, and those kinds of IQ tests that could be administered to economically and quickly to large numbers in schools and industry.

Such tests:

". . . opened the way for a method of classifying intelligence in terms of a standardized measure, with standardization obtained from having as many individuals as possible of various ages take the test.

"The so-called intelligence quotient, or IQ, is a comparison between the mental age [revealed by the test] and the chronological age [of who is taking the test.] . . . As the child grows . . . the IQ varies to only a small extent [thereafter.]"

The encyclopedia goes on to state that "There has been a decline in interest in pure intelligence tests since the 1920s [not exactly true], and a corresponding increase in the number of mental tests that measure special aptitudes and personality factors."

As the encyclopedia established, the IQ tests opened the way for classifying intelligence in terms of a standardized measure.

This was in keeping with the great modernist urge to discover standardization procedures for nearly everything. The average mean of the standard was thought to represent normalcy -- the normal -- as contrasted to the "abnormal."

Depending on which IQ test is being used, the average, normal mean turned out to range between 95 and 110 while an IQ test score of 133 was relatively high. An IQ "score" at about 133 or above was thought to imply potential genius of some kind.

FIVE DEPOWERING DIFFICULTIES REGARDING INTELLIGENCE QUOTIENTS

One of the first difficulties with the IQ thing is its supposed relationship to normalcy, or, as it was often put, to the social norm. As judged against the typical Bell curve, the social norm comprises approximately 80 percent of the society involved.

Thus, in the IQ frame of reference, 80 percent of the social norm reflected IQ scores of about 100.

If the concept of the social norm is transferred over to the concept of the power norm, then the normal IQ score of about 100 reflects the relatively powerless norm. Indeed, the normal of any society are not very powerful.

THIS established that the societal norm consisted of humans that had some intelligence, but not enough of it to enable their escape from the relatively powerless norm into more elevated arenas of activity above the norm.

This, of course, is entirely in keeping with needs of the typical societal power pyramid which, by any means possible, needs to perpetuate a powerless norm among at least 80 percent of its incorporated populations.

The second difficulty: While some researchers of intelligence eventually shifted from IQ research into subcategories of intelligence (such as specific aptitudes and personality factors), almost all of the entire planetary cultures of the twentieth century came to accept that one's IQ was all the intelligence one could hope to have.

In other words, for better or worse, one was stuck with one's IQ "level," and which was not ever going to change very much. The IQ's of individuals were locked in cement, and nothing could be done to change them.

Thus, students need not be provided with education that was too much in excess of their IQ thresholds.

The third difficulty: As stated in the COLUMBIA ENCYCLOPEDIA, "considerable evidence suggests that intelligence is an attribute of the entire personality that cannot be measured adequately in isolation."

If that is the case, which it is, then it takes a rather gigantic leap of rather unfounded faith in order to STANDARDIZE ratios of intelligence via so-called standard IQ testing. This is almost the same as saying that intelligence is probably not what you think it is but standardize it anyway.

This kind of mishmash is of little help to individuals taking IQ tests. The suggestion then is that IQ tests have broad sociological uses but are seldom useful to those tested.

The fourth difficulty, which should be recognizable by now, is that one's so-called IQ score is merely a statistical result of a given test with a given individual in a given environment with given expectations of those conducting the test. In notable fact, different kinds of IQ tests often reveal different IQ scores.

The fifth difficulty is perhaps the worst of all. The term INTELLIGENCE is used all of the time. But great numbers of those using it have never studied its several meanings as established in dictionaries.

STANDARDIZED DEFINITIONS OF INTELLIGENCE

Most dictionaries will define INTELLIGENCE as:

1. The capacity to apprehend facts and propositions and their relationships and to reason about them; [Please note that the term APPREHEND has been discussed earlier in this chapter in relation to SMARTS.]
2. The use or exercise of the intellect, especially when carried on with considerable ability.

The same dictionaries will usually define INTELLIGENT in a somewhat different way, especially when extended through synonyms, and which differences are entirely salient to having or achieving power and activating empowerment:

1. Possessing intelligence;
2. Guided or directed by intellect, i.e. rational;
3. Revealing or reflecting good judgment or sound thought, i.e., being skillful;
4. Success in coping with new situations and solving problems.

SYNONYMS:

CLEVER - implying native (or natural indwelling) ability or aptness and sometimes suggests a lack of more substantial qualities; [Note that clever is an empowerment function, so to speak.]

ALERT - stresses quickness in perceiving and understanding; [Likewise, alert is an empowerment function.]

QUICK-WITTED - implying promptness in finding answers in debate or in devising expedients in moments of danger or challenge; [Likewise an empowerment function.]

KNOWING - implying the possession of special knowledge which may often connote sophistication, secretiveness, or cynicism; [or, it might be added, special smart-like faculties not measured by standard IQ tests, such as keen insight, and fundamental forms of intuition.]

The synonyms for INTELLIGENT listed above are suggestive of functions of intelligence. Those functions can be found in individuals just about anywhere, whether they test at low or high IQ status.

As indicated above, if they are considered carefully, the synonyms for INTELLIGENT are entirely suggestive of fundamental empowerment processes.

DISSECTING THE PSYCHOLOGY DEFINITION OF INTELLIGENCE

The definition of intelligence established in psychology has already been noted. But it is given here once more, and for two reasons that will shortly become obvious.

"INTELLIGENCE, in psychology, the general mental ability involved in calculating, reasoning, perceiving relationship and analogies, learning quickly, storing and retrieving information, using language fluently, classifying, generalizing, and adjusting to new situations."

THE FIRST FAILURE OF THE PSYCHOLOGY DEFINITION

At first take, this definition seems right on the mark, and will remain that way -- until, or if and when, one realizes that it DOES NOT define intelligence.

And indeed, it cannot -- because the same psychology discipline which offered up that definition also is on record as admitting to the fact that:

"The concept of intelligence has proved to be so elusive that psychologists often prefer to define it [simply and superficially] as that which is measured by intelligence tests."

Indeed, the psychology definition above identifies not intelligence per se, but merely provides a short list of what intelligence can LEARN. The psychological definition is thus referring to learned skills, or to categories of performance, rather than intelligence per se. Indeed, intelligence per se may have many innate categories that have not become activated.

With the possible exception of storing and retrieving information, all of the other items on the list are the result of learning on top of innate intelligence.

In general, one has to be taught to calculate, to reason, to perceive relationships, to learn quickly, to classify, to generalize, and so forth.

The faculties for these abilities may be innate in all individuals, but their expression must arise via tutoring, encouragement, and nurturing.

IQ tests based on this definition (as most have been) therefore mostly reflect what the tested has learned. Therefore, such tests do not circumscribe the complete potential panorama of intelligence.

As but one example, the attributes of SMARTS, such as keen insight, cleverness, and acumen, are not included in IQ tests.

THE SECOND FAILURE OF THE PSYCHOLOGY DEFINITION

The second failure of the psychology definition may not ever become visible unless it is pointed up.

The definition states that intelligence is "the general mental ability involved in . . ." etc.

Please note that the word "ability" is given in the singular -- the implication of which is that intelligence is being conceptualized as ONE SINGLE given thing.

Well, in that "The concept of intelligence has proved to be so elusive ..." etc., how, then, is it known that intelligence is one, single given thing?

This definition is somewhat ridiculous -- especially in that even IQ tests DO NOT test for a single, given thing.

All IQ tests are broken up into different categories, each of which tests for a different kind of intelligence: for example, the intelligence to calculate, the intelligence to reason, the intelligence to classify, and etc.

The other option is to wonder if intelligence is not a single thing, but perhaps a series of separate KINDS of intelligences, each of which has a particular sphere of activity.

And THAT topic is, of course, the central one of the next chapter.

ITEM TO EXPLORE

ONE COULD MAKE A LIST OF ALL THE TERMS DISCUSSED AND DEFINED IN THIS CHAPTER WITH THE GOAL OF SENSING WHICH OF THEM ARE EVOCATIVE OF SOME TRIGGERING RESPONSE WITHIN THIS WILL AT LEAST HELP UP-GRADE ONE'S FRAMES OF REFERENCE REGARDING EMPOWERMENT.

```
             EVOCATIVE

               POWER


              to call forth
              to summon up
              to activate
              to inspire
              to create


           SENSITIVE PERCEPTION POWER

      ALERTNESS POWER      DISCERNMENT POWER

               INTELLIGENCE POWER

                  SMART POWER

                  SMARTS POWER

                ACUMEN POWER (1)

        INSIGHT POWER     INTUITIVE POWER

                 KEENNESS POWER

                ACUMEN POWER (2)

                  KNOWING POWER

                LIFE-ENERGY POWER

                   WISDOM POWER
```

FIGURE 16. Deadened evocative power prevents activation of energy and is thus a sure symptom of powerlessness. In self and in relation to others, the deadening also results in non-responsiveness except to gross external stimuli largely emotional and non-rational in effect. Within societal power structures, the many constructive aspects of evocative powers (shown in he figure above) tend to be suppressed from public awareness, largely because they activate ways of escaping powerlessness, and can lead to re-wisdoming that transcends most formats of societal control by the few.

Chapter 21

THE INTELLIGENCES AND THE INNATE POTENTIALS

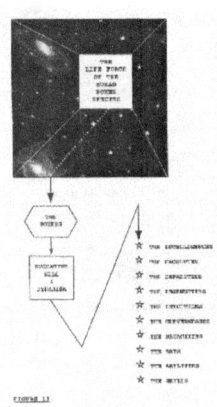

THE FUNCTION of this chapter is to discuss the probable existence of multiple intelligences in order to begin discussing the existence of multiple innate potentials having to do with power and empowerment.

But it is first necessary to have a definition of INTELLIGENCE which gives credible support to the discussions.

To be really serviceable, this definition cannot be imagined out of thin air, because doing so would mean that individuals could invent wild assortments of such definitions peculiar to themselves. There would be no consensus among individuals, and so no one would really know what was being talked about.

As it turns out, there is no need to introduce imagination at all -- because the original English-language definitions of INTELLIGENCE not only have a consensus history but are pertinent and to the point.

However, those original definitions are found only in the OXFORD dictionary of the English language. The OXFORD establishes that our modern definitions have hardly any relationship to the original ones.

The basic distinction between the original and the modern definitions is that the original ones are evocative of empowerment, whereas the modern ones more or less refer only to a rather limited list of skills that can be learned. If ever there was a big payoff regarding the archaeology of nomenclature, this is certainly an example.

THE ORIGINAL ENGLISH DEFINITIONS OF INTELLIGENCE

According to the Oxford Dictionary of the English language, the term INTELLIGENCE was taken from Latin. It appeared at about 1390 and was given the short and simple definition of "the faculty of understanding."

The essential definition of FACULTY was "the power of doing anything."

About 1490, a hundred years later, a second slightly expanded definition had been established.

INTELLIGENCE referred not only to the faculty of understanding but to "Understanding as a quality admitting of degree, specifically with reference to superior understanding, quickness of mental apprehension, and sagacity."

Taken from the Latin SAGIRE (to perceive keenly), the nine original English definitions for SAGACITY were given as:

1. Keen in sense perception, especially that of smell;
2. Acuteness of mental discernment;
3. Having special keenness for discovery of truth;
4. Penetrating and judicious in the estimation of character and motives;
5. Penetrating and judicious in the devising of means for accomplishment of ends;
6. Shrewd; shrewdness; penetration;
7. Keenness and capacity for investigation or discovery;
8. Keenness and soundness of judgment in the estimation of persons and conditions;
9. Keenness and soundness in the adaptation of means to ends.

Somewhat in contrast to the original nine definitions, the modern definitions of SAGACITY are given as:

1. Keen in sense perception [today this definition is given as "obsolete."]
2. Of keen and farsighted penetration and judgment;
3. Caused by or indicating acute discernment.

Why the first definition is considered obsolete in modernist terms is something of a wonderment, since the effect is to eliminate "keen sense perceptions" as an important aspect of understanding.

A careful reading of the OXFORD definitions of intelligence and intelligent reveals no reference to skill or to skills per se. It would be obvious, however, that keen understanding would be necessary in order to proficiently develop given skills in different categories of activity or performance.

It seems that the term SKILL was not given as one of the definitions of INTELLIGENCE until it appeared in Noah Webster's original 1828 American Dictionary of the English Language.

In that dictionary, INTELLIGENCE is simply defined as: "Understanding; skill." Adding the skill aspect is therefore an Americanism.

It is also interesting to note that sagacity as keenness of smell was introduced at about 1607 into English from the French term SAGACE, which refers to "Acute in perception, especially by the sense of smell."

Please note that this French definition does not particularly refer to the physical sense perception of smell, but to acuteness in perception per se.

This definition was quickly converted to slang usage -- i.e., smelly, something that stinks or smells. Indeed, as Shakespeare noted "Something stinks in the state of Denmark."

Indeed, that something "smells like a skunk" in government activities is easily understandable. Things can become rather smelly regarding Wall Street, any bureaucracy, given power structures, and even in the scientific and art worlds.

So, acutely perceiving that something somehow smells is a halfway power point to discovering what does stink.

RECONSTRUCTING THE ORIGINAL ENGLISH DEFINITIONS OF INTELLIGENCE

Since modernist definitions of INTELLIGENCE do not at all INCLUDE the essences of its original definitions, the meaning is that the original definitions have been deconstructed and replaced.

If the original definitions are reconstructed one finds that the definition of INTELLIGENCE at the beginning of the European Renaissance might read something like the following:

INTELLIGENCE - the faculty of understanding necessary to the power of doing anything. Understanding has a quality admitting of degrees of keenness, specifically with reference to superior understanding, quickness of mental apprehension, and sagacity with regard to acute perceiving; keen and farsighted judgment; penetrating and judicious estimation of character, motives, persons, and conditions; shrewd penetration of discovery, truths; keenness and soundness in the adaptation of means to ends."

For a necessary and ready comparison, it is necessary to restate the modern psychology definition of intelligence, since this is the one that has had the most "reality" during modernist times:

"INTELLIGENCE, in psychology, [is] the general mental ability involved in calculating, reasoning, perceiving relationships and analogies, learning quickly, storing and retrieving information, using language fluently, classifying, generalizing, and adjusting to new situations."

At first take, this modern definition seems to cover just about everything necessary to describe intelligence and say that it exists as such.

But it does not. The word "understanding" is not even mentioned in it.

And at this point anyone really interested in empowerment and power might immediately pause and make a groking effort as to how the two definitions differ.

One essential difference needs to be pointed up because it is extremely subtle and might be missed.

The modernist psychological definition more or less makes for a rather short list of PASSIVE skills that can be acquired and perfected by learning processes.

The modern definition is therefore not evocative of too much except skills that are somewhat mechanical. This factor is pertinent to empowerment, because most do realize that one can have skills, but no power.

If examined carefully and thoughtfully, the original definitions are referring to ACTIVE categories of understanding that are realizable via acute perceiving and keen, penetrating, shrewd, sound judgment, and sagacity.

The original definitions, then, ARE evocative of a great number of power factors, and as such those definitions are entirely relevant to empowerment, or to recovering from depowerment.

A point to be considered regarding the foregoing has to do with how much do passive definitions of intelligence contribute to empowerment and to achieving power?

THE POSSIBILITY OF MULTIPLE INTELLIGENCES

As was discussed in chapter 20, there is an idea about intelligence which has been taken so much for granted that its authenticity is seldom inspected or questioned.

This is the idea that intelligence is one single thing, a single unit. It is then supposed that this unit is lodged somewhere in the brain-mind of the individual.

It is even assumed by some that it is possible to leave "the mind" out of this and assume that the physical brain is the framework housing the unit; or that the brain itself is this single intelligence unit.

As a result of this unexamined idea, it has been necessary to fit a rather vast number of human qualities into this single intelligence unit. Not all of those qualities fit too well into the single unit. And so three debates have arisen among researchers.

The first concerns what fits and what does not into the single intelligence unit.

The second has to do with the idea that not just one intelligence unit exists, but that several of them do.

The third involves the idea that there may be more than one "brain" within the whole of the human organism.

For the purposes of the discussions in this book, it is generally accepted that different kinds, types, or categories of power exist.

This leads to the concept that there is not just one overall unit of power, so to speak, but a number of them, and each of which would be linked with particular kinds of intelligence, and with particular kinds of faculties as well.

It can therefore be wondered if one single intelligence unit serves all of the different kinds of powers and faculties.

It is certainly clear enough that there are different kinds of innate potentials within human systems, and that some or many of such potentials never become activated.

If a single intelligence unit served all of the innate potentials, then it would seem that activation of that unit would also trigger all of the innate potentials in some kind of across-the-boards manner.

But by observation, this is not what happens in real life. And indeed, even IQ tests address different categories of intelligence. So the idea of different categories of intelligence is implicit in such testing.

SPECTRUMS OF POWERS AND INTELLIGENCES

It is probably not really necessary to deal with the idea of multiple intelligences, but it is necessary to think in terms of spectrums of powers and intelligences.

A SPECTRUM is thought of as "an array of components separated and arranged in order of some varying characteristic."

The varying characteristics of a spectrum do constitute a continuous sequence or range, and so even a spectrum can be thought of as one inclusive thing in itself.

Nonetheless, the varying characteristics are important because it is only by discovering them that the specific components within the spectrum can be identified and arranged in some aspect to each other.

Power can certainly be thought of as a spectrum, if only because there is a sequence or range of it beginning with Zero Power, or even Minus Zero Power, and then ranging along in a sequence that might culminate with, say, Plus Power One Thousand.

If power can be thought of as a spectrum of many degrees and variations, then it is more or less necessary to think of intelligence in the same way.

Doing so raises the prospect of Zero Intelligence, of course, but that kind of intelligence is something many find occasion to not only to wonder about, but to observe in real-time kinds of ways.

In any event, spectrums have multiples of components, and it is this frame of reference that permits the gradual construction of an empowering overview into the nature of innate potentials.

It would be clear that within such a spectrum, some of the components might be activated, while others of them might not be, in which case they are usually described as existing, but latent and inactive.

It is possible to rephrase the foregoing paragraph as follows: It would be clear that within such a spectrum, some of the components might be powered-up, while others of them might not be, in which case they can be described as powered-down, depowered, or deprived of empowering energy.

The spectrum frame of reference can indeed be applied to just about anything which is made up of a series of slightly different or greatly different components that can be identified because of some varying characteristics between them.

Within the contexts of this book, this includes:

THE POWERS: The innate human factors that can produce an action or an effect.

THE INTELLIGENCES: The innate human powers of mind that can produce or manufacture understanding in different categories of realities and available or unavailable information sets.

THE FACULTIES: (1) All of the innate powers of the human mind that form the basis of all mental awareness and perceptions; and (2) the power of doing anything.

THE CAPACITIES: The innate human powers having to do with maximum energization, production or output.

THE INGENUITIES: (1) The innate human powers of inventing; and (2) the innate human powers of cleverness in devising, combining, designing, or contriving.

THE INTUITIONS: (1) The innate human powers and faculties of attaining to direct knowledge or cognition without rational thought and inference; and (2) immediate apprehension or cognition.

THE CLEVERNESSES: The innate human powers of adroit resourcefulness.

THE SAGACITIES: The innate human powers of keenness, penetration, estimation, and adaptation.

THE ARTS: The innate powers of human ingenuity for adapting all things to human use.

THE ABILITIES: The innate human powers of competence via natural talent or acquired proficiency.

Secrets of Power (I)

THE SKILLS: (1) A learned power of doing anything competently; and (2) learned technical, proficient, and dexterous ability to use knowledge, information, and data effectively and readily in execution or performance.

ITEMS TO MEDITATE UPON

MEDITATE UPON TWO OF THE FOREGOING CATEGORIES THAT ARE MOST ALIEN TO YOU WHILE DOING SO, MAKE NOTES OF YOUR THOUGHTS AND MENTAL IMAGES.

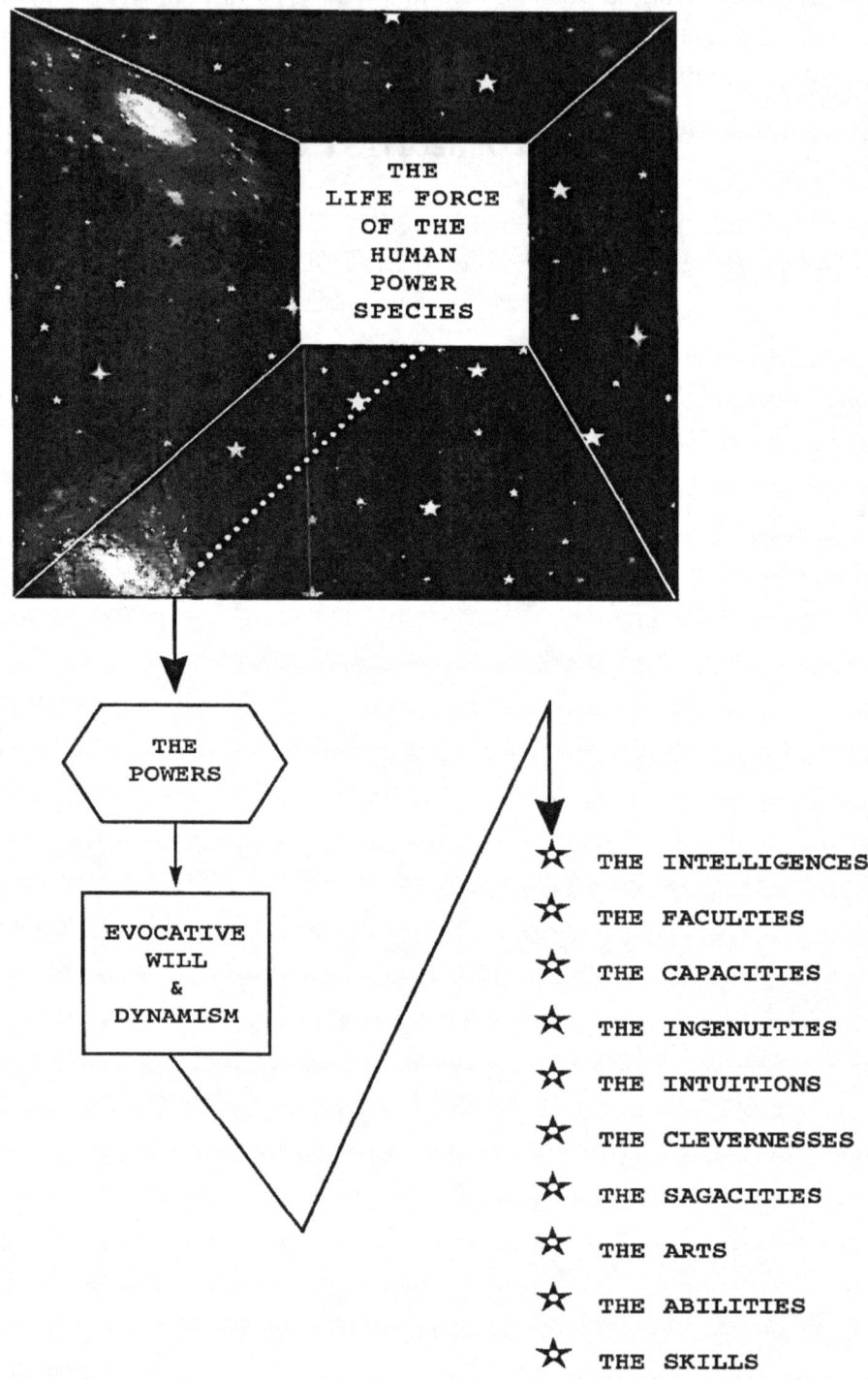

FIGURE 17.

Chapter 22

TWO OF THE PRO-ACTIVE VEHICLES OF POWER: WILL AND DYNAMISM

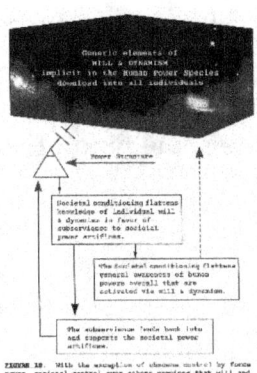

AS THEY have become established during the modernist decades, the conventional concepts pertaining to the nature of human will and will power seem clear-cut enough.

But a more in-depth examination of those concepts reveals a rather miserable assortment of subtle confusions that serve to disarm pro-active realization and utilization of will and will power.

THE DISARMING OF WILL AND WILL POWER

There are two broad results of this. First, it tends to make will and will power relatively harmless in ways that are not easily recognizable.

Second, the disarming efficiently tends to reduce the overall numbers of power contenders who might arise if they DID more completely grok the actual nature of will and will power.

THE SOCIETAL PROBLEM OF WILL AND WILL POWER

An obvious reason behind this disarming is that any given societal power structure cannot really tolerate too much real will and will power emerging among the masses of individuals.

Those masses are supposed to be subservient to the power structure, preferably throughout their subservient lives.

So, if pro-active ideas regarding will and will power begin manifesting among the subservient masses, then the contours of the power structure will inconveniently begin to undergo various kinds of stress.

To the powerful (who probably have become powerful via THEIR will and will power) the will and will power of others is always something to worry about.

Indeed, will and will power can easily be thought of as the top of the line of power -- and few can succeed without them.

So, all pretenses aside, it is rather logical to assume that the powerful prefer that the others NOT activate their own will and will power.

If the powerless did activate their own will and will power, then the matter of who would have control and influence over whom would certainly become something of an unpredictable situation.

The history of the debates and discourses regarding will and will power is exceedingly long and involved, and even a synopsis of it would take many pages.

For the purposes of this chapter, though, it is only necessary to get a good idea that will and will power are enormously significant, and have been throughout history.

The reason for establishing this significance is that awareness of it became generally lost during the twentieth century.

So the twenty-first century started up with deficit understanding regarding the real nature of will and will power.

CLUES TO THE PAST SIGNIFICANCE OF WILL AND WILL POWER

Prior to what became known as the Modern Age, the topics of will and will power had always been of enormous societal and individual interest.

Evidence of this interest is found in the vast number of earlier books on those two topics.

The OXFORD dictionary of the English language contains twenty-four major definitions for WILL as a noun, and fifty-three for it as a verb. This makes a total of seventy-seven definitions, each of which is supported by several identified nuances.

The proliferation of so many definitions establishes that the nature of will was of exceedingly important interest even as the English language began to format at about the tenth century A.D.

During the middle of the nineteenth century, however, interest in the nature of will began a steep decline, and by the middle of the twentieth century investigative interest in the nature of will had almost disappeared.

There are several subtle reasons for this. But a major one can be associated with the nineteenth century shift away from traditional social class systems to more egalitarian social systems.

In the traditional social class systems, only the will and will power of the ruling orders mattered. There was usually no upward social climbing permitted, and such was often overtly forbidden under threat of condign or simply summary punishment.

Even if given individuals in the lower powerless orders managed to develop some will and will power, they were expected to contain their energies in ways commensurate with their social birth class. If they did not agree to this, they would then be eliminated with traditional class-conscious impunity.

The wide-spread rise of egalitarian social systems during the nineteenth century of course dissolved the many social class barriers that had long prevailed in the pyramidal power systems of the past.

Philosophically speaking, the egalitarian hypothesis assumed freedom, equality, and, importantly, equal opportunity of and for All.

In that context, the potentials of will and will power could not be denied to anyone, and it would certainly seem non-egalitarian to do so. THIS context, however, has never been illuminated too much, and it may even be that this paragraph represents the first enunciation of it.

POWER vs EGALITARIANISM

Control, authority, and influence (i.e., power) over others is not exactly consistent with the egalitarian hypothesis.

This means, in part, that egalitarianism can probably be more equally distributed among the depowered and powerless masses which CAN share this egalitarian common denominator.

But on average, the powerful, or those contending for power, are not very much interested in anything too egalitarian because it complicates power positioning and the climbing of power ladders.

Issues of will and will power also complicate the egalitarian hypothesis itself. Many questions can be pondered. For example, can will and will power be thought of as egalitarian or egalitarian-making?

If so, then everyone's quotient for actualizing will power would have to equal everyone else's. This, in turn, would imply that everyone's access to power over others would also have to be equal not just in theory but in fact.

While the powerful might pay lip-service to this in theory, it is naive to think that they would tolerate any serious manifestations along such lines.

The issues of will and will power are thus rife with problems for the powerful and for the scope of egalitarianism. Thus, in both cases, one way of disarming the issues is to disarm the definitions of WILL and WILL POWER by negating their older and precise pro-active meanings and then substituting ambiguous meanings that flatter hypothetical egalitarianism.

A time-tested stratagem is involved here. If it is desired that something important should not be understood as important, then it needs to be redefined so as to appear unimportant.

One can now wonder if this kind of thing has ACTUALLY been pulled off in any all-encompassing socio-cultural sense.

And the remainder of this chapter will be devoted to exploring just that.

HISTORICAL AND CONTEMPORARY DEFINITIONS OF "WILL"

During most of the twentieth century, the conventional definition of will was:

"Desire, wish, disposition, inclination, appetite, passion, choice, determination, self-control, volition." This is taken from a trusty Webster's. But this definition is nonsense if examined closely.

For starters, if one thinks that desire, wish, inclination, or even choice, etc., are synonymous with will, then one might as well think that water flows uphill.

So it is necessary to depart from this modernist claptrap, and examine the original definitions.

In English, three of the more basic and essential definitions first appeared at about 900 A.D., the first of which is NOT found in contemporary dictionaries:

1. The movement or attitude of mind, which is directed with conscious intention to, and which issues immediately in, some action physical or mental;
2. Volition; and
3. Intention, intent, purpose, determination.

For the term VOLITION, most modern dictionaries give the definition of: "The act of making a choice or decision."

In about 1250 A.D., however, the term VOLITIONS (in the plural) had to do with "faculties of resoluteness and resolute determination," which had the characteristic of self-manifesting.

At about 1738, VOLITION was being defined as "The power or faculty of willing."

At about 1836, VOLITIONAL was being defined as:

1. Of or belonging to volition;
2. Pertaining or relating to the action of willing.

Now comes a mix-up. American dictionaries indicate that VOLITION is derived from the Latin VOL + ITIO, meaning to will or wish.

But the more authoritative OXFORD dictionary of the English language indicates that VOLITION came into English not from the Latin VOL, but from the French VOL.

In French VOL does not mean will or wish, but FLIGHT, and which is derived from the Latin VOLARE meaning "to fly, to be nimble, active, motional."

The foregoing is not merely a splitting of nomenclature hairs, because the concepts of to wish, desire, to be inclined, etc., can be seen as somewhat passive against VOL which means to fly, to be active or motional.

In the sciences, if not in American dictionaries, VOLITION is closely connected to motion, as in the cases of VOLATILE and VOLTAGE.

In psychiatry, VOLITION is associated with "significant and relevant impulses." (Note: Psychiatric dictionaries, also refer to "derailment of impulses," and to "derailment of thoughts," examples of which can be observed on a daily basis.)

So, apparently the British English definitions of VOLITION (energetic, motional) have, in American English, been derailed to mean "wish or desire" and which often get not much beyond mere wishing or desiring.

As a test of imagining-power here, one might wonder what will or volition would be if they DID NOT encompass some kind of motional activity or energy.

Furthermore, if will or will power did not CAUSE a result to come into existence, or cause something to happen, then it would be difficult to account for the continuing historical interest in them. After all, whatever DOES NOT cause much to happen is usually of little interest, if any at all.

If causativeness is functionally linked to will and will power, it could be thought that interest in the powerful is great not because of who or what they are, but because they seem to cause stuff to happen. Obversely, interest in the powerless and the depowered is very minimal because they are, so to speak, cause-less.

There are many threads of thinking that can emerge from the foregoing considerations.

But clearly one of those threads might involve the consideration that the feeling of powerlessness is not so much involved with essential powerlessness per se, but rather with cause-lessness.

There is a time-worn phrase along these lines that is familiar around the planet: "I can't get anything going." If true, this is a condition of absent causativeness, which is interpreted as feeling powerless.

As described in chapter 21, it is quite possible to think that one can innately have a great number of powers, intelligences, and capacities, etc. But if they are not active, or have been depowered by socio-cultural conditioning, then cause-lessness can be the result.

One of the central considerations of empowerment is to obtain some idea of what is active and what is not -- not only with regard to self, but to everything within the parameters of one's experiencing thresholds.

DYNAMIKOS

If one is into the archaeology of words, it can be something of a shock to discover that the Greek term DYNAMIKOS means powerful in that language, and that DYNAMIS means power.

The shock comes about when one realizes that the term DYNAMIC is NOT associated with or linked to the conventional definitions of power, will, or will power.

It is clear that the English term DYNAMIC is derived from the Greek terms, and so it is something of a second shock to discover that the meanings of powerful and power do NOT appear in the English definitions. Instead, the English definitions are given as:

Of or relating to physical force or energy;

1. Active [as contrasted to inactive];
2. Marked by continuous and usually productive activity or change;
3. Marked by energy;
4. Forceful, strong [as contrasted to vapid and weak].

Technically speaking, the foregoing are (or should be) the essential definitions of will and will power. And with this, it can be pointed up that if there was ever a case for deconditioning empowerment via language that everyone uses, this is certainly a rather clear-cut example of it.

If this at first is somewhat hard to grok, consider the implications of the following three-step depowerment process:

1. Cut cognitive and educational links between dynamic and powerfulness;
2. Cut cognitive and educational links between will and dynamism;
3. Cut cognitive links between (a) volition as motional-activity-impulses and substitute (b) volition as wish, appetite, or desire, etc.

Everyone has wishes, desires, dispositions, passions, inclinations, appetites, choices, determination, etc. And if those are the definitions of will, then everyone should have will and the rewards of it.

In other words, detach the concepts of the dynamic, and identify volition merely as wish or desire, and ask what one then ends up with. The answer is a societal power structure in which the threat of too much ACTIVE will and will power have been efficiently disarmed -- and VIA, of all things, nomenclature conditioning.

A SUGGESTED RECONSTRUCTION OF THE ESSENTIAL DEFINITION OF "WILL"

As noted earlier, the original definition in English of WILL was: "The movement or attitude of mind, which is directed with conscious intention to, and which issues immediately in, some action physical or mental."

To this essential definition should be added the essential nuances of volition as motional, and dynamic as energetic and active.

By doing this, one can end up with the more efficient and accurate meanings of intention, intent, purpose, determination, power impulses, power flows, and resoluteness.

ITEM TO PLAY WITH

NOTICE AND OBSERVE DYNAMIC PHENOMENA DO NOT INCLUDE ELECTRICITY, ANGER, OR STUPIDITY.

A CLUE TO THIS: REMEMBER THAT DYNAMIC PHENOMENA ARE BUSY CAUSING OR PRODUCING RESULTS OF SOME KIND.

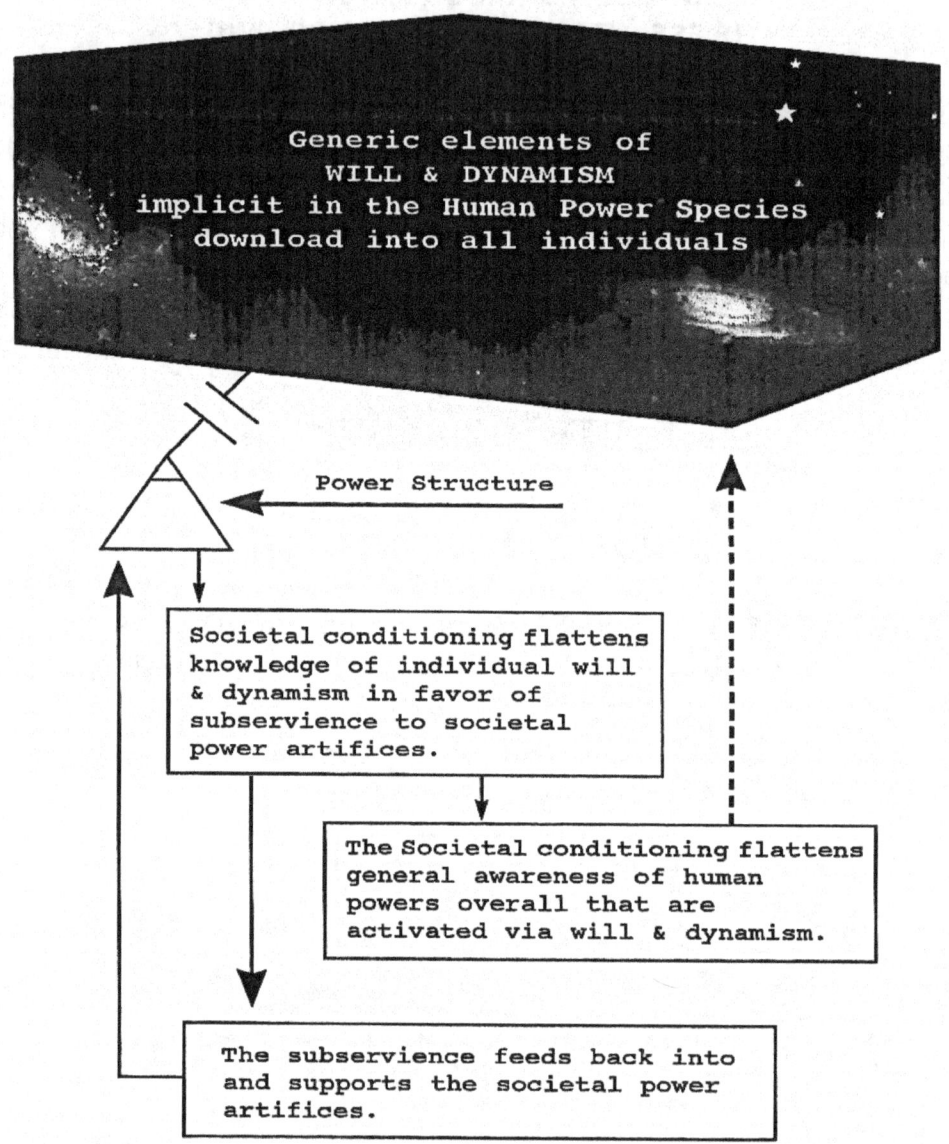

FIGURE 18. With the exception of obscene control by force power, societal control over others requires that will and dynamism of the others must be conditioned into formats resulting in semi-voluntary, semi-hypnotic subserviency to the powerful few. Some writers have analyzed this form of subserviency as "parasitism" by the powerful few of the many. However, none mention that unless this kind of subserviency is broadly achieved, no Pyramidal Power System Artifice can be set up and maintained. Knowledge conditioning that promotes ignorance about the real nature of individual will and dynamism is one of the hidden societal workhorses that flattens general awareness of human powers overall.

PART FIVE
SUBTLE CONTEXTS RELATING TO EMPOWERMENT

Chapter 23

SUBTLE DISTINCTIONS BETWEEN UNFOLDMENT AND DEVELOPMENT

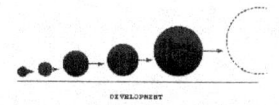
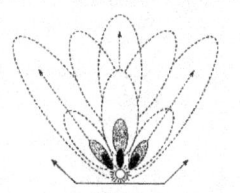

FIGURE 18. A major difference between Unfoldment and Development is similar to the difference between the seed that naturally unfolds into a mighty tree and the automobile engine that is artificially developed in a factory into better and more efficient versions. Development is therefore linear, starting from version 1 and proceeding along to subsequent versions. In contrast, Unfoldment is growth-phase-dimensional in that whatever the "seed" is to grow into intrinsically pre-exists with it. Development is intimately linked to conditions of intelligence-knowledge. Unfoldment personifies phase-shifting of life-energy animating processes, the essential nature of which has not so far been identified. Unfoldment naturally "does it itself," providing conditions are appropriate, but Development "does not do it itself" and requires artificial engineering.

THERE ARE very many distinctions between power that is obvious and power that is subtle.

Subtle power is probably more success-prone overall than obvious power. But those whose awarenesses have been grossly dumbed-down by social conditioning usually can't recognize the existence of subtle power.

And anyway, most who achieve power like it to be obvious to others. So the power limelight is almost always focused on obvious power.

Force power is an example of obvious power. But those achieving power by force usually end up being managed, used, or disposed of by those who are expert in techniques of subtle power. Subtle power is, of course, an adjunct of stealth power, and which in turn is the workhorse of secret power.

There is little doubt that societal power as extensive control, authority, and influence over others benefits very much by keeping attention focused on obvious power, while at the same time preventing general awareness about the nature of subtle, stealth, and secret powers.

One of the subtle "messages" downloading from the above is that if one attempts empowerment only within the visible contexts of obvious power, then those efforts can easily fizzle out along the rocky road ahead.

It is thus that those aspiring to vitalizing empowerment need to have some background knowledge about the many subtle distinctions that can help integrate empowerment with achievement of power.

SUBTLE POWER AND SUBTLE POWER CONTEXTS

There are many misunderstandings regarding the nature of the word SUBTLE, the actual definitions of which are quite surprising, especially with respect to power and empowerment.

On average, this term is used in its depowering modernist meaning of "a fine distinction," and so the first English definitions are given as "delicate, refined."

However, the English term is taken from the Latin terms SUB + TELA meaning "web," and from TEXERE meaning "to weave," i.e., to weave a web.

From this descend the subsidiary English definitions of "cunningly made or contrived, ingenious, artful, crafty, highly skillful, mentally acute, keen."

There are two "messages" to be groked via the subsidiary definitions of SUBTLE.

The first is that attempts to deal with power and empowerment only within their obvious, gross contexts are probably failure-prone.

The second is that the term SUBTLE is a power-term, and as such establishes the real existence of subtle power(s) i.e., the power to weave subtle webs on behalf of empowerment and gaining power.

The term CONTEXT has been used in the paragraph above, and elsewhere in this book. Its English meaning is given as "the parts of a discourse that surround a word or passage and can throw light upon its meaning."

So it might not be imagined that the definitions of SUBTLE and CONTEXT have much in common.

However, the English term is again taken from Latin, in this case from COM + TEXERE, meaning "to coherently weave together by connection."

By the foregoing discussions, it is now at least somewhat possible to grok or intuit the distinctions between the two categories of easily identifiable gross power entities and hard to identify subtle power webs.

By extended meaning, gross power entities are probably always present in subtle power webs, but it would be the power webs that are most significant.

SEPARATING THE SUBTLE CONTEXTS OF DEVELOPMENT AND UNFOLDMENT

One of the first areas that can be examined along these lines involves the important subtle distinctions between unfoldment and development, both of which seem similar enough, but each of which consists of two entirely different kinds of processes.

The essential reason for entering into these distinctions is that those seeking empowerment usually think in terms of developing their power(s) as contrasted to unfolding them.

The principal definition of to DEVELOP (hence DEVELOPMENT) is given as: "To set forth or make clear by degrees or in detail; to EXPOUND."

The principal definition of UNFOLD (hence UNFOLDMENT) is given as: "To open the folds of, to spread out; to EXPAND."

It can be seen right away that to expound and to expand are not the same thing, and that entirely different processes are involved.

This distinction is enormously significant when it comes to concepts of empowerment. The principal reason is that those wanting "to develop" their power would be thinking in terms of setting it forth to others or making it clear by degrees to them.

It is to be admitted that this sometimes does work, especially in the case of this or that kind of force power.

However, those aspiring toward empowerment are probably doing so based on some sense of powerlessness or depowerment within which their power(s) have undergone contraction, shrinkage, or constriction, or have become in-folded, as it were.

In that meaning, the first issue is to open up and expand whatever has become constricted or in-folded so as to have almost no vitalizing activity.

One of the difficulties involved here is that the concept of development clearly refers to making something visible in the outer worlds, while the concept of unfoldment refers to opening up and expanding something that exists within so that it CAN become visible in the outer worlds.

The concept of "development" (of any and all things) is a particular artifact of the cultural West enjoying enormous prestige since the onset of the Industrial Revolution that began in Britain about the middle of the seventeenth century.

The Revolution involved the switch from tools to machines, which led to enormous changes in social, economic, and power structure formats based on the often dramatic development of technological innovations.

As a result, the concept of development became over-luminous, and it began to be applied to all things that hinted of innovative technological potentials or methodological treatment.

One of the central ideas at work within the concept of development had to do (and still does) with inventing or innovating something that did not exist before and set it forth by degrees and in detail so that it became amenable to methodological use and, usually, economic growth.

INNOVATE means "to introduce as if new," the term being taken from the Latin IN + NOVIS meaning "new."

With regard to empowerment, individuals tend to think that they are powerless because they don't have powers, and that they therefore need to innovate them by some new artificial means that didn't exist before.

This is a concept quite different from unfolding what is already there.

DEFINITIONS OF UNFOLDMENT

It is via the foregoing discussion that we finally come to the definitions of UNFOLDMENT.

In English, the verb UNFOLD is a perfectly good word -- but one which has never been applied to the contexts of power and empowerment. It is defined as:

1. To open the folds of;
2. To spread out, expand, open up;
3. To open to view;
4. To make clear by gradual disclosure;
5. To blossom;
6. To develop by increasing or expanding; to gradually make clear to understanding.

But the verb UNFOLD has never been converted into noun forms -- such as UNFOLDMENT, and which would mean the state or condition of being unfolded, opened, expanded, blossomed, etc. In this sense, the processes of depowerment would have something to do with preventing unfoldment of innate powers naturally existing.

UNFOLDMENT AS A PRINCIPLE

Strictly speaking, the term UNFOLDMENT has reference to a principle rather than a concept or idea, and this should be understood so as to better grok the many implications of unfoldment.

The term PRINCIPLE is taken from the Latin PRINCIPIUM meaning "at the beginning" or "first." The English definitions are given as:

1. A comprehensive and fundamental law;
2. The laws or facts of nature underlying the working of an artificial device; and
3. An underlying faculty or endowment.
4. Doctrine or assumption interpreted as being fundamental or comprehensive. [For clarity, this definition refers to principles not based on laws or facts, but which nevertheless sometimes have wide societal usage.]

Ideas or concepts may be constructed with relationship to a comprehensive or fundamental principle. But unless the ideas or concepts are identical to the principle, then at best they are but artificial devices merely juxtaposed to the principle.

As seen in the definitions above, a principle also refers to an underlying faculty or endowment.

In the biggest possible picture, this refers to the underlying faculties or endowments of our species entire.

At the smaller individual level, this also refers to underlying faculties or endowments innate to the individual, but which can either be active or inactive -- can either be empowered or depowered.

THE SIGNIFICANCE TO POWER OF EXPANSION AND CONTRACTION

Most can easily grasp the significance of expansion and contraction regarding power and empowerment.

Power which is contracting is diminishing (in-folding); power which is expanding is increasing (out-folding).

If one feels powerless, then one's sense of power has diminished and contracted -- has in-folded.

If one feels powerful, then one's sense of power has increased and expanded -- has out-folded.

In this sense, the results will consist of an opening-up or a closing-down of one's actual power factors. However, the in-folding of one's power factors DOES NOT MEAN that those factors have permanently been deconstructed.

They have merely become inoperative and could be triggered into unfoldment again.

THE CONCEPT OF TRIGGER POWER

As discussed earlier, the term TRIGGER refers to "a stimulus that initiates a process of some kind."

The term PROCESS refers to "a natural phenomenon marked by gradual changes that lead toward a particular result."

It is fair to mention right away that processes can lead to destructive as well as constructive results.

And in direct aspect to this, it is also fair to mention that in the many worlds of human affairs there exists a great deal of secrecy with regard to which process leads to whatever.

Indeed, knowledge about innate human processes of any kind tends to be considered a competitive and proprietary affair, simply because that knowledge has a great deal to do with accumulating and accessing power.

For example, power holders will certainly want, in subtle ways, to secretly trigger processes that will lead to the destruction of their up-coming competitors. Likewise, the up-coming competitors will want subtly to trigger processes that will lead to the downfall of existing power holders.

In the lingo of powerdom, however, such is not actually referred to as "subtle power processes," but rather misleadingly as "power games."

If one is talking about processes needed to bake a cake, or even the processes of building computers, then there probably isn't too much secrecy involved.

But with the exception of force power, the processes resulting in power, empowerment, and depowerment are an entirely different matter, one that is indeed shrouded in thick and nearly impenetrable intellectual fogs of secrecy.

The intellectual fogs are of course subtly established to derail and prevent empowering impulses not only from unfolding to bigger and better results, but to disarm any knowledge that might trigger the impulses in the first place.

The idea of unfoldment is more at home in Asia than in the European-influenced West where knowledge of unfoldment is culturally avoided.

The most obvious reason for this avoidance is quite simple. The human entity possesses many things that can be unfolded, including the awarenesses, the perceptions, and the mind.

With the exception of the ancient Greeks (whose power structures at least encouraged philosophical unfoldment), the Western ideas of the mind held that it was something to be educationally programmed with whatever information sets were seen as desirable by the societal programmers. This should also be stated as seen as desirable to the societal programmers themselves.

As a result of this social programming, the mind could be contained within and controlled by the parameters of the programming.

The idea that the human mind ITSELF and its innate powers should be unfolded was unthinkable -- if only because an unfolded mind could probably out-think the parameters of the social conditioning.

The prospect of the unfolded mind therefore constitutes something of a nightmare to all societal power structures and programmers.

The best way to alleviate the possibility of this nightmare was to delete any references to UNFOLDMENT itself.

SITUATIONS TO TRY TO OBSERVE

TRY TO OBSERVE AND COMPARE AT LEAST FIVE OUT-FOLDING AND FIVE IN-FOLDING SITUATIONS.

DO NOT JUDGE THESE BY THEIR APPARENT SURFACES INSTEAD, GROK WHAT'S BEHIND OR BENEATH THE SURFACES.

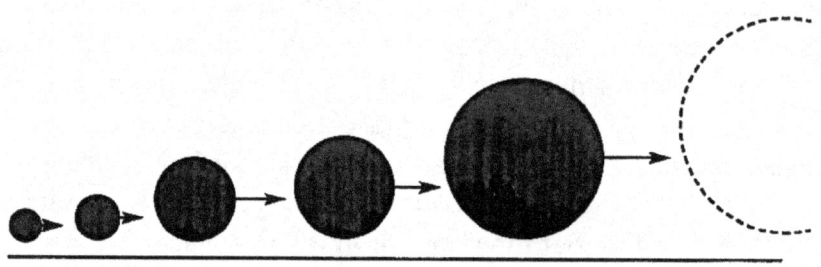

DEVELOPMENT

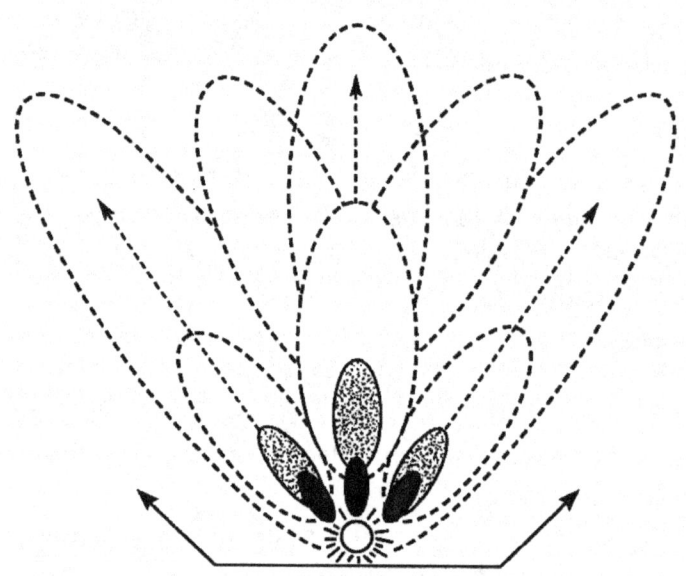

UNFOLDMENT

FIGURE 19. A major difference between Unfoldment and Development is similar to the difference between the seed that naturally unfolds into a mighty tree and the automobile engine that is artificially developed in a factory into better and more efficient versions. Development is therefore linear, starting from version 1 and proceeding along to subsequent versions. In contrast, Unfoldment is growth-phase-dimensional in that whatever the "seed" is to grow into intrinsically pre-exists with it. Development is intimately linked to conditions of intelligence-knowledge. Unfoldment personifies phase-shifting of life-energy animating processes, the essential nature of which has not so far been identified. Unfoldment naturally "does it itself," providing conditions are appropriate, but Development "does not do it itself" and requires artificial engineering.

Chapter 24

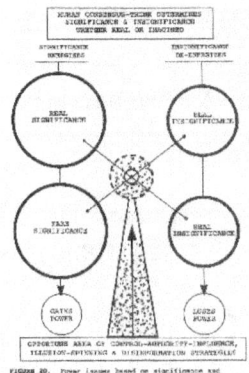

THE DIRECT CONNECTION TO POWER OF SIGNIFICANCE AND INSIGNIFICANCE

IT IS possible by now to GROK that power is not a single thing-in-itself, but is composed of a number of aspects, factors, elements, etc.

Some of the factors are easy enough to perceive, others more difficult. Then there are those which more or less elude observation altogether, and which, in historical references, constitute the inscrutable faces of power.

Those inscrutable faces refer to whatever is not readily understandable about power, whatever seems to be enigmatic, puzzling, obscure, or as something like a riddle.

As might be awkwardly put, discovering that power is "numerous" quite clearly gives substance to the ancient saying that it has a thousand faces.

And so, if one has the patience and commitment to do so, all of the factors or elements considered so far in this volume can be observed and located among the activities of real life.

However, in addition to the most visible aspects of power, there exist various inscrutable and enigmatic factors that are very difficult to identify, especially if one has no clue that they exist in the first place.

And even if one has some idea that they exist, it is difficult to see that they have any meaningful connection to power.

As discussed in the foregoing chapter, one such aspect involves the process principles of out-foldment (empowerment, growth) and in-foldment (depowerment, withering).

The principle of unfoldment is subtle but is quite easy to identify and discuss because most realize that things grow or die depending on whether they are nurtured or not.

It is understood that power accumulates, but the accumulating also can be thought of as growth. So the analogy that power grows is apt.

A CENTRAL, ENIGMATIC, BUT AMAZING THING ABOUT POWER

One of the most central problems about power has to do with why it collects around some life factors or situations but not others.

This constitutes an enigma of the first water.

Indeed, it is easy enough to observe that certain things become empowered while others are deprived of power. This can lead to all sorts of amazement -- depending, of course, on the contents and extent of one's frames of reference.

As but a few examples, power can collect around some, but not all, versions of stupidity, short-sightedness, and even around complete nonsense.

Conversely, and more often, power does NOT collect around some, or even many, versions of demonstrated intelligence, far-sightedness, and complete sense-making.

Power can also collect around, or flow toward, something that has no confirmed reality via proof of authenticity -- such as many ideas, theories, and hypotheses.

Conversely, power often does not collect around what DOES have confirmed reality via proof of authenticity.

Finally, power can collect within scenarios which are entirely unworkable via proven and demonstrated fact and fail to collect within scenarios that are demonstrated to be workable.

One of the major results of all this is that "power is where you find it, but not hardly ever where you might expect it to be."

IS POWER ALWAYS RELATIVE TO SOMETHING ELSE?

The foregoing discussions somewhat establish that power is not a thing-in-itself but is relative to something else.

This also suggests that non-power is not a thing-in-itself but is relative to something else.

One can certainly observe that power is often relative to something else, and so it is worthwhile to be reminded of certain definitions.

RELATIVE refers to those instances of "a thing having a relation to, a connection with, or a necessary dependence upon another thing."

RELATIVISM is defined as "a theory that knowledge is relative to the limited nature of the mind and the conditions of knowing." This general definition can of course be applied to individual minds.

RELATIVITY refers to "the state of being dependent for existence on or determined in nature, value, or quality by relation to something else."

And as has earlier been discussed, if there was nothing to have power over, or in respect to, then it would be difficult either to have or identify power.

So all clues regarding the nature of power lead in the direction of groking its relativity with respect to something else.

Indeed, and to emphasize, if power was a thing-in-itself having no relativity to anything, then no one would know what to develop power in respect of.

One way of enlarging upon this is to image a great void or vacuum having nothing in it except power-as-itself.

The vacuum sits as such -- UNTIL something else comes into it that causes power to congeal, collect, or manifest relative to it.

It can readily be observed that power does not collect around ALL things, whatever they may consist of, but only around SOME things. And after a while, power may uncollect from those things and collect to other things that had no power before.

AN INTRODUCTION TO SIGNIFICANCE AND INSIGNIFICANCE

So why does power accumulate around certain things, but not others? To begin constructing answers to this, it is first necessary to examine the nature of significance and insignificance.

And in order to undertake this examination, it is useful to consider the descriptive analogy of a mighty and powerful storm beginning with a small and insignificant eddy of air at some distant place no one knows where.

At that distant place there would be millions of small air eddies. And so it is something of a question regarding WHY one of them should collect additional forces to it, with the whole then turning into a mighty, powerful gale force.

All small eddies of air are insignificant at first, and most of them don't turn into anything of extraordinary power or force that is difficult to withstand.

The foregoing analogy makes it possible to realize something about power that is usually not clearly pointed out.

If we can withstand something very easily, we usually won't think of it as powerful or as power.

If we have to work to withstand it, then we begin thinking of it in terms of some kind of power which needs to be dealt with and/or withstood.

We usually accept something as HAVING power when it is difficult to withstand, or when we can't do anything about it.

Most of us don't think we have to deal with whatever seems insignificant and so we usually ignore whatever it is.

It is only when it becomes noticeable that an insignificant something is building up into a significant something that we begin to watch or monitor it.

There is some kind of logic in this. But within this logic exists a subtle two-fold problem regarding power which is not entirely logical.

That subtle problem is sort of mind-bending and is as follows: It is not unusual to find that insignificance is being assigned to things that are not insignificant; and conversely, that significance is being assigned to things that are not significant.

It is thus that establishing significance and insignificance merely involves what one thinks or doesn't think about whatever is involved.

And so, there is a general human tendency to attribute insignificance to things that are not insignificant, and to attribute significance to things that are not significant.

This is to say that attributing significance and insignificance to ANYTHING and EVERYTHING is merely a vicissitude of the human mind always busy thinking this way and that about whatever.

At first take, these considerations could seem merely superficial and uninteresting. And so their thunderous significance to power in any of its thousand aspects might not yet be apparent.

The reason for this is that the terms IMPORTANCE and SIGNIFICANCE have been defined in ways that defeat any groking of the exact meaning of the latter term. And one is now invited to pay particular attention to what follows.

CONFUSIONS REGARDING THE DEFINITIONS OF IMPORTANCE AND SIGNIFICANCE

Although the English terms IMPORTANCE and SIGNIFICANCE are used as synonyms, there is an essential and crucial nuance between them which clearly establishes that they should not be thought of as synonymous.

IMPORTANCE is an extension of IMPORT, the principal meaning of which is "to bear or convey as meaning."

IMPORTANCE thus "implies the power of influencing, or the quality of having evident value, either generally or in a particular relation, and often by merely existing."

In contrast, SIGNIFICANCE is an extension of SIGNIFY, the principle (and original) meaning of which is "to betoken, foreshadow, or indicate as something to take place."

In other words, a signification is a PORTENT, the meaning of which is "something that foreshadows a coming event; an omen; prophetic indication or significance."

Strictly speaking, then, IMPORTANCE can bear, carry, or convey meaning.

But significance PORTENDS something.

One of the principal reasons that the definitions of the two terms have been collapsed into each other is that foreshadowing, omens, and prophetic indications have had a lot of bad press during the modernist period of our present civilizations.

The foregoing discussions do not merely represent terminology hair splitting, largely because innate in our species are powers having to do with sensing and identifying factors that foreshadow this or that.

Indeed, no species could be thought of as possessing high intelligence unless it innately contained faculties for recognizing, to one degree or other, what's going to happen.

Moreover, failure to sense what's going to happen can be thought of as one of the definitions of stupidity -- i.e., "slow of mind, unthinking, dulled in feeling or sensation, benumbed, sense-less."

And here it MUST be mentioned that a large part of getting and maintaining power is based on knowing what's going to happen, and in fact such is almost as precious as power itself.

Indeed, if the powerful don't know what's going to happen, then their days assuredly are numbered.

Taking this into consideration, power consists not only of control, authority, and influence over others, but also of artful controlling and concealing foreknowledge of what's going to happen.

A full part of this control over others simply and expediently means that the others should NOT have foreknowledge of what's going to happen.

Thus, ways and means must be devised so that the others become slow of mind, unthinking, dulled in feeling or sensation, benumbed, or sense-less regarding foreknowledge.

One of the possible reasons why ideas of importance (meaning) and significance (portending) have become collapsed into each other is that while it may be OK to find out what things mean, it is NOT okay to find out what they portend. That NOT OKAY aspect, of course, portends gaining empowerment and power.

THE MOST SUBTLE ASPECT OF SIGNIFICANCE

There is a particular quirk regarding the relationship of significance (as defined above) to power and empowerment.

Obviously, (1) discovering meaning and (2) assigning significance are functions of human living and existing, and so both (1) and (2) consist of applications of awareness, perceptions, and cognitions derived from them. Actually speaking, though, meaning has to become understood before anyone can say it has been discovered. And many can read meanings from some information source, but not actually understand them.

So, in sort of a brain-twisting way, it can transpire that meanings can be understood about things that really cannot have those meanings, while things can also have a great number of meanings that never become understood.

THE COMPLEXITIES OF ATTRIBUTING SIGNIFICANCE TO SOMETHING

Something along similar lines can be said when it comes to the matter of attributing significance.

As has been mentioned earlier in this chapter, something can seem significant when it is not, and it is certainly the case that something can seem insignificant when it is not.

This complexity more than suggests that meaning and significance are:

1. What one thinks they are; or
2. What someone thinks they are; or
3. What a group agrees to think they are; or
4. What a power structure thinks (and says) they are; or
5. What a doctrine, educational curriculum, or a hypothesis hold they are.

So one can grok that attributing significance with regard to power and empowerment is a rather complicated affair, because the attributing can consist only of thinking.

And now comes the really strange and astonishing aspect about this.

If people merely begin to THINK that something has significance, then power begins to collect around whatever it is.

Conversely, if people merely THINK that something is insignificant, then power does not collect around it.

Admittedly, those two factors constitute something of a mind-bender, but nevertheless they CAN readily be observed as such if one patiently looks around within human activities.

Somewhat in stark contrast, if people think that something has meaning/importance, then interest may collect around it, but not power or empowerment.

Power and empowerment will not begin to collect around meaning and/or importance unless SOME people also assign some kind of significance to it.

The whole of this discussion may by now have created something of a swirl in one's head and synapses.

But, for some re-grounding here, it is very broadly understood that the insignificant does not represent power, but that the significant probably does.

The quirk that has been introduced in the foregoing discussions involves two factors:

1. Most think that things themselves have significance or insignificance in some sort of fundamental way that is independent of human thinking about them -- and which, of course, can be the case at least in part;

BUT!

2. The ATTRIBUTION of significance to something actually does consist of THINKING that:
   a. This or that HAVE significance; and
   b. Other kinds of this or that HAVE insignificance.

From this it can be deduced that the management and manipulation of significance, whether real or imagined, is a full aspect of all power games, access to power, power acquisition, power positioning, and maintenance of power.

THIS becomes fully understandable in that the insignificant is, well, insignificant, and so whatever it consists of does not stand a chance in any power or empowerment context.

THE SIGNIFICANCE OF THINKING THAT SOMETHING IS SIGNIFICANT

There are two loose ends in this which have to do with:

1. How does something become THOUGHT OF as having significance? and
2. Why is it that significance can be attributed to both the real and the imagined?

These two aspects are sort of wobbly with regard to establishing any kind of certainty, and so it is tricky to address them.

However, one of the more recognizable certainties involved is that power will not collect around or flow to what is thought to be insignificant. That certainty is not astonishing.

But another certainty IS astonishing. If a number of individuals collectively begin to think that something, whether real or imagined, has significance, then power begins to collect around it, even if only weakly at first. THAT is astonishing.

And indeed, when more individuals collectively begin to think-agree that something has significance, then more power will collect to whatever it is -- person, idea, philosophy, facts, theory, hypothesis, real realities, illusory realities, and etc.

Furthermore, when the same begins to be seen as insignificant, then power can quickly depart with a thump.

Within the contexts of this chapter, then, significance equals power of this or that kind, while insignificance equals powerlessness of all kinds.

In this sense, it can be appreciated that power FLOWS TOWARD whatever is thought to have significance -- and FLOWS AWAY from whatever is thought to have insignificance.

This is almost the same as saying that THINKING causes the flowing toward or the flowing away from.

So something regarding empowerment depends on the scope of one's awarenesses and perceptions with respect to sensing and identifying this flowing toward and flowing away from.

There is a single clue here. Significance is attributed to whatever is thought to foreshadow something, while if something is thought to foreshadow nothing, then insignificance is attributed to it.

The English language has a single term for this -- FUTURITY -- defined as: "future; the quality or state of being future; future events or PROSPECTS [emphasis added].

And indeed, future prospects, if seemingly prospective enough, WILL have power flowing to them.

Conversely, whatever is thought not to contribute to future prospects WILL have power flowing away from it.

POWER FLOWS TO TRY TO OBSERVE

TRY TO OBSERVE WHAT POWER IS FLOWING TOWARD AND AWAY FROM EXCLUDE SELF FROM THIS EFFORT SO AS TO AVOID POSSIBLE EGO STRESSES.

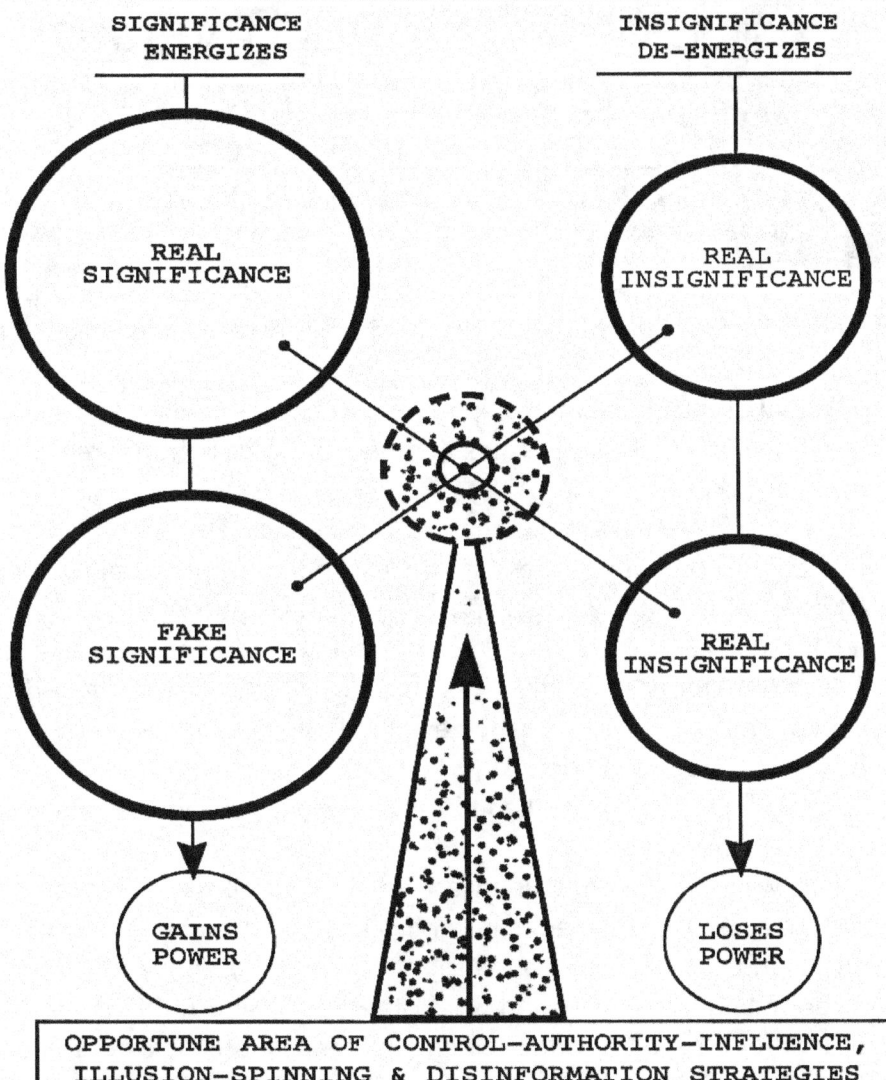

FIGURE 20. Power issues based on significance and insignificance are formidable brain twisters because there can be crisscrossed real and faked versions that are hard to decipher. Communal and consensus thinking are the determining factors: I.E., something gains power if enough THINK it is significant even if it is not, but loses power if enough THINK is insignificant even if it is not. The THINK-THINK crisscross is opportune for illusion-spinning and disinformation strategies, and for management of all forms of control-authority-influence.

Chapter 25

EMPOWERMENT versus THE DUMBING-DOWN OF HUMAN SENSING SYSTEMS

THE CENTRAL topic of this chapter has to do with the dumbing-down of knowledge with respect to the extensive scope of human sensing systems.

But to get to that topic in relationship to power, empowerment, and depowerment, we have to examine certain ancillary issues that help bring to light the reasons WHY the dumbing-down has occurred.

As discussed in the foregoing chapter, the issues surrounding the topic of significance are quite convoluting. There are no less than four principal reasons (factors) for this, and it does take a bit of mental effort to sort through them.

First, significance can be attributed to something that is not significant (i.e., fake significance). In other words, something having no real futurity can be said to have it. Those who accept the alleged significance eventually find out that there is no futurity involved and end up as losers of some kind.

Second, insignificance can be alleged regarding something that really does have significance (i.e., fake insignificance).

Thus, when what has been alleged as insignificant turns out to have powerful futurity, those who accepted the alleged insignificance turn out to be losers of some kind.

Third, the faking of significance and insignificance represent very efficient methods that result in controlling and influencing what others think about things.

After all, if others are to be controlled and influenced, then it is necessary to distort and confuse their perceptions regarding real significance and insignificance.

Fourth, establishing that something is insignificant when it is not is one of the most important methods for inducing and controlling depowerment. The rationale here is quite simple and efficient.

As a natural tendency, people don't devote attention and interest to what they think is insignificant. So establishing something as insignificant when it is not is a very easy way to deflect attention and interest about it. And indeed, if people don't give attention to something or have interest in it, then it is often invisible to them.

The four factors above lead to a very old but recognizable dilemma: if the four factors are considered, then how is one to establish what is real?

Many otherwise elegant philosophical systems have foundered and come to grief because of this. And so, at this reading, one need not necessarily feel too stupid if one experiences difficulties in understanding or groking the whole.

While the issue of significance versus insignificance constitutes a continuing philosophical dilemma, it is not too much of one when it comes to power, empowerment, and depowerment.

The reason, roughly but pointedly speaking, is that power over others is obtained by any and all means possible, and THIS is not a dilemma.

THE SIGNIFICANCE OF ACCESS TO FUTURITY

As earlier discussed in chapter 24, there is a major, if subtle, reason as to why confusions need to be socially engineered about significance and insignificance.

This reason is that what is truly significant usually not only portends but eventuates in some kind of a future, while what is truly insignificant usually does not.

The term FUTURE is defined not only as "what is going to happen," and "an expectation of advancement or progressive development."

As already indicated, FUTURITY is defined as "future events or prospects."

The most probable emphasis is usually on "future prospects" because various kinds of prospects can be derived from future events no matter what they consist of. The "prospective futurity" is therefore always more significant than the "event futurity."

It should be obvious that prospective futurity and power are interrelated.

And if it is, then it is also obvious that the powerful would wish to have control, authority, and influence not only in present time, but even more so with regard to prospective futurity.

And the most obvious reason for control by the powerful of prospective futurity is to enable the powerful to be the first-line major beneficiaries of it.

If the real-life, real-time, implications of the foregoing are patiently meditated upon, then it is unthinkable that the powerful would do anything other than very carefully guard, protect, and prevent wide-spread foreknowledge access to prospective futurity.

IDENTIFYING THE NEED-TO-KNOW FACTOR
WITHIN POWER STRUCTURES

The whole of the prospective futurity thing is, of course, very complex and confusing, so much so that it is difficult to relate it to something individuals can identify with. But there is one way of doing so, if only partially, that most can easily recognize.

If it is hypothesized that foreknowledge and power have direct relationships to each other, then power games are not only games of power, but also games of prospective foreknowledge management, manipulation, and concealment.

If this is so, it must then be hypothesized that access to prospective foreknowledge is almost as important as access to power.

But this is the same as saying that if access to power is very carefully guarded and denied to the many, then access to prospective foreknowledge is almost equally guarded and denied to the many.

And in fact, if one considers the typical structure of a power pyramid in this light, one can discover a significant bit of power-structure anatomy that has never been dragged into the light of day.

This bit, however, is quite well-known in security systems everywhere, but has not been applied to power structures in general.

The "need to know" factor, and in overall power terms it more or less breaks down as follows:

1. Power elites need to know everything, or they will not remain as such for very long.
2. The powerful need to know only what the power elites tell them.
3. The workers supporting and servicing the power structure need to know only what they need to know in order to continue supporting and servicing the power structure.
4. The remainder of the relatively powerless populations incorporated into the power structure need to know nothing -- except, possibly, what they need to know in order to keep them more or less content and not rebellious within the confines of their powerlessness.

In fact, the anatomy of a power structure can adequately be diagrammed not by who's who within it, or by social status, but by how the need-to-know gradients are set up, monitored, managed, and maintained.

If the power structure is examined in this way, it turns out that even many of the merely powerful don't know very much. And if having wealth is, by itself, considered a power factor, then many of the wealthy often know even less.

PROPHYLAXIS REGARDING ACCESS TO POWER AND PROSPECTIVE FOREKNOWLEDGE

So, if power is seen as extremely precious and to be highly desired, then access to it must be guarded, or at least not made easy to obtain.

If ways and means can be set up to prevent easy access to power, then it can be enjoyed by the few who have set up, or endorsed, the ways and means.

The best and most efficient way to manage and perpetuate this kind of thing is to prohibit ALL real information about power, empowerment, and methods of depowerment.

It is thus that the combined total absence of power studies, research, knowledge, and power schools acts like a general prophylactic that prevents, wards off, and guards against the inseminating of power growth among the populations entire.

Indeed, the total absence effectively dumbs-down not only intellectual knowledge about power, but even the awarenesses that are needed to inseminate empowerment.

If prospective foreknowledge has something to do with gaining access to power, then gaining cognitive access to such MUST be treated somewhat along the proven efficient lines of gaining access to power.

Thus, a total absence of foreknowledge training schools must be engineered into existence.

THIS total absence acts like a prophylactic that prevents, wards off, and guards against any real access to foreknowledge.

The hoped-for result of this is that the general populations are artificially dumbed-down IN GENERAL with respect to empowerment of human foreknowledge faculties -- and which faculties are consistently present within our species.

If only randomly, episodes of foreknowledge have naturally blossomed forth within all sorts of individuals since time immemorial, and even among the powerless.

And so, as it turns out, access to power can more easily be contained and prevented than access to foreknowledge. If efficient foreknowledge is combined with efficient stealth powers, then the powerful do understand that there is a special problem here.

THE NATURE OF PROPHYLAXIS

It is worth pointing up an important factor regarding prophylaxis that usually escapes notice.

The concept of prophylactics usually achieves significance only with regard to preventing sexual insemination of egg by sperm.

But in a larger picture of what is involved, humans cannot really prevent anything unless they design and engineer the ways and means to do so.

As it is, most dictionaries define PROPHYLAXIS as: "measures DESIGNED [emphasis added] to preserve or prevent" whatever.

Thus, if foreknowledge can be prevented by information prophylaxis, then power can more easily be preserved at least with respect to foreknowledge.

THE CONNECTION OF DUMMIES WITH REGARD TO POWER

On average, the general concepts having to do with dumb, dumbness, and dummy, usually focus on the idea of natural or inherent stupidity, a term usually thought of as a synonym for dumb. But there are subtle differences between the two.

STUPIDITY is principally defined, without too much elaboration, as "slowness of mind."

But DUMB is principally defined, again without too much elaboration, as "destitute of power" regarding something, and as "lacking some usual attribute," especially in the case of "having no self-propulsion."

Thus, with respect to ANY of the many contexts of power and empowerment, "having no self-propulsion" is almost identical to having powerlessness.

Dumbness and stupidity are most frequently thought of as naturally existing or as inherent. But more to the point of anything significant, both can be engineered into existence via environmental factors, and via social conditioning factors.

If dumbness and stupidity are the result of those two factors, then it is in that sense that DUMB DOWN is defined.

It takes effort of some kind to dumb-down, deliberate effort, the reasons for which are exceedingly hard to identify.

However, there is one definition for DUMMY that signifies something along such lines. A DUMMY is defined as "one seemingly to act for himself but is in reality acting for or at the direction of another or of others."

Here, one may as well add: "acting under the control and influence of another or others."

In the light of the foregoing definitions, it is now possible to hypothesize that stupidity and dumbness can artificially be designed so as to act as prophylactics regarding access to power and foreknowledge.

The best possible result of this designing would eventuate if its targets found themselves "having no means of self-propulsion" relative to access of power and its close associate, foreknowledge.

It would be obvious that "self-propulsion" is a fundamental format upon which any initiating of empowerment basically depends.

LACK OF STUDIES REGARDING INTUITION

It is generally understood that intuition has many uses, meaning that it is some sort of collective of powers, faculties, and intelligences, each of which download different functions.

However that may be, the idea of intuition as foreknowledge predominates -- and it is thus that intuition is doubly damned in relationship to power and foreknowledge.

Intuition is referred to all of the time, at least among the general population, and so it may be thought that a great deal of knowledge has accumulated about it.

In fact, researched information about it is very sparse, even in, of all places, the somewhat organized realms of parapsychology. If one seeks information about intuition, one will find little more than a few brief definitions.

Webster's, for example, indicates that INTUITION is "the power or faculty of attaining to direct knowledge or cognition without rational thought or reference."

The ENCYCLOPEDIA OF OCCULTISM AND PARAPSYCHOLOGY indicates that INTUITION is "that sense of faculty in the human mind by which man knows (or may know) facts of which he would otherwise not be cognizant -- acts which might not be apparent to him through process of reason or so-called scientific proof."

The up-shot of what is known about intuition is that the term exists, but much beyond that is absent, at least in any authoritative sense.

That the reason for this is yet ANOTHER knowledge absence is by now perfectly obvious. Intuition has something to do, as it might be put, with intuitions regarding power and empowerment possibilities and potentials, and with obtaining or accessing prospective foreknowledge as well.

So, if ever there was a candidate which needed to undergo extensive prophylactic dumbing-down processes, here is one that has direct and literal significance.

THE POSSIBLE EXTENT OF HUMAN SENSING SYSTEMS

If intuition were to be better understood and explained, then it probably would have to be conceptualized as being comprised of some kind of sensing systems having to do with "the power or faculty of attaining to direct knowledge or cognition without rational thought and inference."

Although the above definition is found in dictionaries, it is rather misleading.

For one thing, there is no apparent logic to suppose that rational thought and inference cannot figure into intuition.

There is also every reason to suppose that "the power or faculty" is basically composed of interactions of multiple kinds of sensing systems which conventional power authorities of course assert do not and cannot exist.

Furthermore, if one studies history with regard to how past peoples and cultures viewed the existence of sensing systems, two particularly interesting factors can be uncovered or at least extrapolated upon.

1. Our pre-modern predecessors never doubted the existence of what the modern sciences identified as the five physical senses.

2. But the idea that humans possessed ONLY five physical senses did not exist in the past, even among Greek philosophers who advocated a material explanation for the universe.

However, the number and kinds of sensing systems were not particularly well-defined in the past -- largely because people dealt not with mechanisms of the sensing systems, but with their out-put QUALITY.

In other words, people tended to judge sensing (of any kind) by what resulted because of it, even if what was sensed had no connection to the physical realms.

It is clear that our predecessors, even at the start-up of recorded history, accepted the existence of human sensing systems per se. Indeed, the categorization of what IS and what is NOT sensory is therefore of relatively recent origin.

Intuition, and its associated sensing systems, cannot be based only on the five physical senses. For example, the sensing of love, hate, and sexual availability are not functions of the five physical senses, and neither is the sensing of stealth activity, secrecy, duplicity, truth, falsehood, and even the sensing of power.

KNOWLEDGE OF HUMAN SENSING SYSTEMS THAT HAS BEEN DUMBED-DOWN

As might be understood by now, the easiest way of dumbing-down knowledge of something is to undertake ways and means that end up reducing it to insignificance.

If this is successful, then people are likely not to notice it at all, or even want to.

Most people realize that they possess sensing systems that have been dumbed down within the contexts of conventional cultural, scientific, and philosophical terms, but they seldom realize why or how.

However, if the prospective of multiple sensing systems is readmitted into consideration, all individual humans can be thought of as composites of self-propulsion walking, talking, thinking sensing systems.

Within that context, the sensing systems can be said to exist in everyone. It is only their "self-propulsion" that has been dumbed down.

It is entirely probable that the self-propulsion can at least be somewhat reactivated by simply becoming aware of what sensing systems have been dumbed down.

Up until about twenty years ago, the existence of dumbed-down sensing systems would have had to be hypothetically argued via psychical and parapsychological contexts.

It is no longer necessary to argue for the existence of extensive human sensing systems in hypothetical terms. The reason is that knowledge regarding the extensive nature of human sensing systems has dramatically increased -- not in parapsychology, but, believe it or not, in the sciences proper.

It is now clear that the human possesses not just the five standard sensing systems, but very many more of very different kinds.

THE PAST ARGUMENT AGAINST THE EXISTENCE OF MULTI-COMPLEX SENSING SYSTEMS

In order to help grok the list of extended human sensing systems that will shortly follow, it needs to be understood that the scientific argument against their existence centered on a particular aspect.

If sensing systems (such as those having to do with intuition, etc.) were to be admitted as existing, then there needed to be receptors for them.

For example, the eye systems were receptors for light and form. The ear systems were receptors for sound. The nose systems were receptors for smell, the tongue systems for taste, and the skin for tactile impressions or feeling.

And that was the extent of human sensing receptors -- until developments in electron microscopes made it possible to discover other kinds of receptors on and within the human biological organism.

For clarity, a RECEPTOR is defined as "a cell or group of cells that receive stimuli."

A SHORT LIST OF SENSING SYSTEMS RECEPTORS THAT HAVE BEEN DISCOVERED

Please note that the following items are numbered. But this is merely for convenience, and the numbering does not establish any particular priority.

1. Receptors in the nose sensing systems that "smell" emotions, and that can identify motives, sexual receptivity, antagonism, benevolence, etc. (All these are formats of what are commonly referred to as vibe-sensing).
2. Receptors in the ear sensing systems that detect and identify differences in pressure and electromagnetic frequencies (formats of ESP).
3. Skin receptors that detect balance and imbalance regarding what is external to the bio-body (formats of remote-sensing, a mixed form of ESP and clairvoyance).
4. Skin receptors that detect motion outside of the body, even when the body is asleep (a format of ESP).
5. Directional finding and locating receptors in the endocrine and neuropeptide systems (formats of dowsing, intermixed with formats of cognitive ESP or intuition).

6. Whole-body receptors, including hair, that identify fluidic motions of horizontal, vertical, diagonal, even if not visually perceived (as, for example, in the "psychic" factors of the martial art of Aikido).
7. Skin receptors that "recognize" the temperament of other biological organisms (a format of psi "reading").
8. Subliminal sensory systems which locate and identify pitch of sound, a sense of heat across great distances, a sense of frequencies and waves, either mechanical or energetic (all being formats of ESP and vibe-sensing).
9. Receptors that identify positive and negative charged particles at the atomic level. The term utilized for this in psychical research is "micro-psi," but which is rare, but which has been frequently demonstrated especially in the case of C. W. Leadbeater who published OCCULT CHEMISTRY (1908). Thirty years before the invention of electron microscopes, he correctly described sub-atomic particles, many undiscovered, but discovered since. Micro-psi faculties are mentioned as one of the ancient SIDHIS of ancient India (see, for example, YOGA SUTRAS OF PATANJALI).
10. Microsystems transducing of various forms of mechanical, chemical, and electromagnetic energy into meaningful nerve impulses (all commonly thought of as FORMS OF ESP).
11. Receptors that sense gravitational changes (a form of DOWSING).
12. Neurological senses for interpreting modulated electronic information by converting it into analog signals for mental storage, interpretation, and cognition (one of the bio-mind bases for TELEPATHY).
13. Bio-electronic receptors for sensing radiation, including X-rays, cosmic rays, infrared radiation, and ultraviolet light, all of these receptors being found in the retina of the eye (part of the basis for various forms of CLAIRVOYANCE).
14. Receptors that respond to exterior electrical fields and systems (producing forms of CLAIRVOYANCE and AURA "READING").
    Today, the following highly specialized sensing systems are referred to in the new sciences as HUMAN SEMAPHORE CAPACITIES.
15. Skin receptors for sensing perceptions of bonding or antagonism (thought of as forms of INTUITION).
16. Sensing systems for non-verbal "language" communicating (thought of as a form of TELEPATHY or VIBESENSING).
17. Combined sensing systems (neural networks) for making meaning out of at least 130 identified nonverbal physical gestures and twenty basic kinds of nonverbal messages (thought of as INTUITIONAL CHARACTER ASSESSMENT or a particular form of CLAIRVOYANCE).

18. Receptors that trigger alarm and apprehension before their sources are directly perceived (a particularly valuable type of PSYCHIC FORESIGHT, FORESEEING, INTUITION).
19. Sensing systems for registering and identifying nonverbal emotional waves (a form of INTUITION and/or TELEPATHY or CLAIRVOYANCE).

    The following are now known to be associated with the PINEAL GLAND if it is healthy and in good working order.
20. Senses and memory-stores cycles of light and darkness, anticipating them with accuracy as the daily motions of the sun and moon change (a kind of PSYCHIC FORECASTING or FUTURE SEEING).
21. Sensing and responding to solar and lunar rhythms, solar disruptions (flares, sunspots) and moon-caused tidal changes (water or geophysical ones) and can sense "coming" earthquakes and storms (a form of PREDICTIVE ESP especially noted in sailors, farmers, but also in cows, dogs, cats, and snakes).
22. If the pineal gland is fully functional, it acts as a nonvisual photo-receptor (the psychic equivalent being "X-RAY VISION").

The following senses or sensing systems are similar to some already mentioned, but they appear to function upon a completely different basis and are additional to them.

It is now thought that this basis is almost certainly the WATER contained in the bio-body, in the physical components of the nerve systems, and the physical part of the brain.

It is not yet understood how WATER is used this way to create a fluidic but elaborate series of interconnected sensing systems.

One of the best guesses, yet to be established, is that the vibrations of the water molecules link together throughout the entire bio-body and form the equivalent of radar or sonar antennae.

These liquid antenna sensing systems appear to detect the following categories. Divided by categories, they can be thought of as individualized and highly refined sensing systems. All of these categories have been thought of as INTUITIVE.

23. Sense of non-visual wave motions.
24. Sense of non-visual oscillating patterns.
25. Sense of magnetic fields.
26. Sense of infrared radiation.
27. Sense of electrical energy.
28. Sense receptors for local AND distant sources of heat. (This is an unnamed PSI faculty, but one familiar to Amerindians).
29. Sense of geo-electromagnetic pulses, magnetic fields, especially biological

ones (intuitive equivalents unidentified and unnamed).

30. Although the mechanisms are not at all understood, the liquidic sensing receptors apparently are somehow involved in the remote sensing of anything at a distance, however great.

Finally (although there is no "finally" here), we come to sensory systems' receptors spread throughout the entire bio-body, and which apparently feed information into the mind-body interface (if "interface" would be the correct concept).

31. Whole-body receptors (millions of them) to detect pheromones, sexual receptivity, fear, love, admiration, danger, pain in others, intentions in others, etc., (all formerly thought of as inexplicable forms of intuition, ESP or so-called vibe-sensing and/or "psychic reading").

SUGGESTED EXERCISE

AT LEISURE, EXAMINE THE FOREGOING LIST AND NOTICE WHICH OF INDICATE SOMETHING FAMILIAR.

Chapter 26

HUMAN SENSING SYSTEMS, POWER MOTION, AND POWER FLOWS

WHEN INDIVIDUALS have difficulty understanding something, it is usually thought that their knowledge levels and understanding mechanisms are at fault.

But in the case of this chapter (perhaps other chapters as well), the principal reason for the difficulty does NOT involve probable deficits of an individual's understanding capacities.

Instead, the difficulty arises because of the several knowledge vacuums that have been discussed so far.

After all, one can be expected to understand available information, but can hardly be expected to understand something for which no information has been identified and accumulated.

This is to say that the processes of understanding need information to process. If the information is not available, then there is nothing to process.

Further, if one carefully considers the short list of sensing systems receptors provided in the previous chapter, one can easily think of each set as being different.

Indeed, they are different in function and effect, but the whole of them also has one subtle factor in common.

The sets of receptors, each in their own way, detect some kind of motion -- or more precisely put, each in their own way is stimulated by some kind of motion. The receptor sets are therefore specializing motion detectors.

Everyone of course understands what motion is, especially with regard to physical factors. Most may even understand that radio and television receiving equipment are receptors set to detect specific frequencies and wavelengths that are being transmitted from some sending source.

But the general tendency is not to think of radio and television sets as motion detectors, but as things sitting there. In fact, the general tendency is to think about everything in terms of things, not in terms of their motion.

As noted by some investigators, all things, if they are physical, appear to have a fixed quality. And in general. the five physical senses are majorly oriented with regard to this fixity.

The five physical senses can detect physical motion, of course, but generally do not detect motion that is not represented by physicality.

The result of this is that there is a general tendency to THINK in terms of fixity. The term FIXED of course refers to whatever is "securely placed or fastened," to whatever is "stationary," and to whatever is "not subject to change or fluctuation."

FIXITY then refers to "the quality or state of being fixed or stable, "and most people prefer to exist among things and phenomena that have that quality.

There is thus a very big, general, and predominating tendency to appreciate and value fixed things and fixity, even as regards thought, awareness, and perception.

The individual might have five physical sense receptor systems that detect and appreciate the fixity of the physical.

As it has turned out, because of advancing discovery regarding additional receptors, the same individual also has at least thirty-one receptor systems that detect some hind of motion. And in some sense at least, that motion is independent of fixed physicality.

Because of those advancing discoveries, it is probably no longer appropriate to group those thirty-one receptor systems under the general term of intuition. But in that intuition implies acquiring information by other than physical sense means, then that term is generally applicable to most of the thirty-one receptor systems.

Simply put, where there is motion there is also information. And if motion of any kind is detected by this or that sensing system, then the obvious reason for the receptors to exist in the first place is to detect NOT JUST the motion, but what it implies in terms of information.

HUMAN SENSING OF HUMAN MOTIVES

The whole of the foregoing becomes entirely credible if one specific and extremely significant human activity is considered.

Human motives and motivations probably account for a large proportion of most or even all human activities and involvements. Attempting to utilize only the five physical senses to deduce or infer human motives has a very low rate of success.

Yet human motives are identified (intuited) all of the time, and so the sensory receptors that produce such information cannot be associated to the physical five senses.

With this in mind, if the list of thirty-one detector systems is again read through, quite a few of them can be seen to account for this or that kind of motivation detecting.

THE RELATIONSHIP OF HUMAN MOTIVES AND THE ACQUISITION OF HUMAN POWER

Hardly any understanding regarding the panorama of powerdom can be realized if the topic of human motivations is not included at some very basic level.

Indeed, if ever there were two topics that almost completely and intimately integrate, the "marriage" of motives and power easily heads the list -- albeit of course that motives can stimulate other things than power acquiring.

It follows that if acquiring power is seen as precious, then intuiting motives is seen as a very significant armament which must be prevented from falling into the hands, awarenesses, perceptions, and minds of too many.

The best overall way to prevent this requires a threefold methodology:

1. To completely deny authenticity to intuition, and erect a knowledge vacuum around it;
2. To direct human perceptions only to the fixities that can be perceived via the five physical senses;
3. To institute overt or subtle forms of condign punishment when (1) and (2) are "disobeyed."

There is no major societal power structure anywhere in the modern world that advocates and supports free and open inquiry into the nature of intuition. Even modern parapsychology, always hopeful of conventional scientific acceptance, avoids this topic like the plague.

The unavoidable fact is that if intuition is better understood with regard to practical applications (including motives detection), then the certainty that societal power can remain stable becomes increasingly uncertain. This is what the significance of intuition portends if open research into it is permitted.

Intuition is therefore a very sensitive and dangerous issue, so much so that those working within societal power structures will themselves not admit to having some of it.

THE SUPPRESSION OF KNOWLEDGE REGARDING HUMAN MOTIVES AND MOTIVATIONS

If sensing motives via some form of intuition needs to be disarmed, then it turns out that knowledge of the nature of human motives and motivations ALSO needs to be encapsulated within a knowledge vacuum.

It is hard to think that this has been possible, largely because motives and motivations are referred to all of the time. Yet, the nature of motives would belong within the contexts of power studies overall, which, of course, don't exist.

The usual sense attributed to motives and motivations has do with urges, desires, ideas, and intellectual content that fuel or propel motivations. And so interest is fixated on what the contents of those urges, desires, and ideas consist of. If those contents can be intellectually grasped, then it can be thought that the motives are intellectually understood.

THE DYNAMICS OF MOTIVES AND MOTIVATIONS

There is an aspect regarding motives and motivations that is not understandable only via whatever the contents might consist of.

This aspect can be referred to as the DYNAMICS of motives and motivations as contrasted merely to their intellectual content.

The nature of dynamics has been discussed earlier, but to refresh memory, DYNAMIC can briefly be defined as "driving forces and expansionist qualities, and variations in their intensities."

There are many motives and motivations having appreciable intellectual content that can be expressed as ideas, desires, urges, and intellectual goals. However, many or even most of these don't lift off or get anywhere.

To understand and/or grok why this is so, it is necessary to examine needed official definitions of a few terms. Taken altogether, these terms portray why many motives and motivations don't get off the ground or end up in blind canyons. Simply speaking, they don't become empowered, and don't accumulate power to them.

A FUNDAMENTAL ASPECT OF POWER AND POWER-MAKING

When various aspects of power are examined, as they have been in this volume, many of them lead again and again to the concept of motion.

Thus, it is logical to conclude that whatever power consists of, it is not a static thing.

In other words, it is not something at rest, non-moving, or composed of forces in equilibrium.

Equilibrium is akin to fixity and seems to neutralize power. If it goes on too long a sense of powerlessness will develop from within it.

Static conditions ultimately prove to be those of little change, characterized by lack of movement, animation, progression or development -- and hence of little significance that portends futurity.

Technically speaking, there can be no such thing as "static forces" or "static power" -- although those phrases are used all the time to describe when forces or powers cease motion and become stationary.

If a force or a power becomes static, as they often do, they change their state and cease being a force of a power. They can become energies at rest, but an energy which is motionless or static soon loses, well, loses its energy.

In such cases, we like to think that the "potential" energy is still there. But energy, like power, is a strange thing.

When it is not being energy, not being used as such, it tends to dissipate -- as if sort of bleeding off to somewhere else. Much the same can be said of power.

POWER FLOWS

It can easily be observed that when power, energies, or forces do become static, they enter into a condition of non-motion, no change, lack of animation, no development, and "dead" dynamism, as it were.

Dead dynamism is characterized by fixity, lack of driving growth, lack of expansionism, all this equating to no intensity, or to zero intensity.

The best way to achieve a more profound handle on this is to examine what is meant by FLOWS.

In its verb form, TO FLOW is defined as "to move with a continual change of place among the constituent particles."

In its noun form, it is defined as:

1. A smooth uninterrupted movement or motion; and, most importantly
2. A continuous transfer of energy.

The key concepts here are UNINTERRUPTED and CONTINUOUS TRANSFER OF ENERGY. Please memorize them if you are interested in enhancing or unfolding your own power.

AN IMPORTANT DISTINCTION BETWEEN
PHYSICAL ENERGIES AND HUMAN ENERGIES

One of the little-known, thus invisible problems regarding this is that static powers, energies and forces can be observed in modern and post-modern physics and engineering.

For example, in physics STATICS is a branch of mechanics dealing with the relations of forces that produce equilibrium among material bodies.

Water can be stored in tanks and be considered at rest and at equilibrium if it is not also put under pressure. If it is put under pressure, the water molecules will increase their motion, ultimately transforming into heat and steam -- and an explosion.

Stationary charges of electricity can also be produced, resulting in electrostatic energy, which is a changed state of electricity noted for fantastic motion.

So here is a model, a scientific one, indicating that power, energy and forces CAN be contained in a non-motion state or condition. But this model refers exclusively to physical properties.

When this model is superimposed onto human conditions and situations, as it often is, it is mistakenly thought that human power, energies, and forces can be treated likewise and with the same results.

The problem, though, is that the human is composed not only of physical properties, but psychological and motivational ones, and also of the little-understood "life" energies.

And the same laws which seem to govern physical properties DO NOT govern the psychological and motivational properties.

Even so, for the better part of the modern scientific age, scientists thought of the human as a mechanical or mechanistic product of physical properties only, from which somehow resulted the psychological and motivational circumstances which came into play.

Thus, it seemed rational to apply the physics model to human activity or lack of it, and in many categories that model was superimposed on the human, which is also a vehicle for power, energies, and forces which differ considerably from the physical model.

That this was an egregious error in the extreme can become apparent to those who undertake human power studies, and when it is understood that the human is not only a complex series of bio-physical mechanisms, but a psychological vehicle which emanates motivations.

The bio-physical mechanisms are atomic, chemical and electrical in their inherent nature. But human psychology and resulting motivations are quite another matter, indeed.

A larger grasp of all this can be achieved by considering that the human bio-physical mechanisms are preordained, as it were, by factors present in the genetic codes which format the mechanisms, and thus the entire physical body.

These genetic factors are TRANSFERRED from the parents, but themselves are also present in the entire human genetic pool (the human genome) world-wide.

That the genetic factors ARE transferred is a complete indication that the factors are in motion, have energy, and produce the flows which altogether combine into the resulting product, another biological individual.

Each human life would therefore be a simple matter -- if this was all there was to the life situation.

But human life, and especially the living of it, is nowhere that simple.

It is commonly acknowledged, even if grudgingly so, that the human bio-mechanism is also equipped with a psyche that acts more like a BEING than a mere mechanism.

Upon observation, the being is equipped with a variegated psychological profile, and with motivations.

The very great problem here is that it is not at all understood where these come from, and for the most part none of them can be attributed to the bio-mass of the body itself.

And the problem becomes more confounding when it is understood that the indwelling psyche, the psychological profile, and the motivations -- which are what they are of and in themselves -- can also have formative and deformative impact on the bio-mechanical systems.

For example, psychosomatic symptoms, illnesses, and conditions are attributed to factors within the psychological profile, not to the bio-mechanisms themselves.

Thus, it can become quite clear that the psyche, the psychological profile, and the motivations have power, energies, and forces of their own. Otherwise they would not impact either positively or negatively on the bio-mechanical systems.

It is not at all clear whether the bio-mechanisms or the psyche, etc., are primary. But it would be obvious that the human being is composed of at least TWO systems: the bio-mechanistic one; and the other consisting of a mix of the psyche, the psychological profile, and the motivations which emanate from them.

On the other hand, motivations presumably originating in the psyche or the psychological profile often lead to the death of the bio-body. And in such a case, it would be clear which system was primary. You see, motivations often lead to the sacrifice of the bio-body, if they are of that kind.

If we can conclude, as we might, that the human being is composed of two systems, then both consist of power, energies and forces. This is to say that both systems consist of movement or motion flows.

The power and energies of the bio-mechanisms and of the psyche-psychological profile are not easily or immediately recognizable. This is to say that most people have powers and energies they don't recognize or even know about.

And here is the single, and the biggest, clue which can lead to the enhancement and unfoldment of power.

For it can be assumed, and probably correctly so, that a sense of powerlessness is proportionate to the existence of powers and energies which the individual does not yet recognize within self -- and which, therefore, have not undergone the unfoldment processes.

Something of the same can also be said regarding charisma, and various kinds of charisma, which may lie unactivated within self because the individual has not realized they exist within.

If on the one hand individuals possess power, energies and forces within that they don't recognize, on the other hand motivations are usually more identifiable and recognizable.

To comprehend why this is so, we need to look at the meanings of MOTIVE and MOTIVATION.

THE MATURE OF MOTIVES AND MOTIVATIONS

Most dictionaries will give the definition of MOTIVE as "something (as a need or desire) that causes a person to act." MOTIVATION is derived from TO MOTIVATE, which means to provide with a motive.

But these words are derived from earlier words in other languages having to do with MOTOR and MOTION, and which mean:

1. Moving or tending to move into action; and
2. Relating to motion or the causing of motion.

In this sense, motives and motivations may not be identifiable or visible of themselves, but that they result in action brings visibility to them.

Additionally, and surprisingly, it may not matter what the intellectual contents of motives are.

For if motives do not manifest dynamic flows, then they will not manifest. Conversely, if the dynamic flows are present then it probably will not matter too much what the intellectual contents consist of.

In other words, the dynamic flows are themselves the power, not the ideas behind them.

More precisely, the motive or motivation consists of the dynamic energies or forces which result in the action, while the action itself, if powerful enough, will set in motion subsequent activity, often as in the case of a chain reaction.

One of the points being made here is that the motive or the motivation is actually at first a FLOW of energy or force BEFORE it results in whatever action or activity it does.

The motivational flow then results in an action, while the action itself induces subsequent flows among its targeted areas.

When we think of a motivation as an action first and foremost, then we are missing the very important power qualities which precede the action.

You see, power may or may not grow or persist via the action alone -- and indeed the power-strength of the action may be questionable and non-determinative.

Additionally, and perhaps most importantly, the action itself may or may not have power, and this is determined exclusively by how OTHERS respond to it.

As a rule of thumb, OTHERS will respond to motives and motivations only if they sense them as dynamic, or as possessing dynamism.

Dynamism equates to significance and portends something.

Lack of dynamism equates to insignificance and portends very little or nothing at all.

QUALITIES TO OBSERVE

WITHOUT THEIR KNOWING IT, TRY TO OBSERVE OTHERS WITH RESPECT TO THEIR DYNAMISM OR LACK OF IT.

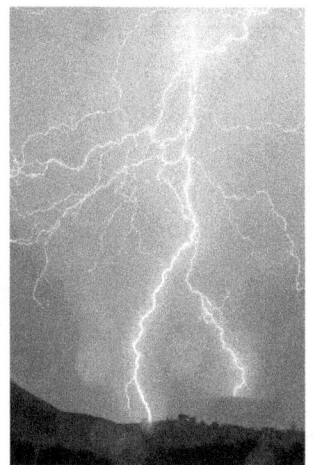

Chapter 27

THE FORGOTTEN CONNECTION OF POWER AND POTENCY

IT IS rather broadly accepted that power has to become manifested in some form in order to recognize it and then to intellectually appreciate its complexities. In other words, power has to be obvious enough to perceive it, so that one can intellectually deal with it in one way or another.

This is true, of course, but only partly so. If one undertakes a study of the very large panorama of power, it can be discovered that some can accurately sense it as existing before it becomes obviously manifested -- and some can accurately sense it as coming or as about to happen before it makes its appearance in any obvious form.

If one attempts to examine the nature of this sensing, it can reasonably be established that many who are trying to climb power ladders do not have it. And neither do many of the temporarily powerful.

Furthermore, it also occurs where it would not be expected to do so -- among the so-called powerless who are assumed to be dumb about almost everything having to do with power and empowerment.

It is thus that yet another very subtle aspect having some portending significance to power can be brought to light.

RECOGNIZING THE DIFFERENCE BETWEEN WHAT WILL AND WILL NOT BECOME POWER

It is difficult to get a handle on this, because the implication is that although many might not exactly know what power is, they can somehow recognize the difference between (1) what is and what is not power, and, more importantly, (2) what will and will not become power.

By extension, this implies that they can somehow recognize what is devoid of power, and what will not manifest as it.

It can first be thought that this kind of sensing could be the same as sensing significance and insignificance. But the difficulty here is that it generally takes a number of individuals to intellectually or emotionally agree about what has significance and what has insignificance. Thus, and as is well known, those kinds of agreements can be mistaken and eventually stand revealed as claptrap.

For clarity, the central interest here has to do with how it is possible to identify power before it happens and becomes obvious.

Any reasonable answer to this question obviously falls more into the category of some kind of intuitive sensing (by any means possible) than into the category of mere and limited intellectual understanding based on what is visible.

POWER AS IT IS IN THE HERE AND NOW
versus
POWER AS IT WAS BACK IN TIME

One of the difficulties in getting a handle on this topic is that people are usually only interested in power as it is being thought of in the "here and now," or as it will be in the immediate future.

A real history of power itself does not exist, of course, because what is taken to be history merely consists of recounting the successes, failures, vicissitudes, trials, and tribulations of the powerful and the epochs in which they lived.

If a history of power itself was ever compiled, it would reveal that power has been thought of, and even manifested, in many different ways.

This suggests that the criteria for power being utilized in any given here and now can be different from those that were utilized back in time.

Although it cannot be known for sure, it seems reasonable to assume that what we today refer to as power was, in the distant pre-historical past, closely associated with the basic imperative of survival per se.

This precisely needs to be stated as survival among, and in spite of, all the threatening odds against it. Indeed, there have always been strong undercurrents of this kind of thing beneath the various kinds of power structures that have been built on top of it.

This can become more clear if one considers the differences between, for example, power structures based in survival, and those based in greed and power only for the sake of power.

In the survival sense, it seems logical to think that the qualities of awareness, vivid observing capacities, cunning, craftiness, enhanced sensing, and perhaps intuitive and inventive intelligence were closely associated with enhancing survival potentials.

Today, such qualities do have relevance to survival. But as has been copiously discussed by now, the qualities listed in the foregoing paragraph are more likely to be considered as enemies not of power itself, but of the powerful few, and of the maintenance of their particular power structures.

In any event, there is an important distinction between power on behalf of survival, and power on behalf of whatever else.

This distinction carries many layers of importance. But a major two-fold importance can be identified.

On the one hand, it seems that power on behalf of survival can only take place in some kind of survival setting and will principally involve individuals and enhancement of their power qualities.

On the other hand, power on behalf of anything else than survival can only take place within some kind of societal setting within which basic survival per se is mostly guaranteed, but within which power positioning is not.

This distinction reflects that shifts in various notions of power have taken place. One of the chief shifts involves the following.

Through time, the importance of power at the individual survival level has been minimized, while the importance of power at the group or societal level has been maximized.

SHIFTS IN POWER CONCEPTS AS REVEALED IN LANGUAGE

Everyone more or less realizes that contexts of power have shifted many times from the minimized individual level to the maximized corporate societal levels.

But what is interesting and even dynamic is that although those shifts can be obfuscated via conventional history rewrite, they none the less stand revealed in nomenclature shifts.

As but one example, this shift away from individual power for the sake of survival to societal power for the sake of power can indeed be identified via the evolving definitions of power in the English language.

In English, the etymology of POWER shows that it was probably taken via French into early English during the eighth century, from the Latin term POTERE which referred to a combination of "to be able" and "potent."

It is this combined concept of "potently able" that early surfaced in English as POER, POEIR, or POUWER, or some phonetic variant.

The term POTENT is most certainly drawn from the Sanskrit PATI, referring to "master."

The Sanskrit is thence taken through Greek and into Latin as POTERE, in which language it referred to being strongly able in some potent sense -- or, as can be said, power-full, or full of potency.

Most modern dictionaries render vague and somewhat impotent definitions for POTENT, and which clearly are not what the ancients had in mind.

For clarity, there are distinctions between (1) whatever affects, influences, and even overwhelms, and (2) whatever DOES NOTHING OF THE KIND.

Whatever does nothing of the kind is certainly impotent. But what the ancients more probably meant by potent is more akin to the modern English terms DYNAMIC or DYNAMISM which, in some major sense at least, refer to the potent quality of power-full-ness.

The earliest English definition of POUWER or POWAR is established as emerging at about 1297. It is given as "Illustration of forms."

This definition is somewhat obscure today. Back then it seems to refer to some kind of relationship or linkage between a king (master) who illustrated, demonstrated, or personified potent power and distributed or delegated active amounts of it to others.

In 1297, POUWER was also thought of in two additional ways:

1. A body of armed men; a fighting force, a host, an army; and
2. Possession of command or control over others; dominion, rule; government, domination, sway, command; control, influence, authority over.

By 1325, however, two definitions of POWAR emerged which we can easily recognize today:

1. As a quality or property, an ability to do or affect something or anything; or to act upon a person or thing; and
2. A particular faculty of body or mind.

Now follows the list of definitions regarding POWAR and associated terms as they evolved during the five centuries between 1340 and 1864.

1340: Authority given or committed; hence, sometimes liberty or permission to act.

1340: TRANSFORM: To change the form of; to change into another form or shape; to metamorphose.

1382: One who, or that which, is possessed of or exercises power, influence, or government; as an influential or governing person, body, or thing.

1388: In medieval angelology, the sixth order of angels in the celestial hierarchy.

1400-50: POWERFUL, Having great power; mighty; potent.

By 1440, another definition had emerged, and which is somewhat commensurate with our thinking today: ability to act or affect something strongly; physical or mental strength; might, vigor, energy; force of character; telling force, effect.

1485: POTENTIAL: Possessing potency or power; potent; powerful, mighty, strong; commanding. (Please note that this definition is now given as "rare.")

1500: POTENT: Powerful, possessed of great power having great authority or influence; mighty; used of persons and things, with many shades of meaning as the power implied is political, military, social, supernatural, moral, mental, etc. (Usually a poetic or rhetorical word, felt to be stronger than powerful.)

1526: A celestial or spiritual being having control or influence: (Please note that this definition is given as "pagan.")

1535: Personal or social ascendancy; influence.

1540: As a verb, TO POWER: To make powerful, strengthen. (This definition is now given as "Rare or obsolete.")

1552: POWERLESS: Without power or ability; devoid of power; helpless.

1556: TRANSFORM as related to POWERFUL: To change in character or condition; to alter in function or nature.

1571: TRANSFORMATE: Someone or something that has undergone transformation, or which has been transformed.

1586: POWERFUL: Of or with regard to persons or things, capable of exerting great force; strong; potent.

1588: POWERABLE, adjective: (Now indicated as obsolete): POWER + ABLE -- hence powerableness, powerfulness; power as a quality.

1586: POWERFULNESS: The quality of being powerful; mightiness; strength, potency; impressiveness, convincing quality.

1592: Of inanimate things: Active property; capacity of producing some effect; the active principle or virtue of an herb, etc.

1596: POWERFUL: Exerting great force or producing great effect; Having power to influence greatly; impressive, convincing, telling.

1661: A large number, a multitude, a "host" of persons (not a military force).

1667: EMPOWER: To bestow power upon, to make powerful, to gain or assume power over.

1674: TRANSFORMABLE: That which may be transformed; capable of transformation.

1681: EMPOWER: To impart or bestow power to an end or for a purpose.

1701: Political or national strength.

1726: A state or nation regarded from the point of view of its international authority or influence.

1727-42: (At the beginning of the scientific age) -- Any form of energy or force available for application to work.

1727-42: POWER-POTENT: The sound expressed by a character or symbol; the meaning expressed by a word or phrase in. a particular context as having force.

1766: POTENTIAL: Possible as opposed to actual; latent; existing in a latent or undeveloped state capable of coming into being or action.

1823: Political ascendance or influence in the government of a country or state.

1841: DEPOTENTIATE: To deprive of power or potency. (I.e., depowerment).

1849: EMPOWERMENT: The action of empowering; the state or quality of being empowered.

1853: POTENTIAL ENERGY: Energy existing in potential form, not as motion; the opposite of kinetic energy.

1855: KINETIC: (Rare) That which excites to motion, or to act; producing or causing motion; potent.

1864: KINETIC: Of, pertaining or relating to, motion; due to or resulting from motion.

1864: KINETICS: The branch of dynamics which investigates the relations between the motion of bodies and the forces acting upon them; opposed to Statics, which treats of bodies in equilibrium.

THE LOSS OF THE CONCEPT OF POTENCY

From the foregoing list, it can be seen that the definition of POWER as possession of command or control over others has been with us since 1297 A.D.

From the same list, however, it can be seen that there are thirty-six other terms and definitions having to do with power and empowerment.

With the possible exception of POTENTIAL, almost all of these have been disassociated from the modern definition of power, and in fact some of them (such as DEPOTENTIATE) have been caused go out of usage altogether.

The one term that links together all of these many definitions and their nuances is POTENT, and from which all of the definitions can be seen as deriving either in full or in part.

And indeed, if that term is used at all today, it is usually only with regard to smell -- as in fragrance, odor, or stink if such are strong enough.

And, by extended metaphor, one can even smell the odors and stinks of skunks in the workings of power structures and situations.

POTENT - RADIANT – RADIATING

The term POTENT can be utilized in many ways, of course, but especially so with regard to whatever STRONGLY radiates something -- again as in fragrance, odor, or stink.

Whatever strongly radiates something is most likely to be referred to as potent.

Conversely, whatever radiates weakly or not at all can be thought of as impotent.

There is thus some kind of scale or measure between whatever is impotent (weakly or not radiating) and whatever is potent (strongly radiating).

But this is almost the same as saying that whatever radiates only weakly or not at all will not emanate power, while whatever does strongly radiate can emanate or have power.

At this point, there is hardly much need to further elaborate upon the nature of potency.

It is more to the point to re-read the short list of human sensing systems provided in chapter 25 -- but now with an eye for groking which of those sensing systems are involved with detecting some kind of radiational potencies.

In conducting this re-read, pay particular attention to 1, 7, 13, 14, 15, and 23 through 31.

SUGGESTED EXERCISES

TRY TO OBSERVE AT LEAST FIVE OR MORE EXAMPLES OF THINGS, INDIVIDUALS, AND SITUATIONS THAT RADIATE STRONGLY OR WEAKLY FOR OBVIOUS REASONS, DO THIS DISCRETELY OMIT SELF FROM THIS ASSESSMENT IN ORDER TO AVOID EGO STRESSES.

Chapter 28

WHERE DO INDIVIDUAL AND SOCIETAL POWERS BEGIN OR START?

VIA EACH chapter in this book, some twenty-seven general aspects of power have been discussed, along with various subtle elements whose themes recur again and again.

As closely as seems possible, the general aspects have been examined within the power contexts of SOCIETAL control, authority, and influence which rather seriously set up and determine the barrier-like distinctions between power and not power.

MISTAKING SOCIETAL POWER FOR POWER ITSELF

Over time and centuries, most of those distinctions have become locked in societal cement -- i.e., have become accepted not only as natural, but as proper, traditional, and authentic. As such, what has become locked in cement is not too much brought into questioning that might shed light on whether the authenticity is real or imagined.

Whether real or imagined, anyone attempting to empower or re-empower themselves will soon encounter a menu of those distinctions, even if they don't realize that they exist. Whether real or imagined, even the imagined are societally maintained as real.

As discussed and implied throughout the text, societal power structures are social artifices set up and intended to result in two obvious functions:

1. To manage the control, authority, and influence over and within the populations involved; and
2. To unequally distribute control of wealth, resources, life necessities, and even the value of human life itself (in that the lives of the powerless and the depowered are not valued as much as the lives of the powerful).

Societal "power" is obviously not power itself, but merely clever USES of it, uses sequestered to the powerful, and largely denied to and prevented among the powerless.

Power therefore does not begin with societal power artifices. While everyone has to exist in tandem with those artifices, it is a mistake to think that power begins or starts within them.

POWER "STARTS" AT THE INDIVIDUAL LEVEL

Power per se obviously belongs to, and is innate within, our species, and whose wondrous complexities, powers, and virtues manifest at the individual level.

The fundamental nature of our species is always in excess of socio-cultural Images Of Man set up for it, and which present highly modified, and usually downgraded versions of human potentials.

These versions always correspond more to the societal artifices than to our fundamental nature, the reason being that the Images are set up and used to achieve and maintain societal control in the first place.

If it is to be thought that power belongs to societal power structures and their managers, then two processes must be instituted:

1. Generic human powers cannot basically be assigned to the individual level, but must cleverly be attributed to something else; and
2. The individual levels must be socially conditioned away from any and all knowledge having to do with individual human powers.

It is thus that those seeking empowerment will encounter an almost complete absence of knowledge regarding human powers in general. If visible and invisible societal factors do not defeat empowerment, that particular lack of knowledge probably will. One cannot really empower something unless one knows it does exist.

The basic outcome of this is that no matter in which socio-cultural situation they live, most humans do not know what their powers actually are.

Those powers are actually quite numerous, and the sole purpose of Volume II is to identify and discuss them in as much depth as possible.

Gaining real information about the full spectrum of human powers has something to do with groking where power(s) begin or start up. As a way to segue into Volume II, that issue is now in part discussed in this last chapter of Volume I.

THE HORROR OF DISCOVERING THAT ONE IS RELATIVELY POWERLESS

At some point as their lives progress, vast numbers of people come to recognize that they are relatively or mostly powerless.

It is rather embarrassing and demeaning to undergo this kind of realization, especially if one suspects that one's powerlessness is recognizable by others.

This constitutes something of a horror, because if one is seen by others as relatively powerless, then it's quite likely that one will ALSO be seen as relatively insignificant.

Existing in some condition of powerlessness might have its life-defacing aspects. But it is far worse to find that others think one is insignificant.

THIS is a rather bitter blow, if and when it comes about -- and needless to say, there is a rather extensive list of obvious and subtle repercussions that can download from that kind of thing.

One notable way of getting around being seen by others as relatively powerless is to somehow to give the impression that one is not.

This can be achieved by seizing upon a number of artifices, one of which involves faking a posture or an attitude which suggests to self, but especially to others, that one is not relatively powerless.

Such posturing is the stuff of soap opera and even good drama, which is why those forms of entertainment are so fascinating. Of course, such posturing is also characteristic of a significant portion of all power games. Indeed, the axiom of "fake it until you somehow make it" was apparently coined with power-posturing precisely in mind.

Behind the scenes of all this, however, a good number of those having some degree of powerlessness begin to wonder where and how power actually begins or starts up.

More precisely stated, people begin to wonder how their power(s) can be started up AFTER they realize they are encumbered with some kind of powerlessness.

Questions along those lines are frequently asked. And so, although modernist societal power structures do not offer any information about the real nature of power, they do provide "reasons" that help confirm why one is powerless, and also help disarm or divert easy access to empowerment.

Those two "reasons" are easily identifiable because they have enormous cultural and societal support and hence are assumed to be authentic:

1. That one is powerless because one naturally never had power(s) to begin with; and
2. That if one is powerless, then as an individual responsible for developing self, the powerlessness is somehow one's own fault.

But if those "reasons" are examined in detail, they prove not to be all that authentic. Some of the reasons why are as follows:

1. On average, individuals become interested in their powerlessness only after they have realized something along those lines does exist.
2. This interest is almost immediately converted into interest regarding power, and how to get more of it. The conversion takes place because power is

seen as significant, while powerlessness is seen as insignificant.
3. Since the interest is now on power (not on powerlessness), it seems logical to wonder where power starts or begins.
4. The two modern socio-cultural "reasons" that account for powerlessness are usually now factored into one's rationalizing processes. In keeping with those two "reasons," this is to say that one rationalizes that one doesn't have power because it was absent to begin with, or one somehow messed up one's self with regard to getting power.
5. Via this rationalizing, one now has two options, both of which again seem entirely logical:
   a. Endeavor to somehow create power which was absent to begin with; or
   b. One can work to straighten out the mess of faults that one has earlier made in one's head.
6. The combination of those two options clearly signifies that AFTER realizing that self is relatively powerless, self is on one's own to do something to rectify it.
7. If authentic power schools existed, the rectification could be expedited. Power schools, however, are absent, and in such subtle ways that even those seeking empowerment don't realize that they ARE absent! If they existed, such schools would nurture the "birth" of human powers.

THE BIRTH OF HUMAN POWER(S)

Power is generally seen as an adult thing, and so it may at first seem slightly counter-productive to bring up the powers of infants.

But indeed, if one is to consider where power begins in societal terms, then, based on all the evidence, the answer is that it probably won't be encouraged to begin at all. Thus, there is no start-up or beginning of power in societal terms, except for those few who can outwit this or that power system artifice.

Power and empowerment cannot possibly start up or begin as one seeks to enter a power artifice but must begin elsewhere and outside of the artifice. The question then is not how to enter a power structure, but where do human powers begin or start up.

And THE basic reality having to do with human power(s) start-up or beginnings is perfectly obvious.

The babe that pops out after prenatal maturation is already possessed of power(s).

It is true that postnatal infants are not immediately seen that way. But in large part this is due to assuming that their initial physical helplessness is also the chief characteristic of their natural, indwelling power(s) and empowering endowments.

Then, piled on top of this essential confusion, is the additional fact that babes are seen NOT as power-humans, but as immature beings that need to be programmed so as ultimately to fit within the cultural and environmental circumstances they have popped out into.

On average, THIS social conditioning takes precedence over all else, and electrically so, with the usual justification that babes are powerless at first.

If the social conditioning, whatever it consists of, is to be reasonably successful, a great number of innate powers need to be canceled out, suspended from functioning, or blockaded by some kind of installed fear.

A WINDOW INTO THE PROBABLE EXTENT OF POWERS OF INFANTS

It is worth noting here that we are talking of INFANTS, not children.

There is of course no clear boundary between infancy and childhood, but infancy is sometimes referred to as that beginning part of life in which the infant is incapable of speech. As most parents realize, this part of life usually doesn't last very long.

An easy, quick, and brief way to get some idea of the inborn powers of INFANTS is to acquire access to the July 1993 issue of LIFE magazine. This issue presents an article entitled THE AMAZING MINDS OF INFANTS (pages 46-52).

"Babies are like little scientists, constantly exploring the world around them, with innate abilities we're just beginning to understand."

They can understand a hundred words (of any language, some 30,000 of them) before they can speak.

At six months, babies recognize their "native tongue," including elements that belong and do not belong to it.

At three months, their powers of memory are far greater than we ever imagined.

At five months, they can add before they can count.

At three months, they can learn and remember visual sequences and simple mechanical tasks.

Babies can comprehend before they can express that they do. This comprehension may exceed expression by a factor as high as one hundred to one.

So, as indicated by the LIFE article, "babies are smarter than you think."

The whole of this may be simply referred to as abilities. But in more crucial fact, they are inborn powers. But whether speaking of abilities or powers, if infants have the highly complex powers discussed in the LIFE article, then there can be no doubt that they also possess others.

The short list of senses provided in chapter 25 gives some hint of what those additional powers might consist of.

IS ONE BORN POWERLESS?

All the evidence accumulated as a basis for the three volumes comprising this series of SECRETS OF POWER clearly reveals that one is not born powerless.

Powerlessness, or being relatively powerless, is thus mostly the result of something other than not having our inborn spectrums of powers, and which are elaborated in Volume II.

AN EXERCISE TO CONSIDER

ASK A NUMBER OF INDIVIDUALS IF THEY WERE BORN POWERLESS OR NOT.

SUGGESTED READING

NOTE: Each of the following sources reveals some explicit or implicit element that can be recognized as being integral to societal power structures, especially those that are pyramidal in format. Most of the sources contain good bibliographies which help extend larger panoramic overviews of societal powerdom. Sources referring to human powers at the species and individual levels will be provided in volumes II.

Adler, Mortimer J., INTELLECT-MIND OVER MATTER. (Macmillan Publishing Co., New York, 1990).

Anderson, Jack, PEACE, WAR, AND POLITICS: AN EYEWITNESS ACCOUNT. (Forge, New York, 1999).

Bennett, James T. & Thomas J. DiLorenzo, OFFICIAL LIES: HOW WASHINGTON MISLEADS US. (Groom Books, Alexandria, Virginia, 1992).

Bennis, Warren, ON BECOMING A LEADER. (Addison-Wesley Publishing, New York, 1989).

Boorstin, Daniel J. HIDDEN HISTORY: EXPLORING OUR SECRET PAST. (Harper & Row, New York, 1987).

Butler, E. A., THE BIG BUCK AND THE NEW BUSINESS BREED. (Macmillan, New York, 1972).

Carrere D'Encausse, Helene, THE RUSSIAN SYNDROME: ONE THOUSAND YEARS OF POLITICAL MURDER. (Holmes & Meier, New York, 1992).

Cetron, Marvin *& Owen* Davies, CRYSTAL GLOBE: THE HAVES AND THE HAVE-NOTS OF THE NEW WORLD ORDER. (St. Martin's, New York, 1991).

Cousins, Norman, THE PATHOLOGY OF POWER. (W. W. Norton, New York, 1987).

Dulles, Allen, THE CRAFT OF INTELLIGENCE. (Harper & Row, New York, 1963).

Ewen, Stuart, PR! A SOCIAL HISTORY OF SPIN. (Basic Books, New York, 1996).

FitzGibbon, Constantine, SECRET INTELLIGENCE IN THE TWENTIETH CENTURY. (Stein & Day, New York, 1977).

Friedman, Thomas L., THE LEXUS AND THE OLIVE TREE: UNDERSTANDING GLOBALIZATION. (Farrar, Straus, Giroux, New York, 1999).

Galbraith, John Kenneth, THE ANATOMY OF POWER. (Houghton Mifflin, Boston, 1983).

Garan, D. G., OUR SCIENCES RULED BY HUMAN PREJUDICE: HUMANLY NECESSARY CAUSAL BLINDNESS PERSISTING EVEN IN SCIENCES. (Philosophical Library, New York, 1987).

Green, Robert & Joost Elffers, THE 48 LAWS OF POWER. (Viking, New York, 1998).

Herodotus, HISTORIES. (Wordsworth Editions, London, 1996).

Hilts, Philip J., BEHAVIOR MOD. (Harper's Magazine Press, New York, 1974).

Horkheimer, Max & Samuel H. Flowerman (Eds.), THE AUTHORITARIAN PERSONALITY. (Science Editions, John Wiley & Sons, New York, 1964).

Horowitz, Irving Louis, THE DECOMPOSITION OF SOCIOLOGY. (Oxford University Press, New York, 1993).

Keith, Jim (Ed.), SECRET ANBD SUPPRESSED: BANNED IDEAS & HIDDEN HISTORY. (Feral House, Portland, Oregon, 1993).

Kohn, Alfie, NO CONTEST -- THE CASE AGAINST COMPETITION. (Houghton Mifflin, Boston, 1986).

Lawrence, James, RAJ: THE MAKING AND UNMAKING OF BRITISH INDIA. (St. Martin's, New York, 1997).

Lebedoff, David, THE NEW ELITE -- THE DEATH OF DEMOCRACY. (Franklin Watts, New York, 1981).

Lichter, Robert S., Stanley Rothman & Linda S. Lichter, THE MEDIA ELITE: AMERICA'S NEW POWERBROKERS. (Adler & Adler, Bethesda, Maryland, 1986).

Maclay, George & Humphry Knipe, THE DOMINANT MAN: THE PECKING ORDER IN

HUMAN SOCIETY. (Delacorte Press, New York, 1972).

Mann, John, CHANGING HUMAN BEHAVIOR: THE FIRST COMPREHENSIVE ACCOUNT OF MODERN ALTERATION AND ENHANCEMENT OF HUMAN BEHAVIOR. (Charles Scribner's Sons, New York, 1965).

Mills, C. Wright, THE POWER ELITE. (Oxford University Press, New York, 1956).

-- POWER, POLITICS AND PEOPLE. (Ballantine Books, New York, 1963).

Mitroff, Ian I. & Warren Bennis, THE UNREALITY INDUSTRY: THE DELIBERATE MANUFACTURING OF FALSEHOOD AND WHAT IT IS DOING TO OUR LIVES. (Carol Publishing Group, New York, 1989).

Nisbet, Robert, THE MAKING OF MODERN SOCIETY. (New York University Press, New York, 1986).

Penrose, Roger, SHADOWS OF THE MIND: A SEARCH FOR THE MISSING SCIENCE OF CONSCIOUSNESS. (Oxford University Press, New York, 1994).

Peters, Charles & John Rothchild, INSIDE THE SYSTEM. (Praeger Publishers, New York, 1973).

Poggi, Gianfranco, THE DEVELOPMENT OF THE MODERN STATE: A SOCIOLOGICAL INTRODUCTION. (Stanford University Press, Stanford, California, 1978).

Scheflin, Alan W. & Edward M. Opton, Jr., THE MIND MANIPULATORS. (Paddington Press, New York, 1978).

Sennet, Richard: THE FALL OF PUBLIC MAN: ON THE SOCIAL PSYCHOLOGY OF CAPITALISM. (Vintage Books, Random House, New York, 1976).

Shattuck, Roger, FORBIDDEN KNOWLEDGE: FROM PROMETHEUS TO PORNOGRAPHY. (St. Martin's, New York, 1996).

Strong, Roy, ART AND POWER: RENAISSANCE FESTIVALS 1450-1650. (University of California Press, Los Angeles, 1984).

Sun-tzu, THE ART OF WAR (Trans, by Ralph D. Sawyer). (Barnes & Noble, New York, 1994).

Suvorov, Vikton, INSIDE THE SOVIET ARMY. (Panther Books, London, 1982).

Weatherford, Jack, THE HISTORY OF MONEY: FROM SANDSTONE TO CYBERSPACE. (Crown, New York, 1997).

West, Nigel, GAMES OF INTELLIGENCE: THE CLASSIFIED CONFLICT OF INTERNATIONAL ESPIONAGE REVEALED. (Crown Publishers, New York, 1989).

Wieman, Henry Nelson, THE DIRECTIVE IN HISTORY. (Beacon Press, Boston, 1949).

Winn, Denise, THE MANIPULATED MIND: BRAINWASHING, CONDITIONING AND INDOCTRINATION. (The Octagon Press, London, 1983).

Wise, David & Thomas R. Ross, THE INVISIBLE GOVERNMENT. (Random House, New York, 1964).

Zweig, Michael, THE WORKING CLASS: AMERICA'S BEST KEPT SECRET. (Cornell University Press, Ithaca, New York, 2000).

A BIOMIND SUPERPOWERS BOOK FROM
SWANN-RYDER PRODUCTIONS, LLC

www.ingoswann.com

OTHER BOOKS BY INGO SWANN

Everybody's Guide to Natural ESP
Master of Harmlessness
Penetration
Penetration: Special Edition Updated
Preserving the Psychic Child
Psychic Literacy
Psychic Sexuality
Purple Fables
Reality Boxes
Resurrecting the Mysterious
Secrets of Power, Volume 2
Star Fire
The Great Apparitions of Mary
The Windy Song
The Wisdom Category
Your Nostradamus Factor

www.ingramcontent.com/pod-product-compliance
Lightning Source LLC
Chambersburg PA
CBHW081719100526
44591CB00016B/2433